MAKING FURNITURE
PROJECTS & PLANS
MARK RIPLEY

MAKING FURNITURE
PROJECTS & PLANS
MARK RIPLEY

DEDICATION
To Monika, Helena and Alice,
with much love

First published 2008 by
Guild of Master Craftsman Publications Ltd
Castle Place, 166 High Street, Lewes, East Sussex BN7 1XU

Reprinted 2010

ISBN: 978-1-86108-560-3

A catalogue record for this book is available from the
British Library.

Photographs taken by Manny Cefai, apart from the following,
which were taken by David Smith: back cover, bottom pic,
pp. 3, 5, 74–8, 170–73, 175–76, 178, 180–84, and
Anthony Bailey: pp. 80–4.

Illustrations by Simon Rodway, apart from the following by
Ian Hall: front cover, pp. 27, 38, 54, 96, 102, 131 and135.

Associate Publisher: Jonathan Bailey
Production Manager: Jim Bulley
Managing Editor: Gerrie Purcell
Project Editor: Gill Parris
Managing Art Editor: Gilda Pacitti
Designer: Chloë Alexander

Set in ITC Stone
Colour origination by GMC Reprographics
Printed and bound in China by Everbest Printing Co. Ltd

CONTENTS

FOREWORD

ark has successfully steered a career as a professional craftsman for over 20 years without compromising his ideals. His furniture is a testimony to his vision, faith and vocation.

Mark's furniture is rooted in the English vernacular tradition: beautiful, understated designs that celebrate wood finely worked. He does not aspire to the vaunted, individualistic designer culture but instead seeks the anonymity of the unknown country craftsman. This is not a false humility but a celebration of the human spirit and the universal values that are embodied in his work. Craftsmanship is a universal language that connects us with our humanity. Kahlil Gibran, the poet, said 'work is love made visible' and Mark's furniture designs are meditations on love.

The projects presented in this book represent a particularly fruitful period of Mark's development as a designer-maker. They can be appreciated on many levels: as practical projects to inspire woodworking endeavours, as a body of work by a leading British designer-maker and a celebration of the human spirit in action.

Enjoy!

Philip Koomen, PhD, FSCD, FRSA

NOTE ON MEASUREMENTS

While every effort has been made to show fair imperial/metric conversions, you are advised to check measurements against the conversion table on page 188 before starting a project. Use either imperial or metric measurements, do not mix the two.

NOTES ON PLANS FOR THE PROJECTS

Bear in mind the following points before using the plans in Part 2 of the book:

Components are usually drawn with no allowance for movement of timber

No rounding of edges shown, for accuracy or clarity

A minimum of ⅛in (3mm) movement gap all round for solid timber panels is advisable.

Drawer frames: where possible, allow a movement gap. In the case of mortice-and-tenon frames, dry tenons can be used at the back of the frame.

Mortice-and-tenon joints: tenons are usually shown full depth in mortices. Allow a gap of ³⁄₁₆in (4mm) between the end of tenons and end of the mortice

Doors are usually drawn as an exact fit in their openings, with no allowance for hinges and ease of movement.

Sheet components such as panels and drawer bottoms shown are ¼in (6.5mm) plywood unless otherwise stated.

Dimensions: where multiple subdivisions of an overall dimension occur, you may need to vary the width or height of a component to fit. Please check all running dimensions against overall sizes before making a project.

INTRODUCTION

THE PROJECTS in this book were made over a ten-year period in my own workshop, and originally published in *Furniture & Cabinetmaking* magazine. The designs come within the broad definition of 'Arts and Crafts' furniture and range from the fairly traditional end of the spectrum to the more contemporary. The section at the end of the book, Speculative Pieces & One-offs, consists of the latter and represents the work I have been doing for the past two to three years. This work has a more distinctive, meditative voice and includes pieces made for contemporary exhibitions.

Part 1, Developing a Design, explains how to interpret the projects and use them intelligently. There is advice on timber selection, on harmonizing the essential elements of furniture design, adapting a project to suit your specific needs, and advice on how to batch-produce chairs.

Part 2 contains 24 varied projects, all complemented by clear photographs and useful diagrams, and each one with a specially commissioned, fully detailed plan.

In writing projects, I try to bear in mind that many readers will be working in small workshops with limited resources. My own early workshops were simply equipped and I worked semi-professionally for a year with no more than a bench, small bandsaw, two or three portable power tools and a basic kit of hand tools. With these I made a wide range of domestic furniture to commission.

For the amateur, expensive, noisy and potentially dangerous machines are, I believe, often unnecessary beyond those I have indicated above. Many timber suppliers offer a machining service and the additional cost of prepared – as against raw – materials is marginal compared with the cost of machinery, when the modest output of the average recreational maker is considered. If you are keen to process your own raw materials, a small planer thicknesser is really all that

is required in addition. Although I am now fortunate enough to have a fully equipped workshop, I have not forgotten those times and have suggested various ways of solving technical problems.

I am assuming that makers reproducing projects will not be professionals and therefore not as pressured by time. I would encourage you to keep your project well within the time available to you, so that it doesn't become a burden, and fully engage in the making process rather than just aiming for the end result.

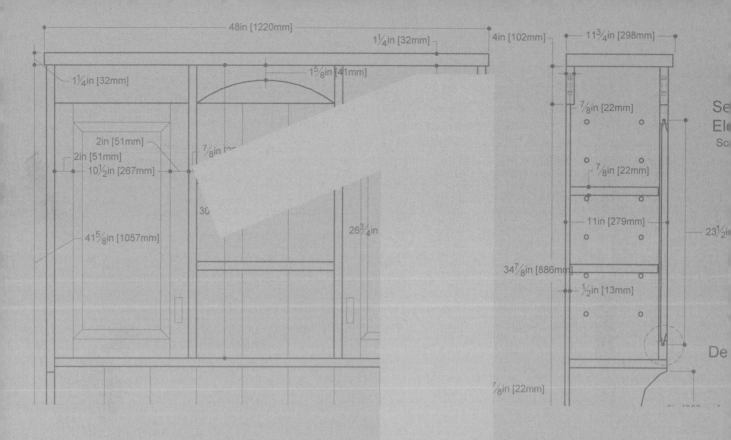

48in [1220mm]

1¼in [32mm]

4in [102mm]

11¾in [298mm]

1⅝in [41mm]

1¼in [32mm]

⅞in [22mm]

Se
Ele
Sc

2in [51mm]

2in [51mm]

10½in [267mm]

⅞in [2

⅞in [22mm]

11in [279mm]

23½i

30

41⅝in [1057mm]

26¾in

34⅞in [886mm]

½in [13mm]

De

⅞in [22mm]

PART 1
DEVELOPING
A DESIGN

ADAPTING A PROJECT

*Integrating the four key elements of furniture design successfully,
while adapting a project to your own needs and tastes*

WITH THE possible exception of the chairs, it is unlikely that you will find a project you want to make in exactly the dimensions you need, so in this section I offer some guidance about developing the designs for your own use. This will also apply to adapting any other design, for example country furniture, or Arts and Crafts furniture. Working from an existing design is a good starting point as this can teach you how it all works.

Furniture design is about harmonizing four elements: structure, function, aesthetics and economy. These are not in any particular order as they are all equally important. One of the reasons I am attracted to Arts and Crafts furniture is that the ethos was very much about integrating these different aspects, and not adding much else. Though decoration was sometimes used, to my eye the most successful pieces were the simplest. The furniture of the Christian communities of Shakers in America was even more refined. Their practical spirituality and the meaning behind it has been an enduring inspiration to me.

STRUCTURE

Structure is about sound construction so that the piece will stand up to everyday use and also take adequate account of the material. In solid wood furniture this

• **Block with slotted screw hole allows for timber movement**

principally means timber movement. Wood expands and contracts across the grain as it responds to changes in humidity. In the temperate hardwoods I use, that movement can be + or – 2%, which on a 39⅜in (1000mm) wide table top is significant. This is usually allowed for by fixing the top on through slotted blocks. Similarly door panels are set loose into grooves in frames with adequate tolerance for movement. The thickness of chair or table legs not only has to be physically strong enough, but also needs to inspire confidence in the user.

FUNCTION

Function presupposes that furniture is made for everyday use and that it should do its job well. The most practical heights for table tops, chair seats and sideboard tops are more or less established and are indicated in the dimensions on the plans.

AESTHETICS

Aesthetics is rather more subjective and I will concentrate on a few basic pointers. Proportion is a principal issue here. The designs featured give an overall sense of this and in adapting a design, it is important to retain consistency. If scaling down a piece, the thickness of rails, sides and top need to be reduced accordingly, otherwise the piece will look clumsy. Drawer front depths and shelf spacing looks better if graduated – deeper at the bottom, shallower at the top, ideally incremental – i.e. each drawer 15% shallower than the one below. If altering the width, expand or reduce proportionately.

ECONOMY

By economy I am not necessarily referring to finance, though – as will be seen in the projects – I am concerned to produce designs that are both profitable and realistically priced. In part this means avoiding unnecessary decoration or structure as I want my

• **Bookcase with graduated shelf heights**

• **Through-wedged tenons**

pieces to follow the principle that 'nothing needs to be added, nothing can be taken away'. If decoration is used, it should be done sparingly. Avoid using more than one moulding design for example, though the same moulding can be used in different sizes.

HARMONIZING THE ELEMENTS

The successful bringing together of these factors is partly trial and error, partly intuition and partly experience. Over the years I have developed an approach to design that is very simple, with few motifs which I use often, and a more or less standardized construction for different types of work: tables, chairs and cabinets. This is not because I am lazy or unimaginative, rather it evolves through working with a clear set of beliefs about design and harmony.

PROPORTION AND DETAIL

So, how do these aspects of design work together? By the time the functional factors of the piece have been resolved into a workable structural idea, elements of proportion and detail can be drawn in. It may be that the structure itself can be used to aesthetic effect, for example with through-wedged mortice-and-tenon

joints, or dovetails. Raised panels in doors are attractive and are structurally sound. Chamfers and simple mouldings on edges are necessary to prevent wear and make the piece more pleasant to use. Handles are essential and have great creative potential, the simpler the rest of the design, the more impact details like handles and hinges have. Making samples of table-top corners, or handles, trying different woods together to see how they work, or making rough scale models of furniture is all great fun and also an inexpensive way of trying things out without committing to the actual piece too soon.

• **Raised panel detail**

• Creating a subtle contrast with ash and oak

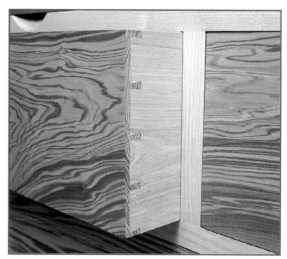

• Olive ash in drawer fronts contrasts with white oak drawer sides, revealing lap dovetails

SELECTING THE WOOD

A vital aspect of aesthetics in woodworking is selection of high quality timber. Generally the grain should follow the direction of the line of a curve as far as is practical. If the colour of the wood is inconsistent, use similar tones for groups of components – door panels, say, or cabinet top, sides and front rails. Grain direction of horizontal components needs to be horizontal.

Vertical grain should point in towards the centre line like an arrow, which has the effect of drawing the eye upwards and around the piece. Timber selection is about unity and harmony rather than uniformity – uniformity is boring, unity feels right. All of these factors contribute to making a piece work and feel 'right'. If it feels 'wrong' people will be uncomfortable with it. They probably won't know why, but furniture makers need to understand the principles of design even if they are not doing the designing.

• Abstract art in wood – semi-burr oak door panels

• 'Bookmatched' door panel and styles

SPECIFIC TECHNIQUES

The projects are generally self-contained, although reading through the book will familiarize you with my approach to making before beginning a project. Pages 104–106 feature a detailed explanation of drawer making not included in other projects, while page 118 explains door fitting in detail.

Finishing is a vital and very personal element of furniture making. I have strong feelings about choosing wood of the colour you want, not staining one wood to look like another. I refer in the

• Hand carving features in this recessed handle

• Hand-planed chamfer on table top

Introduction to enjoying hand making. This is also beneficial to the work itself, as it introduces a sensitivity that machines cannot produce. Although I cut chamfers with a router for speed, I generally take a fine shaving or two with a block plane, to finish the job and to take some of the precision out of it. This 'imprecision' might sound strange when accuracy is so important for good furniture making. Joints need to fit properly – if the gap between a door and cabinet is inconsistent it looks sloppy. However, the use of even a fairly modest level of mechanized equipment can produce results that are just too sharp and precise. A hand-planed chamfer takes very little time and is just not quite perfect: it is more relaxing to the eye, and prevents the work from being soulless.

• Side table with raised panel door and contrasting white and olive ash

BATCH-PRODUCING A CHAIR

Making full-size prototypes of chairs as part of the development process, ensures that batch-produced chairs meet the same exacting standards as chairs made individually

C HAIR DESIGN is a particularly challenging aspect of furniture design, which includes the use of full-size prototypes as part of the development process. It also requires efficient making techniques, as a set of chairs is a time-consuming process to which I apply many of the aspects of design discussed in Adapting a Project. As the sections in chairs are generally small, timber movement is not usually an issue. However, the issue of integrating structure, function, aesthetics and economics apply probably more in chairs than in any other kind of furniture, so these make good case studies. The ladderback chair I am using to illustrate these points, is a direct development from an earlier commission, for which the original pine prototype was made in 1989.

• The pine prototype that started it all

• The new design has a tapered back and a lighter look

THE PROCESS OF BATCH PRODUCTION

Making a beautiful, comfortable chair economically is the ultimate goal of cabinetmakers, and a good start is to adopt a pragmatic attitude to design, considering all aspects of the project at the outset, including the number of hours in which it has to be produced.

Here is an economical approach to making a ladderback chair in a small, modestly equipped workshop.

COUNTING COSTS

There is a great difference between mass production and one-off models, and chairs highlight this difference particularly well. Chairs are often required in large numbers of identical units, so the costs involved in setting up can be retrieved through volume sales. However, they are time-consuming to design and correspondingly expensive to make in short runs or one-offs. Nevertheless, careful specification and planning can generate good designs at prices comparable to top-of-the-range high street products – it is just a question of designing productivity into the piece.

• **The result, a crisp-angled tenon**

At this level, bespoke furniture is a direct alternative to mass-production design. A stock design, that can be made economically from a set of jigs, allows for a quick turnaround and therefore relatively low production cost. It is certainly a very useful item to have in one's portfolio.

PINE MOCK-UP

I had a one-off ladder-back side chair made speculatively which featured tapered legs. I wanted to incorporate these in a new design creating a chair that was lighter and more elegant than some previous examples. I made a full-size softwood mock-up – a three-dimensional 'sketch' of the new design. This was screwed together and strong enough to sit on but enabling modifications to be made easily until a satisfactory result is achieved. The mock-up was used to draw up a full-size rod (drawing) on a sheet of MDF and to scribe off templates for the legs and rails. Although roughly made, the mock-up was accurate.

The rails were also employed in the drawing of full-sized plans for the jigs. There are two pairs of jigs, one for the front and back rails and one for the side rails. The back rail tenon cheeks and shoulders are routed on one side, flipped over and the reverse side is routed.

• **The back jig, used for the angled shoulders of the slat tenons**

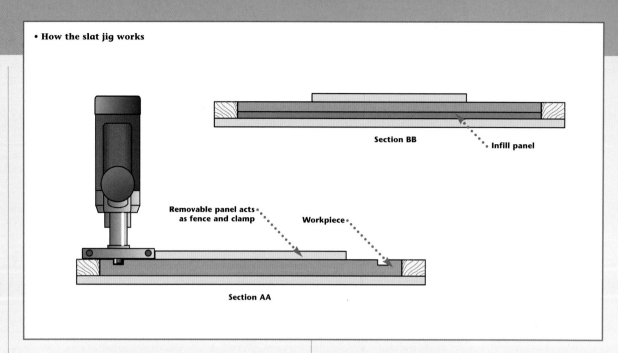

• How the slat jig works

Section BB

Infill panel

Removable panel acts as fence and clamp

Workpiece

Section AA

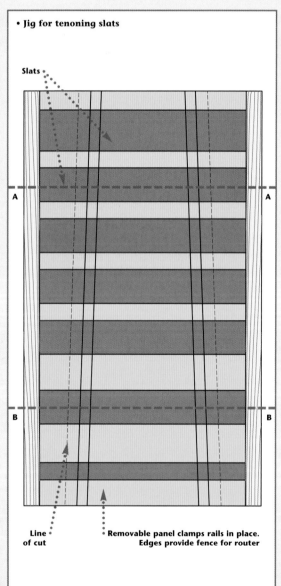

• Jig for tenoning slats

Slats

A · · · A

B · · · B

Line of cut

Removable panel clamps rails in place. Edges provide fence for router

As the back slats follow the same taper, these are also dimensioned on the same jig. The same technique is used for the front rails and stretchers. In both cases, the jig holds the pre-dimensioned components in the correct relative position and a central tapered batten is screwed over the top to both clamp them in place and act as a fence for the router to run against.

DESIGNING THE JIGS

The compound tenons for the side rails and stretchers are cut in left- and right-handed jigs. These provide a base and fence for the router to run against and are mounted in a box designed to hold the components in the correct position. By screwing additional wedge-shaped shims to the router fences, the side rail jigs can also be used to cut the stretcher rail tenons. In total, the jigs took three days to design and make. This included a trial run – which generated yet another prototype – and time spent making adjustments to ensure they worked. It was a good opportunity, though, to use up all those offcuts of man-made boards and lumps of wood not good enough to use, but not bad enough to throw away.

Once the MDF templates have been used to scribe off the shape of front and back legs, they are simply bandsawn and planed or sanded to the line respectively. Obviously a guided router or spindle cutter would be an accurate alternative, but the linishing upper table on my pad sander is very efficient and I opted for this.

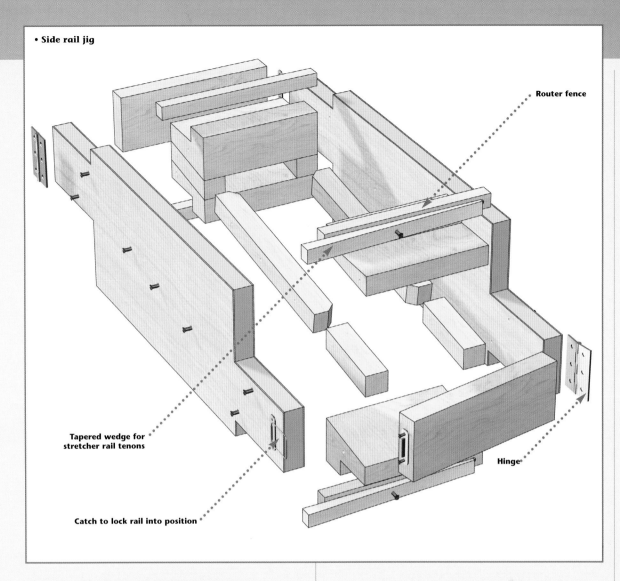

• **Side rail jig**

Router fence

Tapered wedge for stretcher rail tenons

Hinge

Catch to lock rail into position

• **The jig for the compound angled rails holds the components in the correct position, and a router is used to cut the tenons and shoulders**

I spent some time trying to work out a way of jigging up the bevel on the inside face of the back legs. In the event, bandsawing off a marked line on the tilted bandsaw table, and planing in by hand with a smoothing plane, only took three hours for ten pairs, so making a jig would not have been a time-efficient alternative. It is easy to get bitten by the jigging bug and unwittingly spend hours making routing jigs for a job that could be done by hand in minutes.

TAPERED SHIMS

Tapered shims were made to aid the bandsawing of tenon ends. Only one curved support batten is needed to produce the mortices, which are all perpendicular to the sides of the legs. The crest rail curves are again drawn off a template and bandsawn. Although the arrises on the edges of the rails and slats are sanded, all the edges of the legs are chamfered. Those on the legs are routed, as are the stopped chamfers on the rails.

• Cross section of rail jig

Router sits here •

Rail •

Router fence

Hinged end

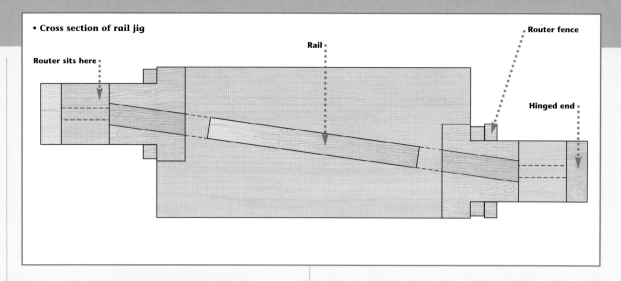

• Plan view of side rail jig

Workpiece sits in here •

Spacers

Hinged end •

Tapered add on fence for stretcher rails • • • • • • • • •

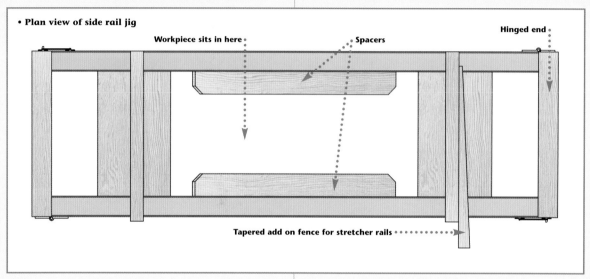

• MDF templates are used to mark out legs and then bandsawn to rough shape

• Positions of joints are marked from these onto the legs

OAK PROTOTYPE

The next task was to make the fully jointed production prototype in oak. If all went well, this would be the first of the set. The job so far had taken two days and we were already up to the point of being clean-sanded, ready for assembly, but temporarily held together with the corner blocks. It even included replacing the odd component that had been spoiled by mounting it in a jig the wrong way. This emphasized what I already knew – to avoid silly mistakes, working methodically is imperative. I was pleased with the performance of the jigs; the joint-making had been completed in good time and all the tenons were easily cut in one day. Despite this, I still hoped to improve on production time when making a batch.

ASSEMBLING

Before assembly, all components are fine sanded and finished with thinned polyurethane. The front and back assemblies are glued up first. Any excess glue can be easily removed after about three hours, by peeling it off the sealed surface with a chisel. The side rail assemblies are glued next. If ever there is a time for believing one does not have enough clamps, it is in the middle of gluing up a set of chairs. As the gluing and assembly process for the front and back frames only takes about 30 minutes, with enough clamps and following a coffee break, it's nearly time to start the next lot. And once you take into account time spent peeling off excess glue, it is more or less a continuous operation.

FINISHING TOUCHES

The all-important corner blocks are roughed out and then hand-planed to fit, before being screwed and glued into place. They are made from 1⅝in (40mm) stock and set ¾in (18mm) below the top edge of the seat rails. The blocks also serve as a base for the seat panels and are of ⅝in (15mm) ply. A ⅛in (3mm) tolerance allows for upholstery and a heavy-duty fabric will give a good push-fit to the seats.

Once the seats are away at the upholsterers, the feet can be levelled off. I use the bench saw – the flattest large surface in the workshop – as a base plate and scribe around each leg with a pencil and a ¼in (6mm) thick block of wood.

• **The back legs are bevelled to meet the slats**

The feet are then trimmed on the bandsaw, planed and chamfered. The finish was built up with two coats of Danish oil and finally burnished with 00 steel wool and waxed.

VERDICT

The price I charged compared favourably with good-quality production chairs but still generated a profit. Given the individual service and one-off nature of the product, I think my customers got a bargain. The unit production time for the standard chair was about 17 hours and it is interesting to note that a one-off carver using the same set of jigs took nearly twice as long as its batch-produced counterpart. Overall, I was happy with the outcome – not just for this commission but for the chance to develop confidence in offering chairs economically in the future.

• **Stopped chamfer detail on the top rails**

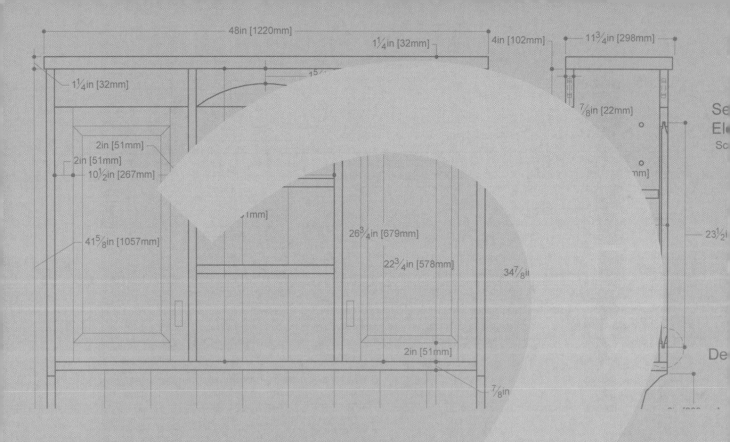

48in [1220mm]

$1\frac{1}{4}$in [32mm]

4in [102mm]

$11\frac{3}{4}$in [298mm]

$1\frac{1}{4}$in [32mm]

$\frac{7}{8}$in [22mm]

2in [51mm]

2in [51mm]

$10\frac{1}{2}$in [267mm]

Se
Ele
Sc

$23\frac{1}{2}$i

$41\frac{5}{8}$in [1057mm]

$26\frac{3}{4}$in [679mm]

$22\frac{3}{4}$in [578mm]

$34\frac{7}{8}$in

De

2in [51mm]

$\frac{7}{8}$in

PART 2
THE
PROJECTS

CHAIRS

CLASSIC DINING CHAIR

This conventional chair reveals some unconventional joint making, which increases strength and reduces making time

A DINING TABLE – especially a simple one – can be very satisfying, because of the relative speed at which a small number of components can be turned into a large and highly functional piece of furniture. While chairs are no less functional, that is where the similarity ends: this traditionally based ladderback design is constructed from some 22 complex components.

STOCK DESIGNS

The design process itself is time-consuming because a chair is not, like many cabinets, a series of two-dimensional faces; it is made up of compound angles and curves that are almost impossible to work out on paper. Models may suffice for communicating the idea of sculptural forms in a cabinet, but chair design demands full-size prototypes to test for comfort.

A designer is unlikely to recoup the development costs of a new chair design in one commission, unless it is for a large number of chairs. Over the years I have developed two stock chair designs which are adjusted to suit. These are constantly evolving, are never produced in the same way twice but provide a starting point from which I can make a prototype for each new generation. This need not take long and may vary from a quick lash-up to check a visual idea, to a pre-production prototype. The latter will include all joints and accurate dimensions, and be used as a three-dimensional working drawing.

These are made in softwood, usually with bandsawn surfaces, and are unfinished. The three or four in my workshop provide a useful talking point, as well as seating, for visitors.

STRUCTURE

The structure of this chair is conventional. Apart from four lower-ladder 'rungs', all the joints are mortice and tenoned.

• **Sturdy construction and timeless design**

THE VALUE OF PROTOTYPES

Prototypes are invaluable, as part of the design process, for working out the visual, ergonomic and structural aspects of a chair. They are also useful when making a set of chairs to an established design, as they will familiarize the maker with their construction, aid the making of jigs and templates and provide a reference point. Remember that this is an exercise in batch production, with any mistakes multiplied. For those unfamiliar with chair making I would suggest the making of a finished softwood 'prototype' as a project in its own right.

• Morticed components stacked in handed pairs – very important!

• Testing for fit – side rail tenon and back leg mortice

Dowels may be an adequate alternative for an occasional chair, but for dining chairs I would not advise them.

The four main sets of joints around the seat are reinforced with corner blocks. When preparing the timber, make enough parts for an additional chair. This allows for natural defects and the odd ... um ... unnatural one.

The back legs are shaped and the mortices marked out. The corresponding mortices are marked on the front legs and the legs put into sets. This is important as there are right- and left-handed legs, so keeping them in order is imperative.

The mortice and tenon in the back leg is a compound joint, further complicated by being set in a curved rail. Cutting angled mortices in the legs is achieved by means of a jig. This holds the leg at an angle to the mortice chisel. A similar arrangement could be used on a bench drill, the joint being drilled out and cleaned up by hand. Double-check each cut to ensure that the mortice is angled in the right direction.

• Front leg morticing jig

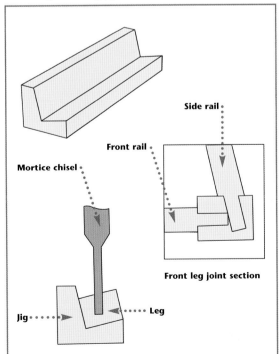

• Back leg morticing jig

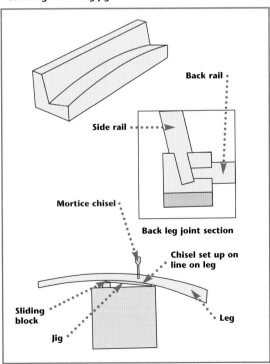

SIDE RAILS

The tenons for the side rails must all be marked out individually using a sliding bevel and square. Again, these are right- and left-handed and must be put in pairs. Concentrate on the top rails first, as the stretchers are marked off later.

Although the cheeks may be cut on a bandsaw, take care not to run through the shoulder of the tenon, especially on the back leg joint. The remainder of the tenon is cut and finished by hand.

A small, flat area is planed over the back leg mortice. Thus the shoulder of the tenon fits onto a flat rather than a curved surface (see below). The outside edge of the leg is sanded to a fair curve at a later stage.

Using a clamp to pull the joint up, assemble the front and back legs and top rail. Each assembly is checked with its partner and any necessary adjustments made to the tenon shoulders until each pair matches.

These top rails are a critical part of the job so must be accurate. The stretcher rails are scribed off the sides of the legs while they are still clamped up, and marked, cut and checked in the same way as the top rails.

The front and back rails are all perpendicular to the legs, making the joints much easier to cut by machine. Remember, though, that the carvers are wider than the

standard version. The top rung of the ladder back should be mortice and tenoned, but the remainder are wide enough to take a No. 20 biscuit. The joints are prepared on the top rung prior to cutting the curve.

A full dry assembly to check that everything fits probably only needs to done on one chair. All the components are sanded, the legs are rounded over to a radius of ⅛in (3mm). An ovolo moulding is applied to the top of the back and the top edge of the rails.

ASSEMBLY

The legs and side rails are glued up first and left in clamps overnight. These are particularly important joints and should be given every assistance. The rest of the chair must be glued up in one well-planned operation.

Corner blocks – as big as possible – are fitted below the top of the rail, to reinforce the mortice-and-tenon joints, and screwed into place.

If carvers are being made, the arms and supports may now be prepared. The shapes of these components are quite complex. Right- and left-hand softwood patterns help to resolve these, and also act as templates for the actual job.

• **Create a flat on the curved back leg for the tenon shoulder**

• **Shape and proportion of corner blocks**

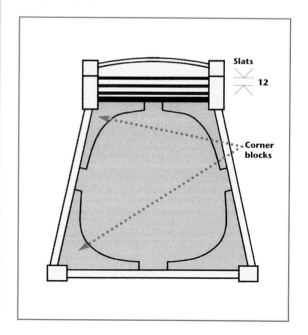

Mortice-and-tenoned crest rail

Biscuit-jointed slats

Big, strong, corner blocks

Notched and screwed arm supports

Mortice-and-tenon construction

The arms are joined to the back legs with stub tenons. A screw is used to give the joint more strength, the hole being counterbored and filled with a pellet. The arm support is fitted to the chair rail with a halving joint and, like the stub tenon, screwed and plugged. The arm and its support are joined with a mortice and tenon joint.

Each of the many joints in each chair must be checked for glue marks before they are finished – brushing on white spirit reveals light patches where excess glue needs to be scraped off.

The chairs are sealed with 70/30 polyurethane/white spirit, burnished with wire wool, and Danish oiled.

The drop-in seat panels are made from ⅜in (10mm) birch ply, and are individually fitted and numbered. An allowance of ³⁄₃₂in (2mm) should be left all the way round the seat panel, after the edges have been rounded over, for the upholstery; although this is a relatively straightforward job, I always use professionals for the upholstery. They have the expertise and access to materials at trade prices, and for a one-off chair may offer an offcut of fabric.

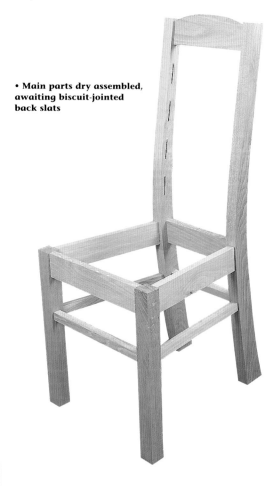

• Main parts dry assembled, awaiting biscuit-jointed back slats

BACK LEGS – ONE APPROACH

A chair's back leg joints are the most important in the structure, taking an enormous amount of stress on a daily basis – and then people do monstrous things like leaning back on them. So when designing chairs it is important to bear these factors in mind. The deeper you can make the tenon, the end-grain component, the better its chances of surviving the racking forces of chair usage, and the more it increases the gluing area.

The conventional approach to the cutting of the back leg mortices and tenons in chairs, used by most furniture makers, is to angle the tenon and have a parallel mortice. This makes for easy setting up on the morticer, but can lead to tenons with short grain, because of the angle at which they are cut, so it pays to be careful when selecting timber for side rails.

Although some time will have to be spent making a jig for the tenons, this will soon reap rewards as most of us rarely make only one chair at a time.

• Back legs on the morticer – note angle and jig

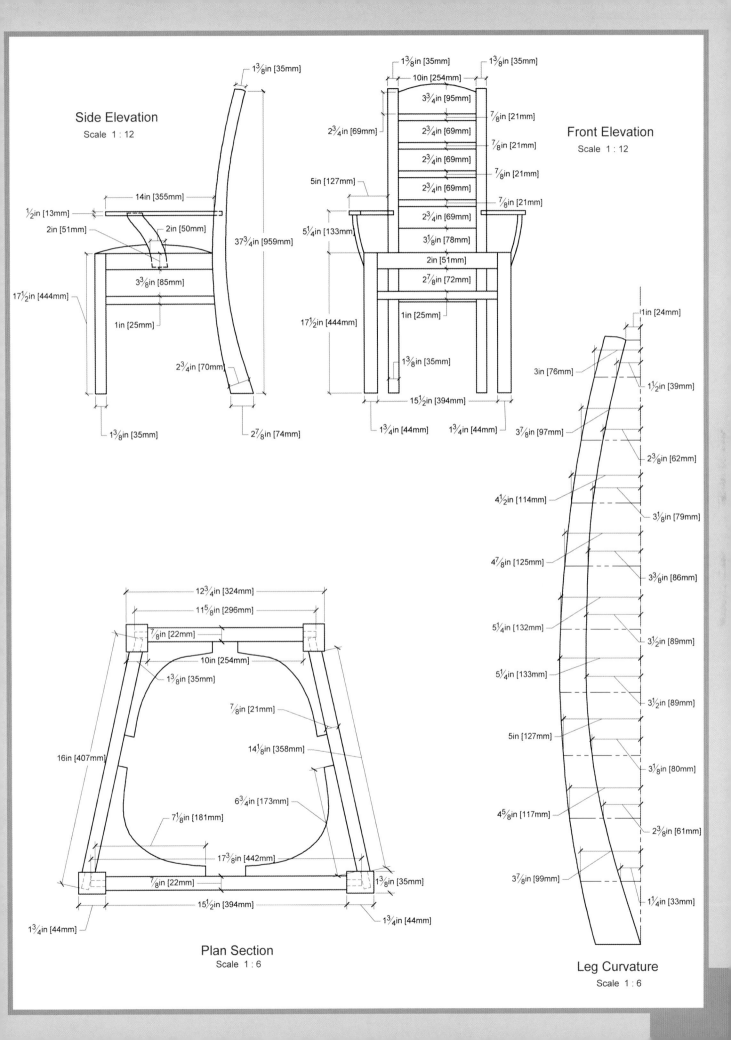

Side Elevation
Scale 1 : 12

Front Elevation
Scale 1 : 12

Plan Section
Scale 1 : 6

Leg Curvature
Scale 1 : 6

LAMINATED DINING CHAIR

Laminating greatly extends the possibilities for design, as this chair reveals

W HEN MAKING a series of pieces for an exhibition I was keen to develop a chair as part of a suite of speculative pieces. In drawing up the design I took the dimensions and proportions straight off a prototype slat-back chair, knowing the ergonomics had been resolved. I planned to remove many of the more time-consuming elements by replacing the stretcher rails with a deeper top frame, the compound joints with mortice and tenons with at least one right angle, and the seven-piece back with a single upholstered laminated panel.

The drop-in seat is replaced with a laminated ply panel which sits over the front legs. As with the slat-back version, the front legs are splayed but brought closer together, which reduces the footprint of the chair, and makes it more compact. In doing this I wanted a more contemporary feel and was interested to see what the response would be. Were people attracted by the apparent comfort of the laminated slats or the classical look of the chair? It would have been interesting to have exhibited them side-by-side, but lack of time and exhibition space precluded this idea.

PLANNING

Rather than make a rough full-size pine prototype as is my practice, I created a scale model and full-size drawings. One reason is that ash (*Fraxinus excelsior*) is an inexpensive wood, so material cost isn't an issue. I also wanted to check the laminations in ash, the number of laminates, planing the taper, and assess the springback, etc. It was also important to try the upholstery, especially on the back. Even a modest amount of padding dramatically affects the comfort of a chair back, as it pushes the sitter forwards and can make the seat feel too shallow and the back more upright. In upholstering the back, in this instance, the aim is to provide a padded cover for the laminated ply-back panel, rather than add significantly to an already adequate level of comfort.

• **Refined over a number of years, this chair has been developed through several versions**

By the time I had made full-size templates and tried some experimental padding on the original slat-back prototype, I felt I had enough information to make a chair that would only require modest design refinements before a set was made – if, of course, I could find someone to commission it!

Although I saved time in various constructional aspects of the design, the back legs are more time-consuming. Preparing the tapered laminates, gluing, cleaning up and shaping the legs takes a while – the first prototype took the best part of a week. As a set, however, this would take much less time.

• **The curved back is shaped to provide good lumbar support**

The shape is copied rather than developed and the scale economy kicks in. There is relatively little assembly and the finishing isn't slowed down by dozens of corners, so I expect this to be an economical design to produce. Assessing how much quicker a set would be is a vital consideration in costing the design rather than costing it on the basis of the one-off prototype.

LAMINATING

The components for the back legs are made from 2⅛in (54mm) stock, planed and thicknessed to around 2in (50mm). The tapered shapes are initially sawn on the bandsaw and planed to the finished size, using a

tapered jig to take the pieces through the thicknesser. This process, which I have read about but not tried before, works well enough. Selecting straight grain is essential to prevent chattering in the planer and to maintain the structural integrity of the laminate. My choice of PVA for laminating is sometimes questioned, although I haven't had problems with creep. One factor is that I leave laminates clamped up for 24 hours before taking them out of the mould. By this time the glue is pretty much dry. The gluing up and basic clean-up of a set of dry laminates takes about two hours, leaving at least six hours a day. If a table is included in the project, it can be constructed during laminate drying time. After removing from the mould, one side of the leg can be planed and run against the bandsaw fence to prepare the basic component.

The seat is a gentle curve and can be made either from two thicknesses of ¼in (6mm) ply, or three thicknesses of ³⁄₁₆in (4mm). I found the back more problematic, and had to cut kerfs in the panels halfway through their thickness, to persuade them to take up the shape.

• **The back curved rebate**

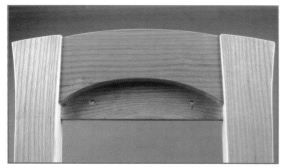

• **End-grain of leg laminations**

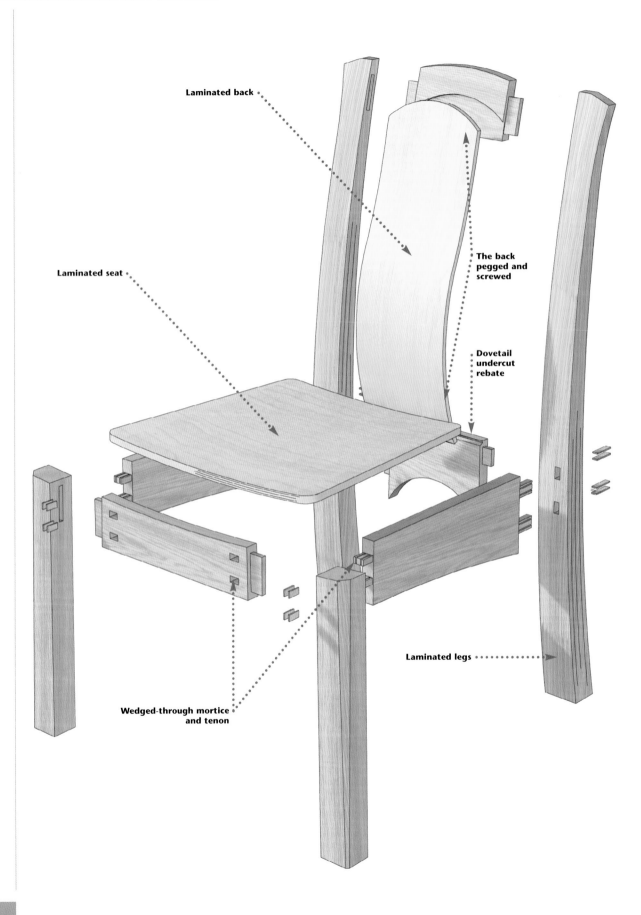

Laminated back

Laminated seat

The back
pegged and
screwed

Dovetail
undercut
rebate

Laminated legs

Wedged-through mortice
and tenon

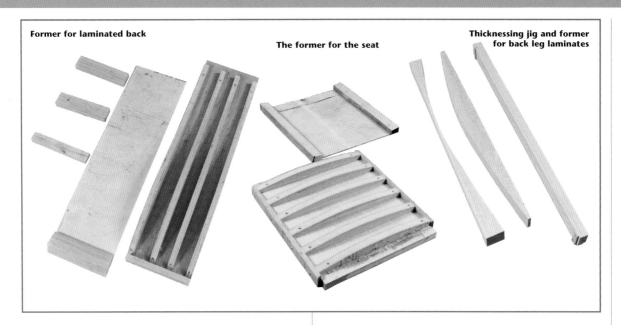

Former for laminated back
The former for the seat
Thicknessing jig and former for back leg laminates

The kerfs must be staggered, to avoid creating a weak point. One side effect of this is that the curve is not fair as it bumps around the kerf points, but, for an upholstered back it is perfectly adequate.

JOINT MAKING

All the rails are shaped, but they begin as rectangular components, otherwise marking out and joint cutting would be very difficult. The mortices are cut with shaped shims supporting the legs at the right angle. After years of making more traditionally constructed chairs, it feels odd to be morticing only one of the front legs.

The side rails are set at an angle in line with the splayed back legs, but the mortices in the back legs are cut parallel to the inside edge of the legs.

Curved support shims are prepared to support the legs on the morticer bed, and the joints are cut partway through from each side to prevent breakout.

• Dovetail-shaped rebate to take the shape of the back

The mortices in the front rail are cut at an angle to the horizontal; a simple tapered shim allows the rail to be held at the required angle to the morticer fence.

Again the joints are cut partway through from both sides. The outside ends of the through mortices are cut, to a slight taper, with a mortice chisel to a marked line. The wedges in the tenon force it into the dovetail-shaped mortice providing the joint with great strength. The tenon cheeks for the front and back tenons were cut on my tenoning jig. This uses a router and can only produce right-angled shoulders. I cut the required angles on the shoulders on the bench saw, with the mitre guide set to the correct angle and stops on the fence clamped to enable safe and accurate holding of the work. The haunches are sawn on the bandsaw and finished by hand.

FITTING THE DOUBLE TENONS

The bulk of the waste between the tenons is removed with a bandsaw, and the joints trimmed to a push-fit. The slits for the wedges are cut at an angle.

• Wedged-through tenons on the back

That means that the wedges, when fitted, are perpendicular to the end of the tenon. The tapers on the front legs can be bandsawn and planed; the tapered chamfer is cut on the planer, with the fence set at 45°, beginning the cut with the foot of the leg on the outfeed table. Several small cuts are preferable to a few hefty ones.

The chamfer is finished with a hand plane. Shaping the back legs again begins with the bandsaw, cutting to a line marked off a template. I finished the shaping with a spokeshave and bench plane. Both back rails are rebated to take the back panel. A simple template is made for the router guidebush to follow, to form the curved rebate. This must be done before sawing the top curve, while there is still something to clamp the template to.

The bottom rail rebate is routed and undercut with a dovetail cutter to take the angle of the back panel. Finally, the side and back rail curves are sawn. The curves for the seat are scribed directly off the laminated seat panel and sawn.

• **Side view showing the back profile**

Bevelled inclines are marked onto the side rails from these curves. After sanding all the components, slight chamfers are planed on all the arrises with block planes and a spokeshave.

ASSEMBLY

A full, dry assembly is made to check that everything fits. This is a good time to shape the back and seat panels. I find that allowing for the tolerance on upholstered panels tends to be a bit of a guess. The fabric on this panel is thick, pure wool and rather heavier than the fabric I initially planned. In the event, it took two of us wrestling with it on the floor to persuade it to go in; what we call 'a snug fit'.

I recommend sanding the edges off ply panels before sending them to the upholsterer – used sanding belts are ideal for this.

The finish is thinned polyurethane applied before assembly; avoid areas to be glued and cut back with a palm sander. There are four gluing operations: back legs and rails, side rails to back legs, front rail and front legs. To achieve accurate fit with the wedges, thickness a strip of wood to the exact width of the mortice, and bandsaw wedges off this. Getting them to go in straight when the joint is clamped up can be tricky, as space for tapping them in with a hammer is restricted. After assembly I clean off the joints with a belt sander, which I find the best way to achieve a good result. To level off the feet, put the chair on the bench saw and, checking that the seat is level front and back, scribe around the feet with a small strip of wood and pencil. These are planed in as necessary and the feet are chamfered.

After cleaning up the chair, apply another coat of polyurethane, especially to cover the areas sanded in the cleaning-up process. Finally, a couple of coats of neutral Black Bison Liberon wax are applied using a ScotchBrite pad, and then buffed off. The back is fitted with No. 6 screws and the holes plugged with $\frac{9}{32}$in (7mm) pellets. Fixing blocks are attached to the insides of the side rails to screw the seat on.

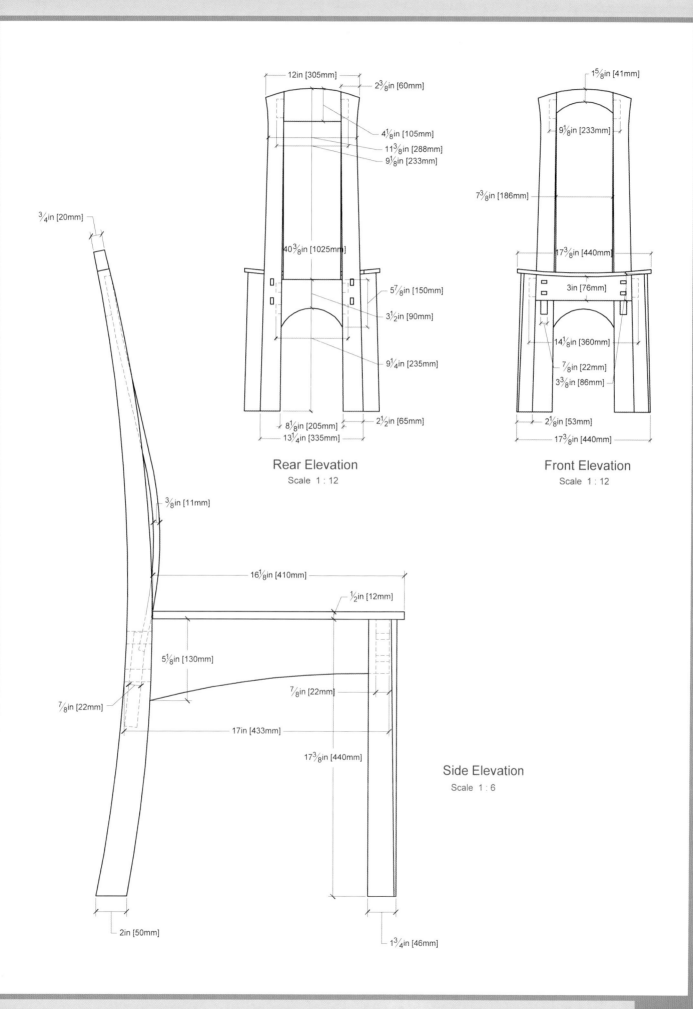

12in [305mm]
2³⁄₈in [60mm]
4¹⁄₈in [105mm]
11³⁄₈in [288mm]
9¹⁄₈in [233mm]
40³⁄₈in [1025mm]
5⁷⁄₈in [150mm]
3¹⁄₂in [90mm]
9¹⁄₄in [235mm]
8¹⁄₈in [205mm]
2¹⁄₂in [65mm]
13¹⁄₄in [335mm]

Rear Elevation
Scale 1 : 12

1⁵⁄₈in [41mm]
9¹⁄₈in [233mm]
7³⁄₈in [186mm]
17³⁄₈in [440mm]
3in [76mm]
14¹⁄₈in [360mm]
⁷⁄₈in [22mm]
3³⁄₈in [86mm]
2¹⁄₈in [53mm]
17³⁄₈in [440mm]

Front Elevation
Scale 1 : 12

³⁄₄in [20mm]
³⁄₈in [11mm]
16¹⁄₈in [410mm]
¹⁄₂in [12mm]
5¹⁄₈in [130mm]
⁷⁄₈in [22mm]
⁷⁄₈in [22mm]
17in [433mm]
17³⁄₈in [440mm]
2in [50mm]
1³⁄₄in [46mm]

Side Elevation
Scale 1 : 6

BREAKFAST CHAIR

An all-wood chair that is both comfortable and economical to make

• **The thinking behind this chair was to make bespoke chair-making more affordable**

FOLLOWING SEVERAL enquiries about kitchen dining suites, I was prompted to consider making a practical, all-wood chair. My aim was to produce four chairs within a normal working week of 40 hours. The chair had to be comfortable, compact and economical to produce, a contemporary design, and capable of adaptation to individual client requests without re-jigging the frame.

DESIGN

The principle advantage of this construction is the strength of the joint in the deep back section – rather a crunch point for a chair. Removing the need for stretchers also makes the design look cleaner.

The kick-out on the back legs makes it difficult to tip back on these chairs which would, of course, be bad for them. Both the seat and splats are sprung to gentle curves, enough to add significantly to comfort.

The frames are 2⅛in (54mm) ash throughout, with the rails resawn to thickness. The seats are brown oak and sawn to ½in (12mm) before thicknessing to ⅜in (10mm) for gluing-up.

Three sections are used for each seat and the joints, biscuited. The timber is face and edged and, to enable the most economical selection, thicknessed to the biggest sizes the wood will allow.

LEGS

As they are the most difficult, the back legs are marked off first, using a template. These were marked ⅟₆₄in (2mm) oversize, with an extra 1⅛in (40mm) at each end to allow for fitting to the spindle template, of which more shortly. Some of the front legs can come out of the back leg offcuts, while shorter lengths can be used for rails. The back splats are bookmatched. Having resawn the various rails and splats, everything can be thicknessed slightly oversize, to allow for settling and final truing-up before marking out can begin. Even in well-seasoned timber, some stresses are likely to be relieved by resawing, and these need to be allowed to do their thing. A couple of days in a warm workshop will probably do.

The front legs are tapered and this can be done in any number of ways. A spindle jig could be set up for this, or a tapering jig for the bench saw.

Cutting the slight tapers on the back legs is less straight-forward because of the curves. I cut these on the surface planer, starting the cut with the foot of the leg in front of the cutter. Screwing a simple handle onto the foot of the legs – using the same hole that fitted them to the spindle jig – keeps this operation safe.

SHAPING BACK LEGS

An MDF template is made for spindle-shaping the back legs. Two curves are cut into a single template: one for the front profile, the other for the back. An extra 1⅝–2in (40–50mm) is left on each end of the leg blanks to allow for screwing to the template. The wide template does not flex and gives you plenty to hold on to a long way from the cutters.

I used a 5in (125mm) four-knife rebating block with the scribing cutters removed, together with a guide on a ball-race bearing. A cage guard was set up; mine unfortunately doesn't have an extraction port but I'm not sure how effective it would be anyway.

Lead-in and lead-out points are essential and I simply used strips of 2 x 1in (50 x 25mm) wood, rounded the ends on the bandsaw and clamped them to the spindle table. The work is fed towards the cutter block, running against the lead-in point and carefully offered up to the cutter. With a firm grip and steady feed, run the leg along the cutter until the lead-out point comes into play and the work is run out along it. Most care needs to be taken when feeding in and out. The finish from the four-cutter block was good, similar to that from a two-knife planer, so needed some sanding.

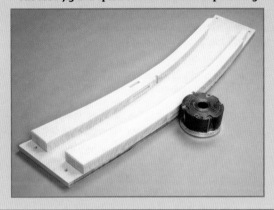

• **The MDF jig and spindle block used to shape the legs**

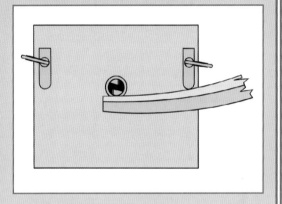

• **Lead-in and lead-out blocks or points are essential**

Remove ⅛₄in (1mm) with each pass and finish with a finer setting along the whole length of the leg when the required taper is reached.

MORTICES

The template used to mark out the back legs also serves as a rod for marking out the mortice and crest rail positions; only one mortice is needed in each front leg. The front, back and side rails are marked for mortice and tenons, and a sliding bevel is set for the angle of the splayed front and back legs, to mark the shoulders of the front and back rail tenons. This setting is also used to mark the through mortices on the front rail.

• **Through tenons are used for the front joints**

• **The splats are screwed to the back rail**

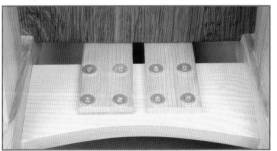

• The splats are tenoned into the crest rail

• Front rail joints before glue-up

A template is made to scribe off the shape of the side rails and the position of the curved shoulder at the rear of the side rails. Even though the tenons will be cut on the spindle moulder against a stop, this marking out helps to keep track of what you are doing and prevent angles being machined the wrong way round.

A tapered batten the same ratio as the splay on the legs is prepared, and the front and back rail ends are cut so that the tenons will be parallel to the shoulders. The pieces are set out so that, at this stage, all the tenons are the same length. All the mortices, including the double through-wedges, are cut on the morticer, and the same tapered batten is used to shim the front rail to the right angle, with the mortices cut partway in from front and back to prevent breakout.

No shims are needed for the front legs as the mortices are parallel to the front. Curved shims are needed for the back legs in two planes:

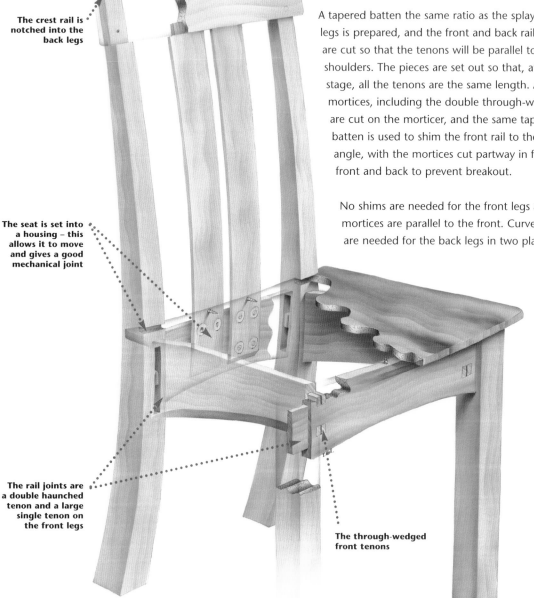

The crest rail is notched into the back legs

The seat is set into a housing – this allows it to move and gives a good mechanical joint

The rail joints are a double haunched tenon and a large single tenon on the front legs

The through-wedged front tenons

• The side rail mortices and tenons

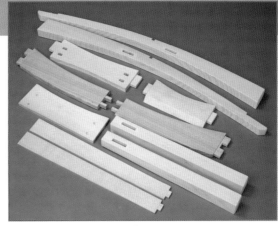

• Everything ready for the glue-up

firstly, to support the back of the leg on the morticer table while cutting the twin mortices for the side rails, and the connecting trench for the tenon haunch; secondly, to shim out the front of the leg from the fence while cutting the single back rail mortices.

TENON BLANKS

I cut the tenons on the spindle moulder, but the rails are quite wide and the joints could be cut with the router, running the fence along the end of the rails.

The indispensable tapered shim is pressed into service again to pack out the rails to the right angle for tenoning. A plywood sub-table with fence and cam-lever hold-downs makes an invaluable addition to the main sliding table on the spindle moulder, giving plenty of support for the work right up to the cutters.

TENONS AND WEDGED MORTICES

Tenons

A routing jig is needed to cut the curved shoulders at the rear of the side rails. This is screwed to the side rails at points that will be cut away when the rails are shaped.

A template follower is fitted to the router and the depth of a twin-flute cutter set to the tenon cheek. The distance between the shoulder and the jig is sufficiently small to allow the curve to be scribed straight off the leg template. The haunches are bandsawn and the waste between the tenons removed with the router running against the ends of the tenons.

The front rail tenons are again spindle-moulded or routed and inset ⅛in (3mm) from the sides. The tenon cheeks are bandsawn; work from the top down, cutting all the top cheeks, then reset for the next cut. The waste is removed with a router, again running the fence against the ends of the tenons.

Wedged Mortices

The mortices in the front rail need to be wedged and are marked using the sliding bevel, with lines ¹⁄₁₆in (1.5mm) outside the mortices. At this stage, all the joints are checked for a good fit and labelled.

• Tenons cheeks were cut on the bandsaw

• The wedge slots were also cut on the bandsaw

• Cutting the curved tenon shoulders on the rear of the side rails

• **The back leg mortices and the back rail joints**

The tapered shim can be screwed to this, with a sacrificial strip clamped between the work and the shim to prevent breakout. With the out-feed fence on the spindle set back, the in-feed fence is set so that the twin tenoning discs project by the length of the tenon. By clamping the rail in place on the sub-table up to the in-feed fence, the work is led into the cutters to cut the angled tenon.

TEMPLATES

Templates are prepared to mark out the shapes of the front, back and side rails, and seats. As I had made a full-size mock-up that screws together, I could remove the required piece, draw around, and replace it.

These shapes are simple and easy to cut on the bandsaw, then sand, so I did not make moulding jigs for them, but if someone were to order 30 chairs, for a chapel say, it would be worthwhile spending a couple of days jigging it all up.

The front legs and rail assemblies are dry-fitted to mark the curve for the sprung seat, and bandsawn when still assembled. The notches for the crest rails are marked and bandsawn into the back legs, the top of which are angled to relieve the corner.

The crest rail/splat joints are small mortice and tenons; ⁵⁄₃₂in (4mm) wide mortices are routed into the crest rails and the splat tenons bandsawn to fit and a taper is cut on the leg side of the splats. The crest rails must be shaped and sanded, and drilled for fitting to the back legs.

CHAMFERS

A full dry assembly is made to check everything out. The crest rails are scribed in to ensure a good fit on the front of the leg.

At this stage, the chair seats are sprung into shape with a couple of small G-clamps holding a batten over a block of wood. This is offered up and the notches that will let the seats into the back legs are marked off. The seat notches are cut with a tenon saw and the waste chiselled out.

Tapered chamfers are planed on the outside corners of the front legs and a ⅛in (3mm) chamfer routed all round the back legs. A deeper chamfer is routed to the outside lower edges of the side rails.

The remaining arrises are slightly eased off with a sanding block, before sanding all surfaces to 120grit on the linisher, sealing and palm sanding to 240grit. The seats are Danish oiled and the frame sealed and waxed.

ASSEMBLY

The assembly sequence begins with the side and front rails. These are clamped up and wedges fitted. At the same time, the back leg and rail assemblies and splat/crest rail assemblies, can be glued up. When dry, the wedges and projecting tenons are sanded off and the surfaces sealed.

The side frame/front rail assembly is glued to the back leg assembly and then the front legs are glued on, with the crest rail screwed into position. The splats are gently drawn into position on the inside of the back rail with G-clamps and screwed in place.

The seats are sprung into position and screws fitted into the splats and the front rail, set 2⅜in (60mm) either side of the centre and close enough together to prevent the seat from splitting. No glue is used to fit the seat, leaving it free to expand and contract over the front legs and in the back leg notches.

All the screw holes are fitted with ⁵⁄₁₆in (8mm) pellets which I made no particular attempt to hide. No one I have spoken to about this design has objected to them and most people seem to think they are an attractive feature.

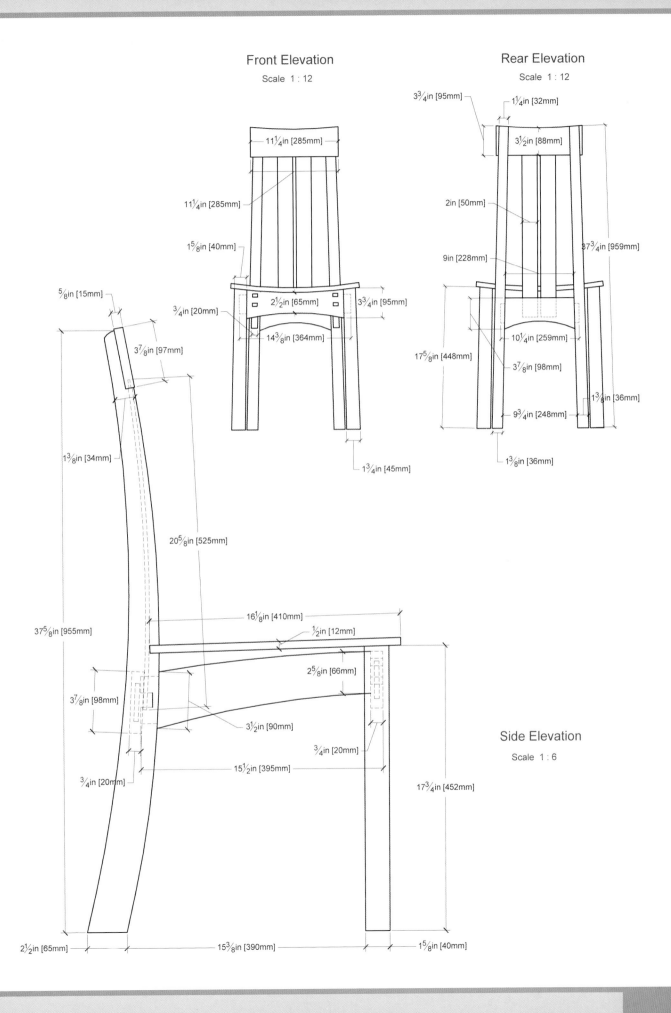

Front Elevation

Scale 1 : 12

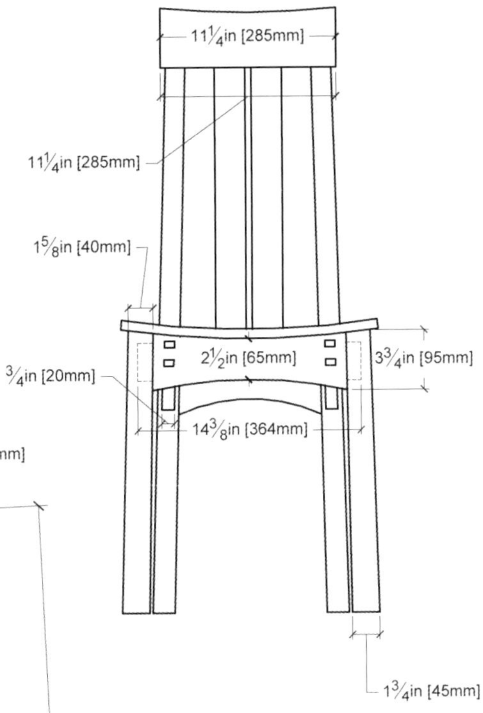
11¼in [285mm]
11¼in [285mm]
1⅝in [40mm]
2½in [65mm]
3¾in [95mm]
¾in [20mm]
14⅜in [364mm]
1¾in [45mm]

Rear Elevation

Scale 1 : 12

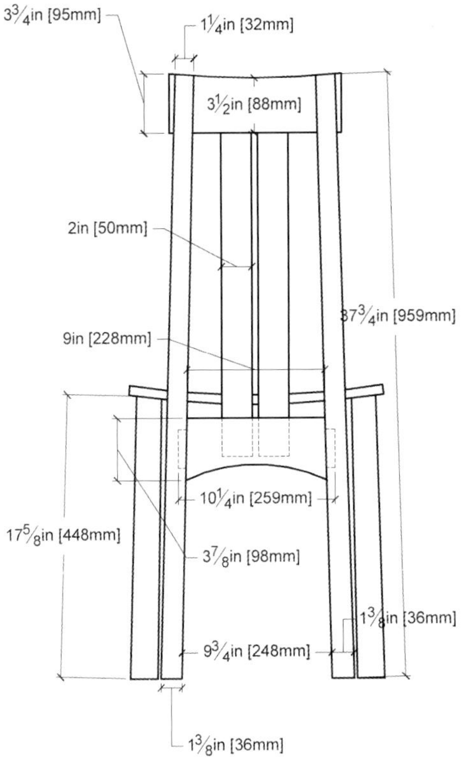
3¾in [95mm]
1¼in [32mm]
3½in [88mm]
2in [50mm]
37¾in [959mm]
9in [228mm]
10¼in [259mm]
17⅝in [448mm]
3⅞in [98mm]
1⅜in [36mm]
9¾in [248mm]
1⅜in [36mm]

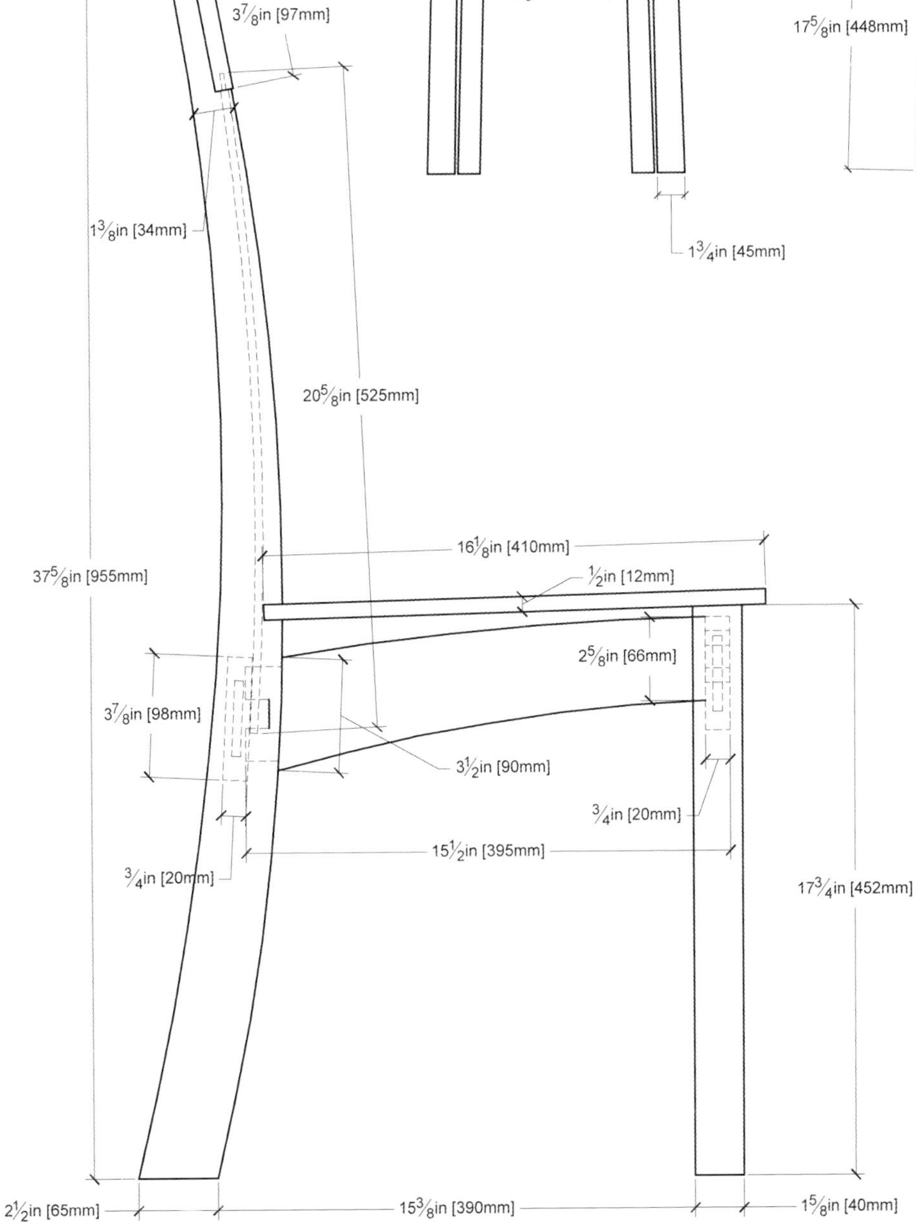
⅝in [15mm]
3⅞in [97mm]
1⅜in [34mm]
20⅝in [525mm]
16⅛in [410mm]
½in [12mm]
37⅝in [955mm]
2⅝in [66mm]
3⅞in [98mm]
3½in [90mm]
¾in [20mm]
15½in [395mm]
¾in [20mm]
17¾in [452mm]
2½in [65mm]
15⅜in [390mm]
1⅝in [40mm]

Side Elevation

Scale 1 : 6

ARTS & CRAFTS CHAIR

This set of oak chairs is part of the same suite as the spectacular 'Craftsman Style' dining table in oak on page 80

• **The legs are parallel on their inside faces, but the outsides are tapered.**

• **The flexible sawn back slats mould themselves to the back of the sitter**

I MADE THESE chairs – part of a commissioned suite – after seeing some contemporary interpretations of Gustav Stickley's work.

DESIGN

A more vertical back than my usual chairs was specified, with a shallower curve in the lumber support; this is comfortable and also encourages one to sit up straight! There is a conspicuous use of through-wedged mortice-and-tenon joints, and pegs in brown oak to contrast with the French oak frames. The legs are parallel on their inside faces but the outsides are tapered.

MAKING FURNITURE

BACK LEG SHAPING

Using a spindle moulder

An MDF template was made of the leg profile; this served as a template for making the spindle-moulding jig and as a rod for marking out the joints.

The back legs are bandsawn from planed blanks ⁵⁄₆₄–⅛in (2–3mm) oversize. These are clamped to an MDF template cut to the precise shape of the outside and inside of the legs.

The template is about 7in (180mm) wide, and is fitted with toggle clamps to firmly fix the leg in place. Mould one side, then fit the leg to the other side of the template to finish the profile. The advantages of this – rather than simply making a template the same shape as the leg – are that no screws are needed to fix the workpiece to the template, and it gives you plenty to hold onto without getting your fingers near the cutter block.

Clamp blocks to both ends of the spindle table to provide points to feed the work into and off the cutter block. I used a 5in (125mm) rebating cutter with a bearing guide in preference to a ring fence. This is a system that router users will be familiar with, but on a bigger scale and correspondingly able to handle larger work.

The final job in shaping the back legs is to taper them from top to bottom on the surface planer and after morticing.

• **The spindle jig for shaping the legs.** Note the registration blocks

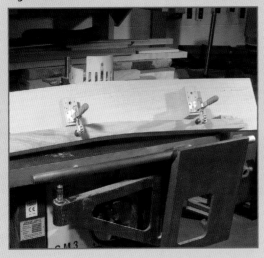

• **A rebating block with a bearing guide is used,** similar to a routing technique

This is only slight, but gives the chair a more sophisticated feel and, in conjunction with the inverted curve in the crest rail, it helps to create the sense that the chair back narrows towards the top.

The flexible sawn back slats mould themselves to the back of the sitter. The seat is notched around the back legs, butting up to the base rail, leaving a detail of the top of the base rail between the upholstery and the back slats.

CONSTRUCTION

The vertical legs make construction easier, as no angled tenons are used except in the double through-wedged joints, where the side rails join the back legs. Even here, the construction is simplified by the more vertical back, as the shoulder of the side rail is straight, rather than curved. The latter requires a jig to rout the curved shoulders, so this design saves that operation.

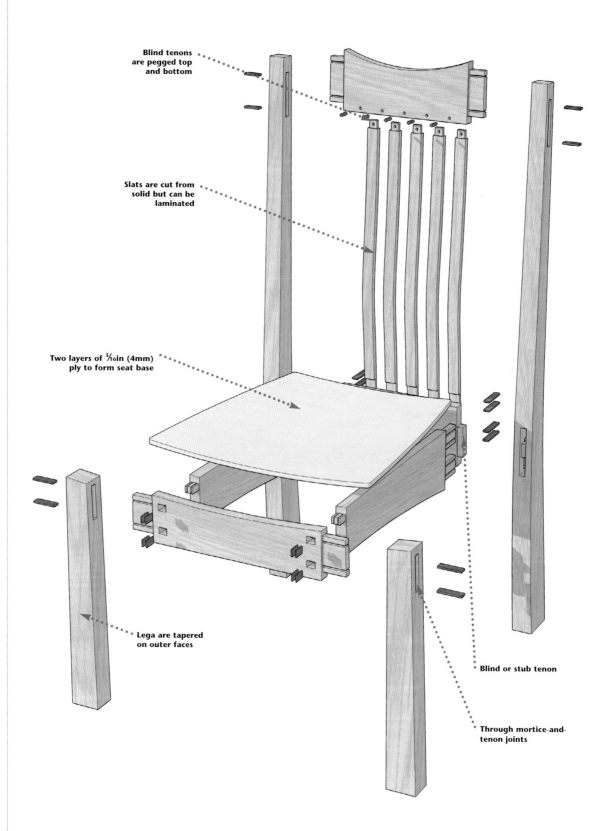

**Blind tenons
are pegged top
and bottom**

**Slats are cut from
solid but can be
laminated**

**Two layers of 3/16in (4mm)
ply to form seat base**

**Lega are tapered
on outer faces**

Blind or stub tenon

**Through mortice-and-
tenon joints**

MORTICING

For a job of this nature, involving six chairs, I find a bandsaw and a bench-top morticer are essential to keep the project moving at a reasonable pace. Although the outlay for even a basic morticer might seem a luxury if you are not selling your work, the cost in relation to the time saved and the quality/value of the finished furniture makes it more than justifiable.

One advantage of batch making is that jigs for various operations can be used effectively. The back legs require chocking at the right angle on the morticer, and offcuts from cutting out the leg blanks come in handy here. Once set up for one leg, all six can be morticed, the template reversed, and the other six done. The through mortices are cut from both sides of the joint to prevent breakout.

When the machining is complete, the outsides of the mortices need to be opened up by hand to form a wedge, or dovetail shape. When fitted, the wedges will open out the tenons to fill the tapered mortice and create a joint with the combined strength of a dovetail, and mortice and tenon.

TIMBER SELECTION

French oak was used throughout with brown French oak for the wedges, pegs and plugs, to accentuate the constructional details, and ⁵⁄₃₂in (4mm) WBP (weather-and-boil-proof) ply was used to laminate the seats.

MARKING OUT

The cutting list for the legs and rails is prepared. These are all cut as rectangles to enable easy joint making, and shaped after the joints are fitted. The joints are marked out on the first chair and checked carefully. These are then used as a rod for the subsequent chairs.

HAND FITS

There is a haunch joining the twin tenons into the back legs, which is routed between bandsawn cuts.

• **The back joints of chairs can be the most stressed joint, so a double tenon does make a lot of sense**

• **The back slats are tenoned into the underside of the crest rail, screwed and plugged at the bottom**

The twin through mortice and tenons into the front rails are also bandsawn and routed to fit. Stub tenons are cut on the base rail and single through-wedged tenons fit the crest rail and front rail to the legs.

TENONS – SPINDLE MOULDER

As the only angled tenons are on the rear of the side rails, these can be cut simply by packing them out with a tapered shim. On the spindle moulder, tenons can be cut with slot cutters. My 6in (150mm) diameter cutters will cut 2in (50mm) long tenons, adequate for most furniture applications, including these chairs. Spacers are used to set the thickness of the tenon. These are stacked and the spacers themselves can be held together and checked against the mortice as a guide, but a trial tenon will need to be cut and offered up to the mortice before going ahead with all the joints. Once set up, all the joints will be exactly the same, something I never quite achieved with routing jigs or bandsawn tenons, and with perfectly matched shoulders.

RAIL SHAPING AND LEG TEMPLATES

I did not make a prototype for this chair, as it was developed from existing designs, examples of which I had to hand in the workshop. However, having made the joints for all six chairs, I modelled the shaping on No. 1 first, gradually working the curves and tapers down until they felt right from all angles and the other five were copied from No. 1. A mould for laminating plywood chair seats was used to form the seats; this is a two-part mould – a curved base and a plywood caul – that is clamped over the two ⁵⁄₃₂in (4mm) ply sheets. I also tried the seat and clamped the back slats in place to check for comfort and detailing. This is the

phase of making where visitors are pressed into trying and commenting on the design and comfort of different chairs. A cushion is used to simulate the feel of the upholstery.

FINISHING

With the shaping of all six chairs complete, they can be disassembled and sanded in preparation for finishing. A mixture of roughly one-third Danish oil, one-third polyurethane and one-third white spirit was applied, allowed to dry and cut back. I use a spirit-based matt polyurethane varnish. The joints could be masked off but careful application with a smallish brush makes this time-consuming process largely unnecessary. The slats are sanded and sealed at this stage.

ASSEMBLY AND FITTING

The back assemblies are glued up first, followed by the front rail and side rail assemblies. When dry, the double through-wedged tenons in the front rails are cleaned up, and the front-side assemblies can be fitted to the back leg assemblies. Finally, the front legs can be fitted. Each glue-up requires fitting wedges, which should be prepared in advance from a strip of brown oak thicknessed to fit the mortices. The most efficient programme of gluing will depend largely on how many sash cramps are available.

The slats are tenoned into the crest rail and scribed off against the base rail. They are notched around the base rail, and screwed and plugged.

• **Slot cutters are used to cut the tenons**

• **The advantage of using a spindle to cut tenons is the accurate repeatability**

• All the tenons are through-wedged with contrasting brown oak

• Tenons through the front rail, as opposed to going into the leg, makes for very strong construction

At their base, the slats are cut to follow the curve of the base rail. Before fitting, the slats are sorted into sets of five where the curves are most similar, and the tenons marked while they are aligned. The tenons are pegged with brown oak dowels after assembly; ³⁄₁₆in (5mm) square strips of brown oak about 6¾in (170mm) long were roughly chamfered with a Stanley knife and hammered through a steel plate with a ³⁄₁₆in (5mm) diameter hole drilled into it. Once cut to about 1³⁄₆₄in (27mm) lengths, one end can be slightly tapered to ease the pegs into ³⁄₁₆in (5mm) holes drilled through the crest rail and slat tenon. These are glued and hammered into place.

FINISHING AND UPHOLSTERY

Upholstery is always difficult to judge, even on a simple seat like this, and variations in foam density of ¼in (6.5mm) in thickness make a substantial difference to the feel and appearance of a chair. The thickness of foam and type of fabric determine how much allowance needs to be made around a drop-in seat to give a good fit. Even reducing the depth of a seat from front to back by a tiny amount can make a surprising difference. In this case, 2in (50mm) foam was used and pulled really tight by the fabric to give a firm seat.

• The seat mould – the seat is made from two sheets of ³⁄₁₆in (4mm) ply

• The seat in the press

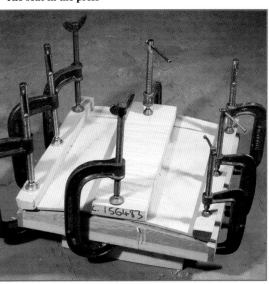

• A finished seat blank on a dry assembled chair

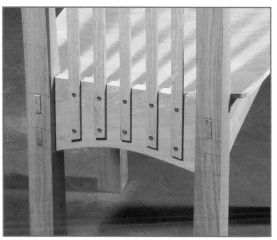

• Detail of slats, where they meet the base rail

I was happy with the result and felt the chair complemented the Arts and Crafts feel of the matching table faithfully.

The exterior of the chair is now sealed with the same polyurethane and Danish oil mix, and cut back. A further coat was applied after the back slats were fitted and finally a clear beeswax was applied with a synthetic wire wool pad.

Finally, the seats were fitted to the frames with screwed blocks.

• The haunches on the tenons are cut out on the bandsaw

• The haunches are cleaned up using a router

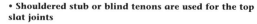

• Shouldered stub or blind tenons are used for the top slat joints

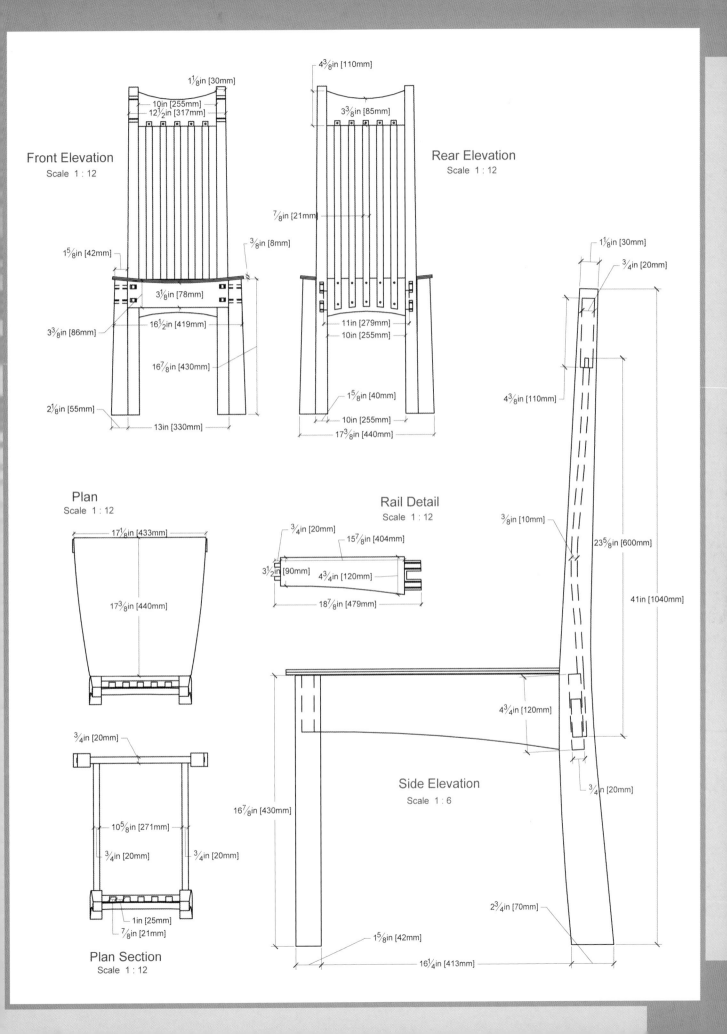

Front Elevation
Scale 1 : 12

1⅛in [30mm]
10in [255mm]
12½in [317mm]
1⅝in [42mm]
⅜in [8mm]
3⅛in [78mm]
3⅜in [86mm]
16½in [419mm]
16⅞in [430mm]
2⅛in [55mm]
13in [330mm]

Rear Elevation
Scale 1 : 12

4⅜in [110mm]
3⅜in [85mm]
⅞in [21mm]
11in [279mm]
10in [255mm]
1⅝in [40mm]
10in [255mm]
17⅜in [440mm]

Plan
Scale 1 : 12

17⅛in [433mm]
17⅜in [440mm]

Rail Detail
Scale 1 : 12

¾in [20mm]
15⅞in [404mm]
3½in [90mm]
4¾in [120mm]
18⅞in [479mm]

Side Elevation
Scale 1 : 6

1⅛in [30mm]
¾in [20mm]
4⅜in [110mm]
⅜in [10mm]
23⅝in [600mm]
41in [1040mm]
4¾in [120mm]
¾in [20mm]
2¾in [70mm]
16⅞in [430mm]
1⅝in [42mm]
16¼in [413mm]

Plan Section
Scale 1 : 12

¾in [20mm]
10⅝in [271mm]
¾in [20mm]
¾in [20mm]
1in [25mm]
⅞in [21mm]

TABLES

HAYRAKE TABLE

A reworking of the Arts & Crafts 'hayrake' idea for modern living

THIS ENGLISH oak (*Quercus* sp.) dining table was commissioned for a large riverside cottage on the Thames. The client required an extension, from approximately 83in to 118in (2100mm to 3000mm). This involved adding two leaves and was easy to accommodate from an engineering point of view. The top is drawn out to cantilever over the ends of the fixed frame.

The 'hayrake' stretcher arrangement is associated with the Arts and Crafts movement and this, together with heavy sections, pegged mortice-and-tenon joints, and chamfers, gives the table a strong, uncompromising feel. Proportion is just as important in this type of work as in more delicate furniture, and I spent a lot of time resolving the design. An 1/8 scale model was made and later oversized components were gradually worked down until they felt just right.

TIMBER PREPARATION

My main concern was finding clean, sound 4in (100mm) stock for the legs. I prefer air-dried stock for anything over 2½in (63mm); kiln drying often causes 'honeycombing' (not visible until the board is opened up) – the fibres pull apart inside the timber if it dries out too fast, an effect similar to cutting through a honeycomb. If present it can render a board more or less useless.

• The hayrake stretcher table was a favourite with members of the Arts and Crafts movement, particularly with Sidney Barnsley

The boards I had selected registered a consistent 9–10% mc (moisture content) throughout their thickness, when sawn through, which is fine. The surface of the boards had 'catspaws' on it. These are clusters of very small knots which, in moderation, I quite like. As this is subjective, I did check the client agreed with me before committing myself, and she didn't want a solid oak table that looked like veneered MDF. I feel just the same about solid wood, so I could see we were going to get on.

The top was prepared from 2⅛in (54mm) stock, some of it a bit uneven but it planed down to a clean 1½in (38mm). As the top alone weighs about 220lb (100kg) I was pleased it was not thicker. For one thing it looks right and, secondly, the leaves themselves are quite heavy and would be awkward for one person to fit if they were much thicker. The top boards were quarter sawn and 9% mc, though kiln dried. Hayrake and top frames were also 2⅛in (54mm) stock, though I ended up using some 1in (25mm) already in stock for the long side rails. This matched perfectly and allowed greater freedom in selecting for the top.

As the side rails are braced by the runner guide assembly, nothing was lost structurally and the project still came nicely within budget.

TIMBER SELECTION

Quarter-sawn stock is advisable for extending table tops, as the main tops and leaves have relatively little or no supporting framework to keep them flat. In order to ease timber selection, the grain usually runs across rather than along the top on extending tables. Even if the wood was available to create a very large top, with the grain running long ways, the grain would only follow through when the table was fully extended with the leaves in the right order.

Timber selection is obviously important to the overall appearance of a table, but balance rather than blandness is the aim. Production line, solid wood furniture looks uniform because all the products need to match each other, and the samples in the catalogue. People also need to be able to buy pieces from the same range at different times. As makers of one-off furniture we can be more creative with timber selection and finishes.

CONSTRUCTION – FIRST STAGE

The leaves needed to be made up of boards of equal width, namely two times 9in (approximately 225mm). The main tops are made up of 9in wide boards as well, with the two outer panels being graduated down to form the required overall length. The tops are butt jointed and fitted with biscuits. Both faces are planed flat with a jointer plane and the edges trued up but left slightly oversize for final calibration after fitting to the frame.

TOPS – SETTING UP

I prefer wooden alignment lugs to the solid brass 'bullets and sockets' that can be bought for the purpose, as I find those awkward to fit and in use they can cause damage to the edges of the table leaves. My wooden shop-made ones are effectively oversized biscuits set in to ¼in (6mm) slots routed into the edge of the table tops. The grain runs across the lug to stop it breaking off. The slots for these are routed from the underside of the table top, so when everything is assembled, the underside of the top is flush.

When the leaves and tops are pushed together, the edges can be cut straight and true by clamping a long batten in place as a guide for either a portable circular saw or a router.

The top is skimmed off with a sharp jointer plane and all the configurations tried to ensure everything fits, then the top removed for sanding and chamfering. The butting edges are sanded and slightly rounded over to a radius of about ¹⁄₁₆in (1.5mm). There are two reasons for doing this: firstly, it makes the extensions more comfortable to handle – a heavy leaf combined with a sharp arris is potentially quite dangerous; secondly, the top will inevitably move around a bit and be subject to wear, and a slight round-over is a lot more forgiving than a sharp edge that is worn or does not quite line up.

THE FRAME

The frame – legs and top rails – are marked out for haunched mortice-and-tenon joints. The legs fitted comfortably under my morticer for a ½in (12mm) mortice. These joints are too deep to cut with a router, and biscuits are certainly not strong enough in this context. If a morticer is not available, the bulk of the mortice waste can be removed with a drill and the sides and ends cleaned up by hand. Drill ⁵⁄₁₆in (8mm) holes for the pegs in the legs and clean up any breakout inside the mortice. I use my Startrite 352 bandsaw set with a standard ¾in (19mm) skip-tooth blade to cut tenon cheeks and the bench saw aided by the sliding carriage to cut the shoulders. This is efficient and accurate.

• **Underframe construction with extension leaves off**

Whatever equipment you have, it is useful to devise a system for frequently repeated jobs – such as mortice and tenons – so time is not wasted reinventing the wheel for each project. It's also interesting to see how versatile simple machines – such as a bandsaw, jointer, planer and portable router – can be when used in conjunction, often curtailing the need for more sophisticated and expensive equipment. This is particularly relevant in one-person, one-off workshops where profit margins are small and overheads need to be minimalized.

CONSTRUCTION

Clamp up the frame dry and, having checked all is square, push the ⁵⁄₁₆in (8mm) drill bit in to mark the position of the holes in the mortices. Label each joint so they can be reassembled in the same position. Do note, though, these are the positions of the holes in the mortice, not the tenons. For the draw pegs to work, the hole in the tenon has to be offset by about ³⁄₆₄in (1mm) in the direction of the tenon shoulder. When the tapered peg is hammered in, it will 'draw' the joint up tight. While the frame is clamped up, the exact size of the hayrake can be measured and a template made in MDF of the stretcher framework.

HAYRAKE STRETCHER

The hayrake stretcher arrangement is remarkably efficient, as it transmits force in all the right

directions while causing minimal interference with leg room. The drawback is it is quite difficult to do. The joints are all draw-peg mortice and tenons. Dovetails join the ends of the stretcher rails to the legs, but the main assembly comes first. All components are machined well over length initially. The right-angled T-members are mortice and tenoned first, and are through-wedged as well as pegged. Once prepared and dry assembled, the 45° angled Y-rails are marked out, by laying them on the assembly and marking directly off the frame.

The mortices are cut perpendicular to the rails and bored for pegs, as per the main table frame. I cut the tenons using the mitre guide on the table saw. This was laborious and if I were to repeat the job I would make a router jig. The complete dry-fit of the hayrake will be the acid test of your joinery skills. There's not really anywhere to go with this, it either fits or it doesn't. Hence the value of a full-size template.

LEGS

The inside corners of the table legs are scribed onto the ends of the hayrake frame. The dovetails slide in and must all go in one direction. A routing jig, a simple plywood right angle, is clamped in position and, using a template follower on the router base,

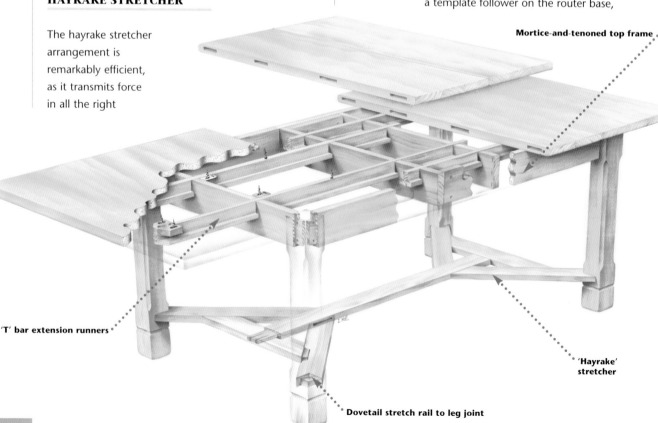

Mortice-and-tenoned top frame

'T' bar extension runners

'Hayrake' stretcher

Dovetail stretch rail to leg joint

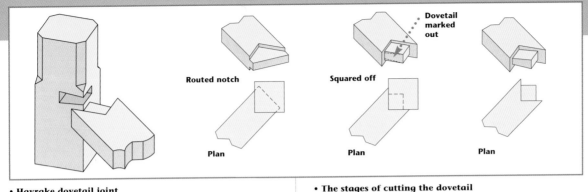

Routed notch

Plan

Squared off

Dovetail marked out

Plan

Plan

• Hayrake dovetail joint

• The stages of cutting the dovetail

notches are machined onto the hayrake ends. This is the first stage of cutting the dovetail joints. The sides of the notches will butt up to the sides of the legs. The remainder of the dovetails are cut by hand, pared down to the marked line with a chisel. The positions of the dovetails are scribed off the stretcher frame onto the legs and the joints notated. Remove the bulk of the waste from the dovetail sockets with a plunge router, then pare to the scribed line by hand. Check each joint in turn for fit, then do a complete dry run of the whole table frame. Notches are marked for the guide rails in the end frames and centre frame members. Construct a simple biscuit-jointed box to fit the central rails after the main table frame has been assembled.

FRAME

Once the hayrake framework and dovetails for the legs are cut, the whole frame is dismantled and fine sanded. The chamfers are routed using a bearing guided 45° chamfer cutter. The underside of the top rails and the edges of the legs are all stopped chamfers and are marked for length before routing. The ends of the stopped chamfers are trued up with a chisel, either using a guide block or free hand to a marked 45° line.

On the hayrake the chamfers are continuous. The 90° and 135° angles are finished with a chisel. The 45° corners are finished with a small fishtail carving gauge. A V-grooving cutter is used to rout the detail around the feet. The legs are clamped together and one side

of all four legs is routed in one pass. This operation is repeated for all four sides. A heavy chamfer is machined around the bottom of the legs to allow for easy movement across a carpet and give a slight visual lift.

The bases of the guide rail notches are cut with a morticer but a router would do as well and the remainder removed on the bench saw.

After a final check, the frame is ready for assembly. The long top rails and legs are first glued into two sub assemblies and the end rails and hayrake assembled in a third operation. The guide-rail box is screwed in to complete the frame. Once everything is cleaned up, coat the whole frame with white spirit to check for glue marks which will show up as pale patches. The top of the frame is planed flush. The T-section rails are made up allowing a ³⁄₃₂in (2mm) margin above the top of the frame. These are then fine sanded and waxed and checked for fit. Any high spots in the notches will be shown up by the wax and can be eased off.

TOPS

Once the rails are moving in and out freely, the tops can be planed to a tolerance of ³⁄₆₄in (1mm). It's important that any future movement in the frame or table top, or settling to the floor, does not cause the top to bind on the frame. The tops are fitted with screws on the inside ends of the guide rails and slot screw blocks on the outside ends. An expansion plate

• Leg detail

• Draw dowel detail on mainframe tenons

• Wooden lugs on extending leaves

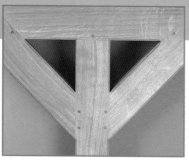

• Hayrake stretcher with draw-dowelled joints

• Slotted block on end of guide rails aids expansion and acts as stops

• Lever fitting for locking tops together

is fitted at the centre of each guide rail. These also act as stops, preventing the tops being pulled out too far.

FINISHING

I'm under no illusions about the working life of a family dining table and have finished this one accordingly. A piece of furniture like this should be associated with friends, children, enjoyable meals and celebrations, not endless anxiety about damaging the precious thing. Consequently I gave it three coats of polyurethane: the first two thinned with white spirit, the final one applied with a rubber and full strength. These were gently cut back between coats and Danish oil was applied with a cloth on a daily basis until delivery.

GLUING THE HAYRAKE

To enable the assembly to be clamped up, glue 45° clamping blocks in place. The edges of the rails are sanded prior to gluing up but the faces are planed and sanded after assembly. Likewise, the chamfers are routed after gluing up and the pegs are turned. These are slightly tapered along their length and brought to a point at the narrow end to enable them to find their way through the holes without causing any damage. Before I had a lathe I did this job by hand, whittling ⅜in (9mm) square stock with a Stanley knife. Given the time, though, it's rather pleasant doing it by hand. The 'T's are glued, pegged and wedged first.

Originally draw pegs were used to pull in joints and hold them with neither glue nor clamps. There are some excellent examples over my head, as I write, in the roof beams of my workshop that have been there for at least 200 years. However, I use glue and clamps. It's reassuring, though, even when a frame is clamped up, a draw peg will still produce a satisfying additional squeeze of glue from the joint. The pegs are sawn flush and the hayrake is hand planed flat and sanded once the glue has set.

• Clamping the dovetail joint

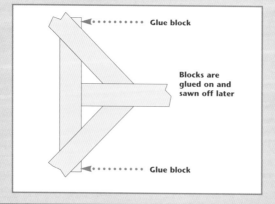

• Gluing up the hayrake

Glue block

Blocks are glued on and sawn off later

Glue block

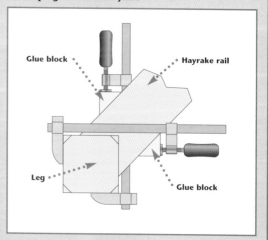

Glue block — Hayrake rail

Leg — Glue block

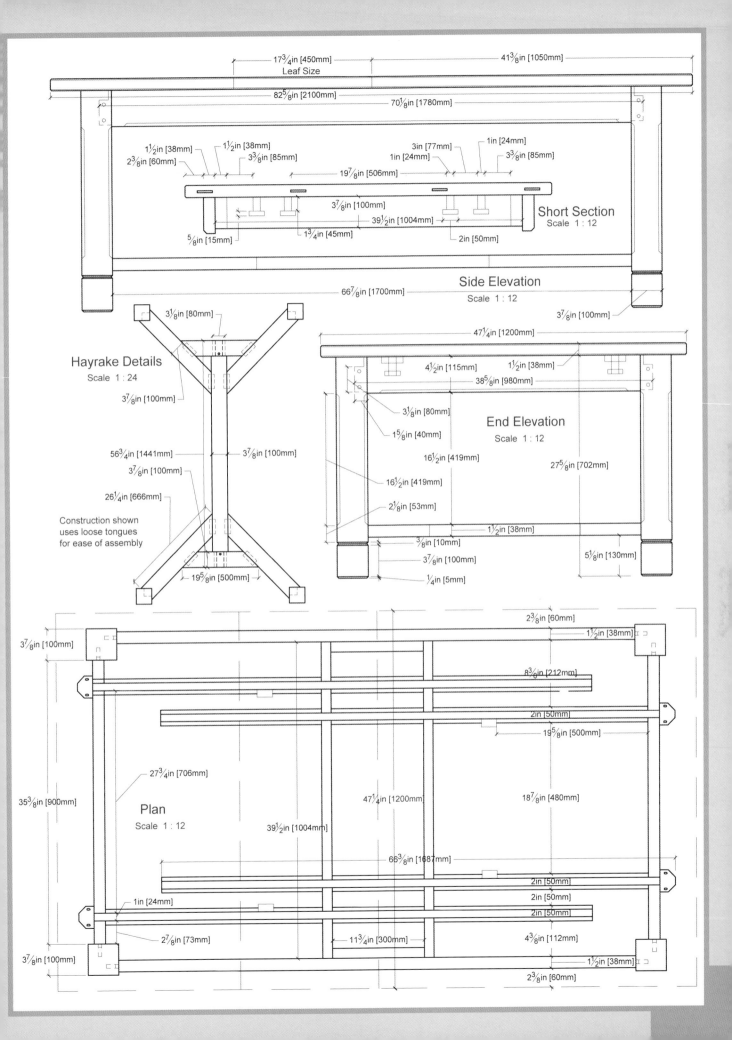

17¾in [450mm]
Leaf Size
41⅜in [1050mm]
82⅝in [2100mm]
70⅛in [1780mm]

1½in [38mm]
1½in [38mm]
2⅜in [60mm]
3⅜in [85mm]
3in [77mm]
1in [24mm]
1in [24mm]
3⅜in [85mm]
19⅞in [506mm]

Short Section
Scale 1 : 12

3⅞in [100mm]
39½in [1004mm]
⅝in [15mm]
1¾in [45mm]
2in [50mm]

Side Elevation
Scale 1 : 12
66⅞in [1700mm]
3⅞in [100mm]

3⅛in [80mm]
Hayrake Details
Scale 1 : 24
3⅞in [100mm]

47¼in [1200mm]
4½in [115mm]
1½in [38mm]
38⅝in [980mm]

3⅛in [80mm]
End Elevation
Scale 1 : 12
1⅝in [40mm]

56¾in [1441mm]
3⅞in [100mm]
3⅞in [100mm]
16½in [419mm]
27⅝in [702mm]
16½in [419mm]
26¼in [666mm]
2⅛in [53mm]

Construction shown
uses loose tongues
for ease of assembly

1½in [38mm]
⅜in [10mm]
3⅞in [100mm]
5⅛in [130mm]
19⅝in [500mm]
¼in [5mm]

2⅜in [60mm]
1½in [38mm]
3⅞in [100mm]
8⅜in [212mm]
2in [50mm]
19⅝in [500mm]
27¾in [706mm]
35⅜in [900mm]
Plan
Scale 1 : 12
47¼in [1200mm]
18⅞in [480mm]
39½in [1004mm]
66⅜in [1687mm]
2in [50mm]
1in [24mm]
2in [50mm]
2in [50mm]
2⅞in [73mm]
11¾in [300mm]
4⅜in [112mm]
3⅞in [100mm]
1½in [38mm]
2⅜in [60mm]

COFFEE TABLE

Neoclassical columns and plain detailing create a timeless table

THE CLIENT for this coffee table project was the daughter of a former neighbour in a village where I once rented a workshop and cottage. Although they now live in the New Forest, the family was keen to commission me for three pieces: a coffee table, a chest of drawers and a corner cabinet – the New Forest suite. Most of the preliminary work was done by correspondence and telephone conversations and the table design – turned legs, shelf and an overhanging top – was largely suggested by the client.

TIMBER AND CONSTRUCTION

With the exception of the table legs, the whole job was made from 1in (25mm) prime quality French oak. The legs were laminated from 2⅛in (54mm) boards.

TURNING THE LEGS

My first woodwork teacher had an 'experimental' approach to woodturning. His demonstrations were usually prefaced by 'stand back gentlemen, I have not tried this before'! At one demonstration he turned a bowl blank from a whirling square of 2in (50mm) thick mahogany from the face side in one pass. He used a parting tool that sent big triangular sections flying off in all directions.

The little I know about proper turning was learned from the instructor in the woodwork shop of a rehabilitation centre for people with visual impairments, where I was working as an assistant instructor. My skills are still rather limited and depend far too much on abrasives.

The main problem with this design is keeping a crisp corner where the round section meets the square. Once all four legs have been turned, they are put back on the lathe to be accurately matched and finished. The legs are coated – excepting masked areas for the tenon shoulders – with thinned polyurethane. The turned section can be cut back on the lathe and brought up to a full oiled finish.

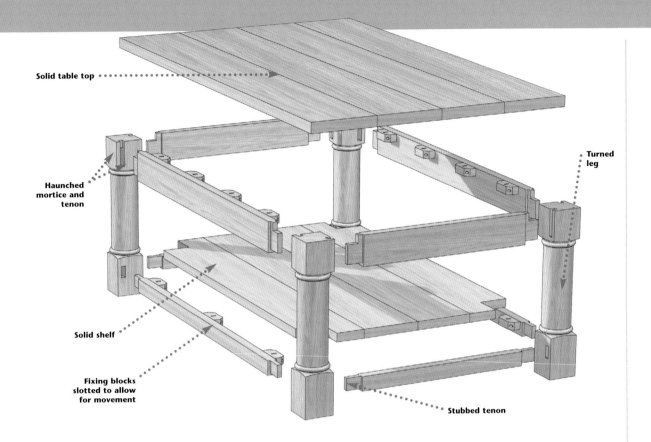

Solid table top

Turned
leg

Haunched
mortice and
tenon

Solid shelf

Fixing blocks
slotted to allow
for movement

Stubbed tenon

My trust in boards more than about 2⅜in (60mm) thick is limited as they are inclined to crack. Careful matching and jointing produced a result which, while not invisible, is certainly not obvious. All the joints were arranged to run along the length of the table.

LEG SECTIONS

The square sections at the top and bottom of the legs are not as wide as the diameter of the turned beads (if they are the same, the top and bottom would look disproportionately heavy). To achieve this the blank is prepared with reduced square sections at both ends, and a thicker square for the turned section. This is best achieved with a well-tuned bandsaw and finished with a skew-angle rebate plane. It is important to cut the haunched mortices before preparing this relief, otherwise supporting the leg in the morticer becomes awkward. I also prepare the tenon cheeks at this stage. My router tenoning jig continues to produce good, but slow, results.

TOP AND SHELF PANELS

The top and shelf panels are glued up at the same time as the leg blanks, faced off and sanded. The frame rails are also planed and dimensioned.

Everything is left longer than the final required lengths so the length of the frame, in proportion to the top and shelf, can be altered. It is usually adequate to judge the fine-tuning of these measurements from scale elevation drawings, and I was not prepared to do a full-size mock-up of the whole table.

• A neat chamfer to take the sharp arris off the edges

• Slotted fixing block to allow for movement of the shelf

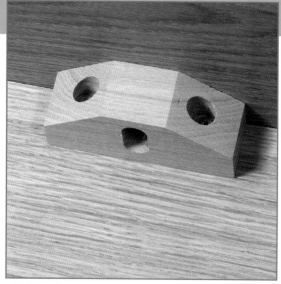

• Similar blocks are used to fix the top

Proportioning the leg turnings, however, did begin with a full-size pine mock-up. Apart from resolving the visual dynamics, it was also an opportunity to work out the sequence of turning operations.

• Mark Ripley polishes the coffee table with its final coat of oil

DRY ASSEMBLY

A dry assembly of the frame is set up next. The shelf is measured and the notches marked out. These should be able to tolerate expansion across the width and, for neatness, a corresponding relief on the adjacent faces. I allowed ⅜₆in (2.5mm). The notch is cut on the bandsaw, sanded and the edges are chamfered with a file.

The bead details at the base of the table legs mean the shelf is captive and has to be inserted during assembly. Consequently, all the parts need to be finished before gluing up.

FINISHING

All surfaces are sealed with two coats of thinned polyurethane, cut back between coats, and a third applied to the table top. Three coats of Danish oil are applied at 24-hourly intervals. After two or three days, the whole piece is lightly burnished and given one final coat of oil.

The shelf and top are fitted with small blocks made with a cross-grain slot. These slots are routed in 2¾ x 7in (70 x 175mm) strips of wood. They are then cross cut on the bandsaw to 1⅛in (30mm) widths and bored with a ⅛₆in (4mm) hole and ⅜in (10mm) counterbore to sink the screw head. The corners are bandsawn and the piece sanded on all sides. Central blocks fitted to the end rails do not need to be slotted.

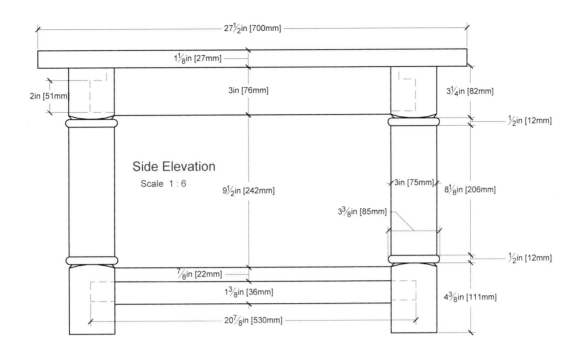

Side Elevation
Scale 1 : 6

27½in [700mm]
1⅛in [27mm]
3in [76mm]
2in [51mm]
3¼in [82mm]
½in [12mm]
9½in [242mm]
3in [75mm]
8⅛in [206mm]
3⅜in [85mm]
½in [12mm]
⅞in [22mm]
1⅜in [36mm]
4⅜in [111mm]
20⅞in [530mm]

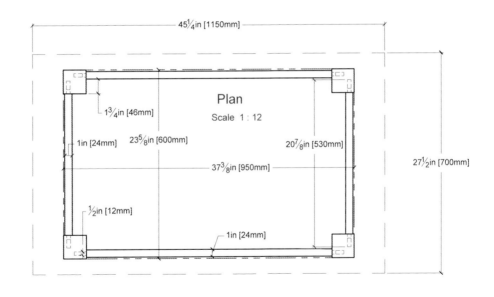

Plan
Scale 1 : 12

45¼in [1150mm]
1¾in [46mm]
1in [24mm]
23⅝in [600mm]
20⅞in [530mm]
37⅜in [950mm]
27½in [700mm]
½in [12mm]
1in [24mm]

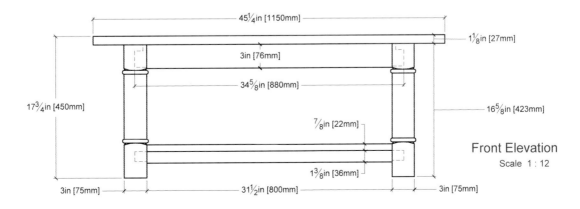

Front Elevation
Scale 1 : 12

45¼in [1150mm]
1⅛in [27mm]
3in [76mm]
34⅝in [880mm]
17¾in [450mm]
16⅝in [423mm]
⅞in [22mm]
1⅜in [36mm]
3in [75mm]
31½in [800mm]
3in [75mm]

LARGE OCCASIONAL TABLE

Advanced joint-making techniques and sophisticated design feature in this oak centrepiece

• **The upwardly curving arch gives lift to what is actually quite a low table**

THIS PROJECT renewed a long association with a large country house in southern England that was used as a retreat centre for many years, but recently changed ownership. I had completed several projects for the previous owners, including two chapel refurbishments and the furniture for two rooms used for solitary retreats. The whole house had been significantly modernized, but its use for retreat, prayer and reflection was continuing. My intention when designing the furniture was to connect the traditional construction of the space with a contemporary feel and spiritual simplicity (Four-door Cupboard, on page 114, is part of the same commission).

The design for the table is derived from a large refectory table I made in 2001. The principle difference is the stretcher rail arrangement. The upwardly curving arch gives lift to what is actually quite a low table for a centrepiece.

TIMBER

The project is made from French oak (*Quercus robur*). All the stock was waney edged in 1in and 2in (25mm and 50mm) boards. As the suppliers offered a machining service, I asked them to thickness the 1in (25mm) boards to ⅞in (22mm). They selected flat boards for this, and the result was an economical one from my point of view.

The legs for the table are made from some 3⅛in (80mm) thick boards left over from a project that was cancelled a couple of years ago, now workshop-conditioned to perfectly match the humidity of the chapel.

FRAME JOINERY

All the components are initially prepared as rectangular blanks. Much of the shaping is undertaken later, which makes marking out and joint-making much easier.

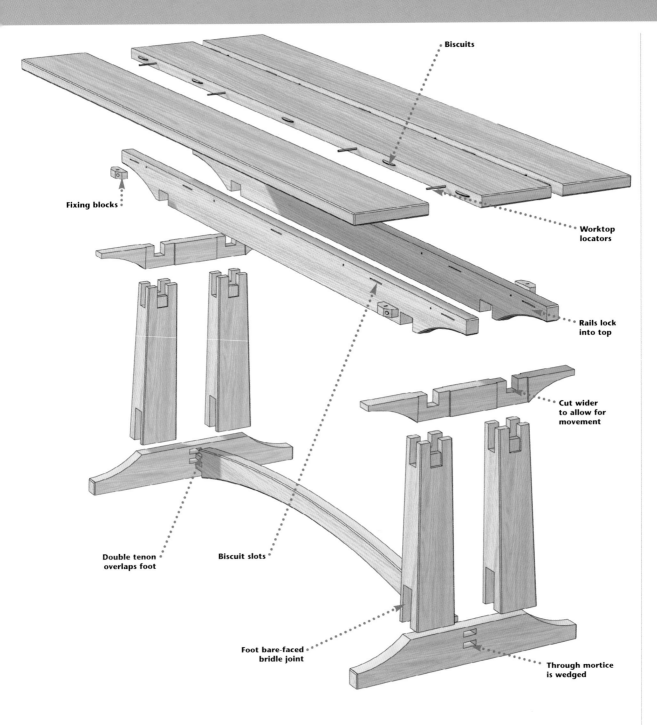

Biscuits

Fixing blocks

Worktop locators

Rails lock into top

Cut wider to allow for movement

Double tenon overlaps foot

Biscuit slots

Foot bare-faced bridle joint

Through mortice is wedged

However, the legs can be tapered at the outset, as the joints are cut using the inside faces as a working face. The end frame assemblies are marked out first, but before doing this, the bevels on the feet and top bearer rails need to be planed.

Two types of bridle joint are used in the leg assemblies. Firstly, the feet are joined to the legs with bare-faced bridle joints – as the leg tapers upwards it is not possible to slide the foot into a joint. At the top though, this is not an issue and one pair of full T-bridle

joints are used. These, in turn, are intersected by smaller cross halvings where the long top rails join the leg assemblies. The stretcher rail is jointed with through-wedged mortice and tenons.

Marking out is a straightforward process but needs to be performed in a systematic way to avoid mistakes or confusion; mark and make each stage of the joint making as you go: end frames, top rails and stretcher rail. Each stage is dry fitted and shaped before moving on to the next phase.

SUB-CONTRACTING MACHINING

There are various problems with sub-contracting machining, the primary one being that someone else is doing the selecting – something which most of us would probably regard as unacceptable. Another problem is the consistency of the machining quality itself with tearout or inaccurate edge planing. It can also be very expensive.

The planing of whole boards, however, is economical and actually helps with selection as you can see exactly what you've got before breaking out a cutting list. All that is required then is to surface and plane down to the finished thickness to remove any slight unevenness in the board. This not only saves a lot of time at the preparation stage, but radically reduces the amount of waste generated – a definite advantage, given that the disposal of trade waste is becoming an increasingly expensive problem.

LEG ASSEMBLIES

The joints in the legs are marked and scribed with a marking knife. I cut the bulk of the waste out on the bandsaw, running the inside face against the fence as all the joints are parallel to these. Paring back to the scribed lines with a wide chisel finishes the joint.

• **The top has the stretchers locked into it with bolts – you can just see the two strips here**

• **The foot has a gentle chamfered curve**

Obviously, there is no joint making as such in the feet, but it can be useful to fine-fit the joint by carefully planing the side of the feet.

The top rail shoulders are scribed directly off the legs. The waste can be removed with a router worked against fences clamped to the rail. Alternatively, you could do this on a bench saw, as I did. These joints can be fine-fitted by planing the sides of the legs until they drop down to the final depth.

TOP RAILS

The long, top rails are fitted over the top of the bridle joints in the tops of the legs. This looks like a Chinese puzzle by the time it is completed, but is actually simple enough if taken step by step.

One complication, however, is that the rails have to drop vertically onto the leg assemblies because once the stretcher rail is fitted they incline inwards. The faces of the bridle joints therefore have to be cut at an angle to the face of the legs.

• **The stretcher has a double wedged tenon which overlaps the end rail**

• **The worktop bolts that lock the top together**

This is achieved with tapered shims providing a support for a router. In fact, there are two shims, one for the inside of the leg, the other for the outside. To allow for movement in the top, the joint is cut about ⅛in (3mm) wider than the thickness of the top rails. These joints only locate the top rails – the top assembly is attached to the base frame with slotted blocks. The sides of the joints can be cut on the bandsaw, working from the inside edges of the legs, as they are vertical. After this, removing the waste from the top rails themselves is fairly straightforward using a circular saw.

STRETCHER RAIL

With the leg and top rail joint making complete and set up dry, mark out the shoulders of the stretcher rail. Select the wood for the stretcher rail carefully: the grain should follow the curve as closely as possible – it certainly shouldn't be fighting it. Complete joint marking before cutting the piece to shape. To make sure that the shape itself worked, and that the joint shoulders were exactly right, I prepared a plywood template. The double curve of the rail and the spaces it encloses can only be worked out three-dimensionally. Fences clamped to the rail enable a neat job to be performed by the router when it comes to cutting the joints.

The through mortices in the foot rails are cut on the morticer with wedged shims keeping the bevel against the fence. To prevent breakout, first cut two-thirds of the way from one side, flip over – remembering to turn the shims around – and cut from the other side. Open up the outside of the mortices by ⅛in (3mm)

• **The top bridle joint**

with a hand chisel to create a tapered mortice. This provides a space for the wedges to force the tenon into. The tenons are scribed directly off the mortice positions. As the tenons at this stage are parallel to the bottom of the stretcher rail, they can be cut on the bandsaw running the rail against the fence. Much of the waste between the tenons can also be removed on the bandsaw. The shoulders are finely cleaned up by hand.

Cutting the slots for the wedges is surprisingly difficult as the top of the rail, which is not slotted, gets in the way. In any event this should not be done until the dry-fits are finished; the sides of the tenon are inclined to snap off when taking joints apart.

CURVES

A number of curves are sawn at this stage – the scalloped relief on the feet, the long top rails and bearer rails, and of course, the stretcher rail. As with the top and bottom faces, the curves on the feet and bearer rails are bevelled. This is created by canting the bandsaw table to the correct angle using a sliding

• **The chamfer detail follows on the top edges**

• **Detail showing the interlocking of the top**

The curves are finished with a spokeshave. A dry assembly now, with the table tops set in place, gives an impression of the finished piece.

TOPS

The top panels are narrow enough even for my small planer thicknesser to prepare without having to use butt joints. These are fairly close to quarter sawn. I am not sure that I like large expanses of quarter-sawn oak and I have had one customer complain about all those medullary rays. If it is just off quarter sawn, you have nearly all the structural advantages of stability with a more subtle appearance. I have to admit that the joints between the tops – worktop locators threaded through the top rails – are a little unorthodox but they are very effective.

Boring the 1⅜in (35mm) holes to take the nuts and 'washers' has to be performed using a pedestal drill. The slots for the threaded rods are routed. Once bolted together, the top can be faced off and the edges aligned and chamfered. They need to be removed to plane the small chamfer on the inside edges of the tops and top rails and for finishing. Chamfers are also worked on the corners of the frame components.

FINISHING

The whole table is disassembled and sanded in preparation for finishing. A coat of thinned polyurethane is applied to all of the surfaces that will not be glued and cut back with a palm sander. This procedure shows up flaws in the surface while it is still easy to do something about it and provides a barrier to glue, which makes clean-up much more straightforward, and produces a fine surface for subsequent oiling or waxing.

ASSEMBLY

The end frames are glued up first. I considered pegging the bridle joints in the feet originally, but this is a huge gluing area and I decided there was little structural advantage. Also, I wanted to keep the whole piece as uncluttered as possible. The only other glued component is the stretcher rail; this needs to be clamped either side of the tenons to allow them to protrude through the foot rails and to provide access to fit the wedges.

Angled clamping blocks are taped to the bottom rails to aid the glue-up. The wedges are cut from a strip of wood the same thickness as the tenons. With the rail glued and clamped, the wedges are glued and tapped in with a hammer, taking care to align them properly. Cleaning up the dried joint is a real pleasure – all the work is revealed as a decorative structural detail.

Final finishing is a matter of preference. The base has three coats of neutral finishing wax while the top is built up with Danish oil and burnished.

I used synthetic wire wool saturated with Danish oil for a final burnish. When wiped dry with a cotton cloth, it leaves a beautiful low-lustre finish.

• **The table *in situ***

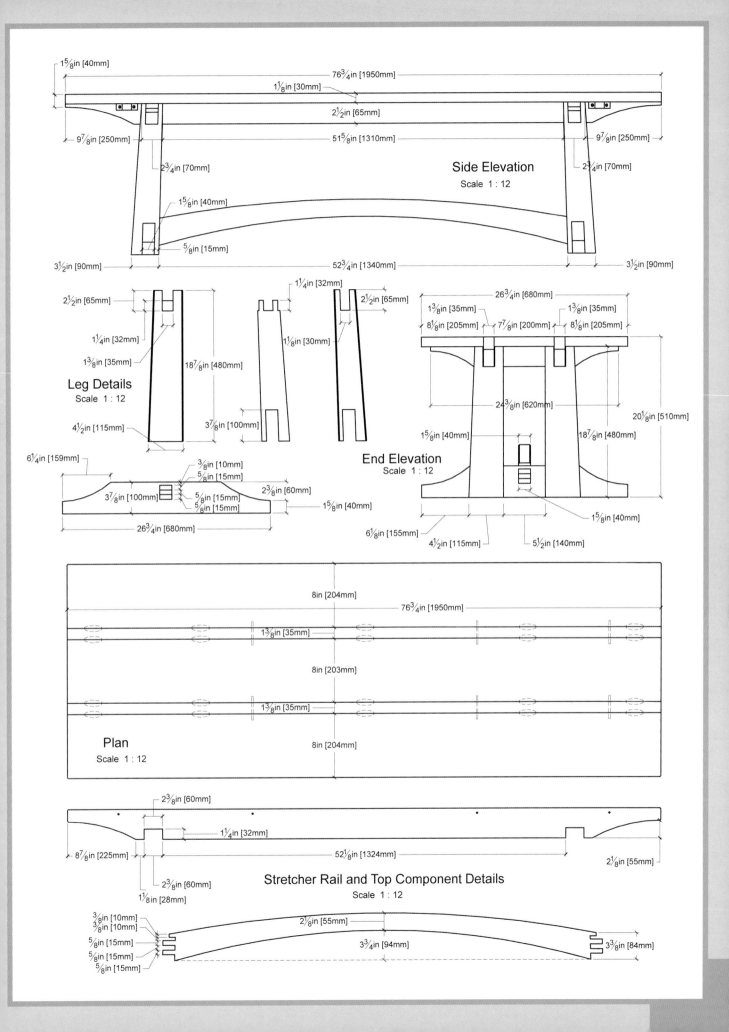

1⁵⁄₈in [40mm]

76³⁄₄in [1950mm]

1¹⁄₈in [30mm]

2¹⁄₂in [65mm]

9⁷⁄₈in [250mm]

51⁵⁄₈in [1310mm]

9⁷⁄₈in [250mm]

2³⁄₄in [70mm]

Side Elevation
Scale 1 : 12

2¹⁄₄in [70mm]

1⁵⁄₈in [40mm]

5⁄₈in [15mm]

3¹⁄₂in [90mm]

52³⁄₄in [1340mm]

3¹⁄₂in [90mm]

2¹⁄₂in [65mm]

1¹⁄₄in [32mm]

2¹⁄₂in [65mm]

1¹⁄₄in [32mm]

1¹⁄₈in [30mm]

1³⁄₈in [35mm]

18⁷⁄₈in [480mm]

Leg Details
Scale 1 : 12

4¹⁄₂in [115mm]

3⁷⁄₈in [100mm]

26³⁄₄in [680mm]

1³⁄₈in [35mm]   1³⁄₈in [35mm]

8¹⁄₈in [205mm]   7⁷⁄₈in [200mm]   8¹⁄₈in [205mm]

6¹⁄₄in [159mm]

3⁄₈in [10mm]
5⁄₈in [15mm]

3⁷⁄₈in [100mm]   5⁄₈in [15mm]
5⁄₈in [15mm]

2³⁄₈in [60mm]

1⁵⁄₈in [40mm]

26³⁄₄in [680mm]

24³⁄₈in [620mm]

20¹⁄₈in [510mm]

1⁵⁄₈in [40mm]

18⁷⁄₈in [480mm]

End Elevation
Scale 1 : 12

1⁵⁄₈in [40mm]

6¹⁄₈in [155mm]

4¹⁄₂in [115mm]

5¹⁄₂in [140mm]

8in [204mm]

76³⁄₄in [1950mm]

1³⁄₈in [35mm]

8in [203mm]

1³⁄₈in [35mm]

Plan
Scale 1 : 12

8in [204mm]

2³⁄₈in [60mm]

1¹⁄₄in [32mm]

8⁷⁄₈in [225mm]

52¹⁄₈in [1324mm]

2¹⁄₈in [55mm]

2³⁄₈in [60mm]

1¹⁄₈in [28mm]

Stretcher Rail and Top Component Details
Scale 1 : 12

3⁄₈in [10mm]
3⁄₈in [10mm]
5⁄₈in [15mm]
5⁄₈in [15mm]
5⁄₈in [15mm]

2¹⁄₈in [55mm]

3³⁄₄in [94mm]

3³⁄₈in [84mm]

CONTEMPORARY 'SLAB' TABLE

A heavyweight table that comes apart for ease of transport

• **The finished table, with complementary chairs in oak. Chairs of the same design are featured on page 30**

Chairs of the same design are featured on page 30

CONSTRUCTION

The construction of the table is unconventional. It comprises seven components: two tops, a top rail and four slab legs. These are all joined together with threaded stainless steel rods set into counterbored and plugged holes. The elliptical end profile created by setting a round plug into an angled surface echoes the elliptical handles used in furniture I designed and made for the same room a year previously.

O NE OF MY clients saw a laminated-back chair (see page 30) and a slab-end-style coffee table which I had exhibited in a show, and commissioned eight chairs and a refectory table, based on those designs.

In order to make the design work ergonomically, the table needed to be at least 94½in (2400mm) long but the client thought 87in (2200mm) was the maximum the room could take. I was pleased that they wanted a static table, as opposed to an extending one. An extending table is a different challenge, but a static table has a directness and simplicity that I find appealing as a design opportunity.

However, we were left with the problem of accommodating the legs of the sitters, especially at the ends. It was the client's idea to turn the slab legs inwards, and the design was developed through scale models, as it was difficult to visualize two-dimensionally.

The first realization was that inclining the legs and deepening the top rail created a very strong and simple structure, which obviated the need for a lower stretcher rail and left foot room unrestricted.

In practice, the table accommodates eight comfortably, as the chair was conceived as a more compact design than its predecessor, and had a smaller footprint, while maintaining the seat size and comfort of the back.

• **The central stretcher beam is an integral part of the top**

MAKING FURNITURE

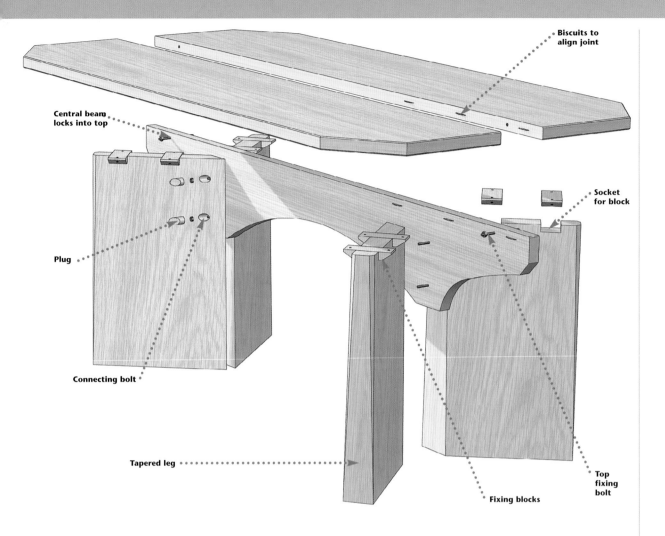

Biscuits to align joint

Central beam locks into top

Socket for block

Plug

Connecting bolt

Tapered leg

Fixing blocks

Top fixing bolt

TIMBER

The thick sections of the components, especially the legs, require careful selection at the buying stage if expensive waste is to be avoided. I was fortunate in finding well-dried 4in (100mm) thick boards with one square edge and about 12in (305mm) clean timber before the sap. 10ft (3000mm) lengths of this allowed the legs to be prepared with little waste;

• Only seven components make up the very direct, simple concept

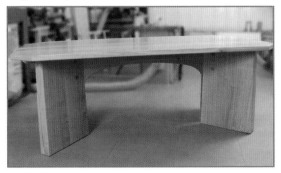

given the cost of prime 4in (100mm) oak, this was just as well. I also knew that there was plenty more in case of mishaps.

The 2in (50mm) for the tops and frame was also carefully selected, but with more allowance for selecting planed stock for the table top, I would like to have made the top from two 20in (510mm) widths; that, however, proved unrealistic. There is a single joint in each leg and in each half of the table top.

I am still coming to terms with metric measurements when buying solid timber. I suspect the relatively recent increase in the amount of French oak being brought in means that importers have started using the metric system for selling as well as buying. Some anomalies, such as 1in now being sold as 27mm mean that if, like me, you are used to mentally converting wood into usable board feet, you effectively get nearly 10% less than you expected.

• **Biscuits help align the top while bolts hold it all together**

More than once I have thought I had been sold short, when careful checking with a calculator and tape measure revealed that, strictly speaking, I hadn't.

PREPARATION

The first stage in making is the hard graft of machining the raw material into components. While ripping the 4in (100mm) board to sizes that I could handle, I burned out my portable circular saw!

The tops and rail were prepared into six planed boards, thicknessed to 1⅞in (48mm) allowing for final selection and planing of the four table-top members when they settled, one for the rail and one spare. I had someone with me on work experience for one day, and made use of the extra set of muscles to further plane and thickness the components.

• **Underneath, note the slot which takes the top fixing bolt and is covered by a capping piece**

MAKING TOPS

The tops are fine-thicknessed and made with biscuited butt joints, faced off and sanded. The edges are dimensioned and sanded all round.

LEG TAPER AND CONSTRUCTION

The leg stock was quarter sawn and of even colour, making the setting out for gluing easy. By making stopped cuts two-thirds and one-third along the board and then turning the piece around and planing in the opposite direction, a clean result can be produced safely. This process has to be carried out twice on each face to achieve the required taper.

Once the butt joints have been prepared, biscuit joints are cut off each face to produce a double row of biscuits in each joint.

After gluing, the faces are sanded. I used a pad sander with a batten supporting the narrow end to make the surface parallel with the sanding belt. The bevels were sawn on the bandsaw and planed true by hand.

Tapered chamfers on the outer edges are again cut on the surface planer. These components are heavy and, like any heavy woodwork components, are easily damaged yet need to be made to accurate dimensions. Obviously care needs to be taken in machining and lifting during such jobs.

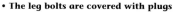

• **The leg bolts are covered with plugs**

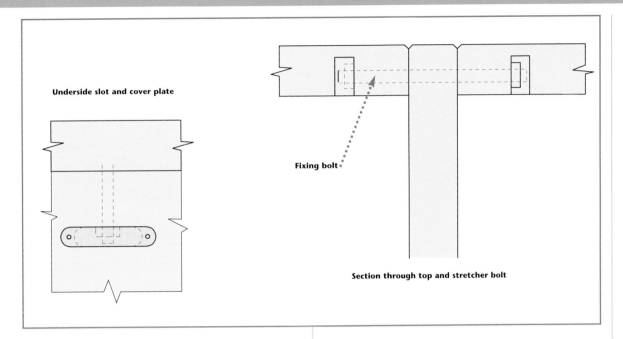

Underside slot and cover plate

Fixing bolt •

Section through top and stretcher bolt

STRETCHER RAIL

The legs and tops were set up on the workshop floor, and the stretcher rail positioned and supported between them. Fine-tuning of the positions of the legs and the cutaway corners on the tops can then be tried and tested. I tried out all seating positions with the prototype chair, in order to establish the optimum distance between legs, then the inside bevels were re-checked for alignment, and fine planed. The positions of the legs on the rail, then the curves, were marked, sawn to shape on the bandsaw and

finished with a spokeshave. The corner reliefs are then sawn with a portable circular saw and hand planed to finish.

BORING SET-UP

The positions for the top/rail bolts are marked on the table edges and rail. Routed slots cut on the underside of the tops give access for fitting the washers and nuts, and tightening them with spanners. These slots are 1⅛in (30mm) deep by 1⅝in (40mm) long with a further ½in (12mm) each end at ⁵⁄₃₂in (4mm) deep.

• The fixing blocks are screwed into sockets

• One of the bolts that locks the legs in place

Biscuit slots are cut in the table edges and rails to aid alignment. I used an 8mm (⁵⁄₁₆in) threaded stainless steel rod throughout and drilled ⅜in (10mm) holes with the hole slightly reamed with a countersink to make rod fitting easier.

Setting up for the legs/rail uses a similar technique to the top/rail joints with the complication that the leg joints are drilled at an angle. These were drilled freehand after careful marking. The holes in the rail are ½in (12mm) diameter to allow for rail movement. The nuts are fitted with socket wrenches.

LEGS/TOP BLOCKS

Fixing blocks are let into the tops of the legs to which the tops are screwed. I made a simple jig to rout a recess in the legs.

The eight blocks begin as a strip which is fitted to the recess. The central holes are marked and drilled before the individual blocks are cut off and tapered. Holes are drilled into the angled faces and countersunk before the blocks are sanded.

PLUGS

The plugs for the legs are individually turned on the lathe, beginning with a 5 x 1in (125 x 25mm) square blank, to allow enough length for easy handling. Initially the blanks are turned to cylinders and then to a taper and checked for fit. The bevel is marked from the table legs, and each one is individually fitted and numbered. The plugs project by ⁵⁄₆₄in (2mm) with a chamfer filed onto the outside edge.

Covers for the table-top slots are again made in a single strip before cutting off and fitting. They are drilled and countersunk to take No. 4 screws.

ASSEMBLY

At this stage a full assembly is set up. Cutting the threaded rod to length is done with a hacksaw and the ends are chamfered on a linisher, using an old belt to remove sharp edges and burrs and ease the fitting of the nuts.

- First the blocks are screwed to the tops of the legs. The assembly sequence is to set up the legs of one side, and place them in position on the floor.

- Push threaded rods with nuts and washers fitted to one end. The rail slides onto these and the opposing legs are fitted and bolted in place. The bolts are tightened with two inexpensive socket spanners.

- Next, the biscuits are fitted to the divider together with the threaded rods. Both tops are placed in position, and the washers and nuts fitted. When the alignments are correct, the nuts can be tightened.

- The ends of the table top and rail can be finely trued. The assembly will not be glued. The table is very heavy and yet in its knock-down form, I had no trouble delivering and setting it up single-handed.

Once the assembly has been successfully set up and numbered, it is taken apart for chamfering of the top edges, rail and feet.

FINISHING

The whole job is fine sanded and sealed with thinned polyurethane, three coats on the top cut back between coats, and one elsewhere.

A palm sander with 240grit silicon carbide paper prepares the sealed surfaces for three coats of Danish oil, then all that's left to do is a final assembly.

I recommend a bi-monthly dressing of teak oil on table tops. I've found that polyurethane is flexible, so it does not chip or craze and has excellent heat and moisture resistance. It also has UV protection and wood does not darken as much as it does under a pure Danish oil finish.

The legs and frames do not need quite so much work – a sealing coat of polyurethane and two to three coats of Danish oil will suffice.

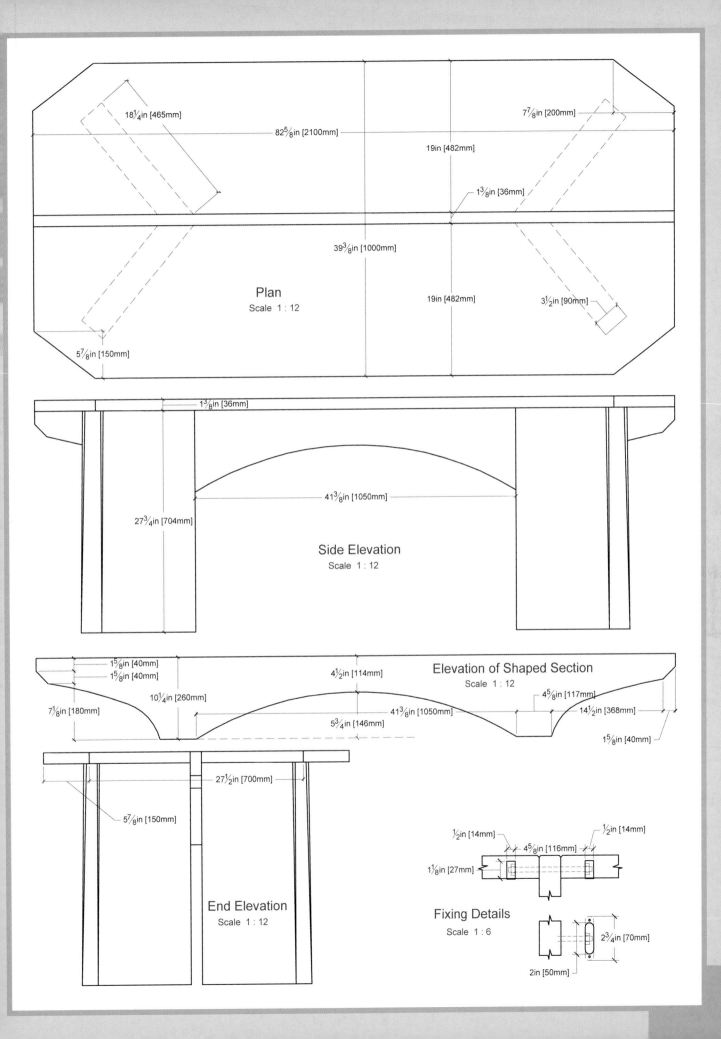

Plan
Scale 1 : 12

18¼in [465mm]
82⅝in [2100mm]
7⅞in [200mm]
19in [482mm]
1⅜in [36mm]
39⅜in [1000mm]
19in [482mm]
3½in [90mm]
5⅞in [150mm]

Side Elevation
Scale 1 : 12

1⅜in [36mm]
41⅜in [1050mm]
27¾in [704mm]

Elevation of Shaped Section
Scale 1 : 12

1⅝in [40mm]
1⅝in [40mm]
4½in [114mm]
4⅝in [117mm]
10¼in [260mm]
7⅛in [180mm]
41⅜in [1050mm]
14½in [368mm]
5¾in [146mm]
1⅝in [40mm]

End Elevation
Scale 1 : 12

27½in [700mm]
5⅞in [150mm]

Fixing Details
Scale 1 : 6

½in [14mm]
½in [14mm]
4⅝in [116mm]
1⅛in [27mm]
2¾in [70mm]
2in [50mm]

CONSOLE TABLE

Recessed handles set off this traditionally constructed side table

• **Designed for use in a gallery, this table had to complement other furniture in the room**

• **The solid shelf is supported by a stiffening batten**

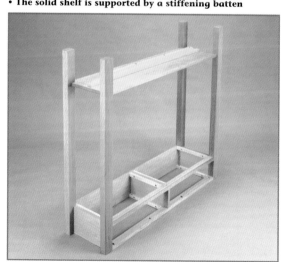

THE CLIENT who commissioned this table was looking for a piece to occupy a space in a room conceived as a gallery. Most of the time, however, it was used as a dining room, so the table was designed to complement a very simple, natural oak dining suite. As befits its gallery usage, the room is painted white and is very well lit, providing an unusually clear space to present the furniture. The client was keen to maintain the rectilinear design of the existing furniture, so I was allowed only the two shallow curves in the recessed handles, which perhaps gives them extra power.

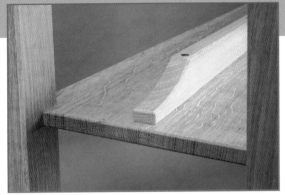

• **The shelf is tenoned directly into the legs**

TIMBER

French oak (*Quercus robur*) was used, mostly 1⅛in (27mm) boards and some 2⅛in (54mm) for the legs. I do not have the space for a proper timber store, and usually select and buy for specific projects, but inevitably a small stockpile develops. I made this table from an unprepossessing pile in the workshop, which yielded some good timber. As the timber was well conditioned and much of it part-machined, producing the cutting list was fairly straightforward.

THE DESIGN

To keep the design as simple as possible, the shelf is not set on a frame, but is tenoned directly into the legs, and a rail is screwed to the underside to provide additional stiffness, which is only visible from a very low viewing angle. The ends are set in from the legs; this creates a more three-dimensional look and makes the inside of the ends flush with the insides of the legs. A solid central divider is fitted between the front rails and back panel, leaving only the fitting of kickers to complete the cabinet for drawer fitting. Ends, back and bottom front rail are all mortice and tenoned, and the top rail is lap dovetailed into the front legs. Although working to a budget, we could afford traditional drawers with hand-cut dovetails.

The drawer linings were resawn from 1⅛in (27mm) and put in stick. A single piece is prepared for the drawer fronts so that the grain will run through and single biscuit joints run through both the top and the shelf.

JOINTS

These were all marked out together, in the order they were to be made:

• Leg mortices
• End panel, back panel and front lower frame tenons*
• Shelf tenons
• Top rail lap dovetails*
• Divider notches

* The rails are marked out so that the legs are ¾₄in (1mm) closer together at the front than they are at the back. In addition, the divider is planed to a slight taper, with the back being ⅟₅₂in (0.5mm) narrower than the front.

When assembled, the two openings for the drawers will open out slightly towards the back, easing the drawer fitting. Before assembly, the top rail also has transverse slots routed into it which will take screws for the top. This is done with the router running against a fence clamped across the rail, and supported at the back by the lower rail which is the same thickness. A ⁵⁄₃₂in (4mm) slot is machined for the shank of the screw, and a ¹¹⁄₃₂in (9mm) counterslot is routed for the head.

• **With the top removed, showing the internal arrangement of the kickers**

• **The back rail is double-tenoned into the legs, with a haunch in the middle**

The legs are double-morticed with a connecting haunch. These were cut on the morticer, the haunch being cut in a second operation with different depth setting. The haunch is finally cleaned up by hand. The base tenons are the same length as the thickness of the shelf.

TENONS

The tenon cheeks for the back and end panels are wide enough to be cut with a router, running the fence along the end of the work, but I cut them on a Sedgwick SM3 spindle moulder that I had recently installed. Unfortunately, this machine is no longer produced, and I had to wait for a secondhand one to become available. With a sliding table and a couple of tenoning discs, this cuts tenons for most furniture-sized applications. Needless to say, this is a great advantage compared to routing or bandsawing tenons, both in terms of speed and consistent accuracy.

The haunches were bandsawn and finished to length with a router. The bandsaw was also used to cut the tenons in the shelf, which is a kind of one-and-a-half tenon arrangement. Once again, the bandsaw is

• **The top rails are also slotted, and the divider is screwed and plugged**

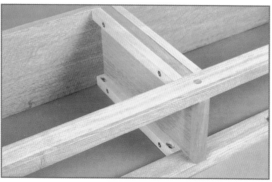

employed to cut the dovetails in the top rail, with the socket scribed off the finished dovetail. The socket part of the joint is initially sawn by hand and the bulk of the waste removed with the router, before cleaning up by hand. A skew-angle carving chisel is very useful for getting into the corners and, because you can use it either way up, you only need one of them, rather than a left- and right-handed version of a bevel-edged skew chisel.

A full dry assembly is set up at this stage and the divider can be fine-tuned. This is screwed at the back and through the front rails. Pellets are set into the back and underneath the lower front rail after glue-up.

ASSEMBLY

All surfaces are now sealed, with the areas that are to be glued masked off. The slightly unorthodox shelf construction means that gluing up has to be done in the right order: end panels to legs first, followed by the shelf, lower top rail, and back panel in a second single operation. Pre-sealing the surfaces not only makes finishing very much easier but also allows the excess glue to be peeled off when it is almost dry. The divider is fitted when the glue-up of stage two is finished. With a hand plane, the top of the frame was trimmed flush and the top checked for fit. There is a ⁹⁄₁₆in (15mm) overhang at the back so that the top sits against the wall while the legs clear the skirting board.

KICKERS

Eight kickers were made; they are drilled for screw holes into the cabinet ends and divider. The top ones are also slotted to take the screws for the top and allow for movement in the top panel.

• **Looking from the base showing the slotted holes in the kickers, to allow the top to expand and contract**

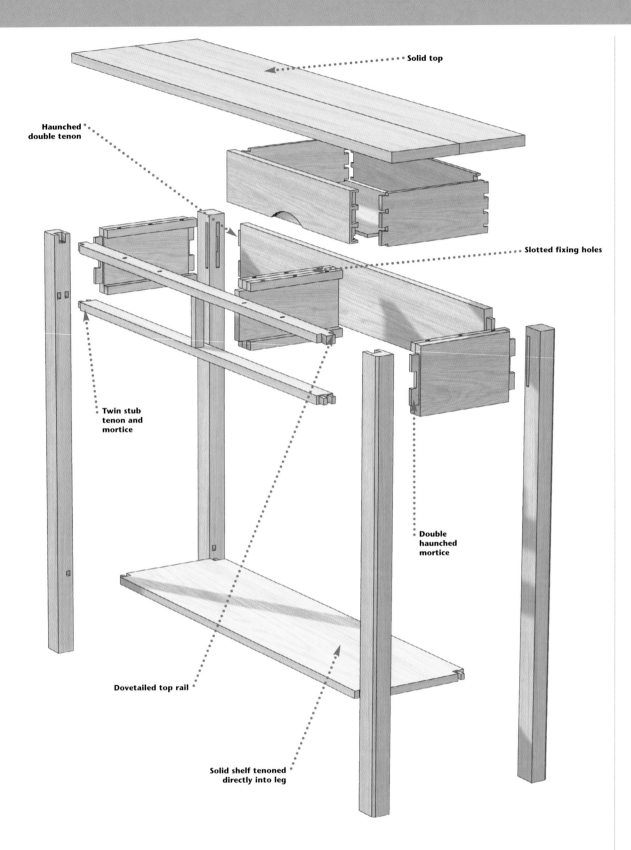

Solid top

Haunched double tenon

Slotted fixing holes

Twin stub tenon and mortice

Double haunched mortice

Dovetailed top rail

Solid shelf tenoned directly into leg

These slots were machined with a router using the same ⅜₂in (4mm) and ¹¹⁄₃₂in (9mm) cutters that were used for the top rail slots. Because of the narrow section of the kickers, it is much easier

to rout the slots into a ⁹⁄₁₆in (15mm) thick board, and rip saw them to width afterwards. The kickers were then screwed in place in readiness for drawer making.

• **The slots for fixing at the leg end**

DRAWERS

The drawers are traditionally constructed, except for the bottoms, which are veneered. This has the advantage that no projection of the drawer bottom is required at the back and, as the cabinet is quite shallow, this helps to maximize the depth of the drawers. In fact there are no stops – the drawer simply hits the back of the cabinet.

The recessed handle is ⁹⁄₁₆in (15mm) deep in a ¹³⁄₁₆in (21mm) thick drawer front. This left precious little room for the groove to take the drawer bottom. To overcome this, the groove was routed to ³⁄₁₆in (5mm) deep either side of the handle and down the sides. Behind the handle the groove is shallower and the bottom is notched to allow for that. Drawer slips would have been a possible alternative but the time permitted by the budget, which meant the whole job had to be completed in one working week, didn't allow enough time. The drawer sides, back and

• **The solid drawer fronts are lap dovetailed in the traditional manner**

• **The top rail is dovetailed into the legs**

interiors were waxed with neutral Liberon finishing wax. The handles are routed using a simple template and template follower. First a ¼in (6mm) diameter cutter is used to remove the bulk of the waste, then the same template is used with a dovetail cutter to undercut the handle and provide the finger pull.

FINISHING

The piece was fine sanded and checked for residual glue marks, then it was given three coats of Danish oil, with more applied to the top. Some observant readers may notice that the lower rail is lipped. This is because, in spite of appearing to be the same colour as the rest of the frame, it came up much lighter than I expected when finished. I concluded that I couldn't live with it as it was, so routed back ³⁄₁₆in (5mm), and glued in a lipping. This had to be inset to fill the area revealed by the recessed handles. The time this took was well worth it for my peace of mind. Finally, the piece was burnished with synthetic wire wool.

• **The drawer pulls are routed out of the fronts**

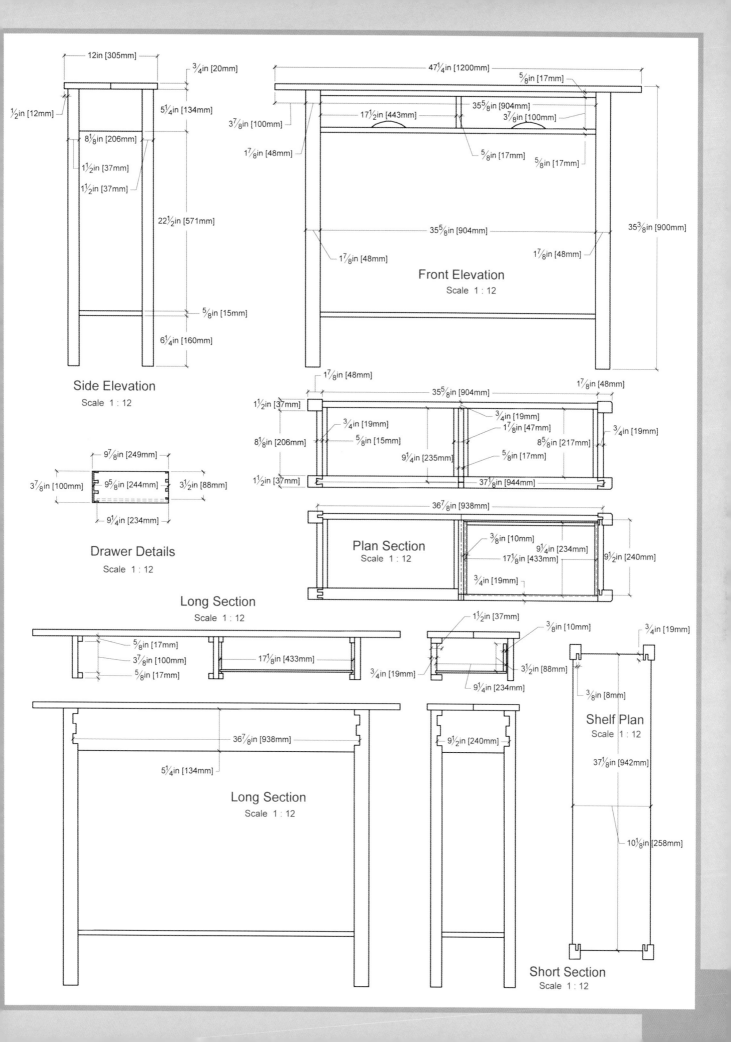

12in [305mm]
¾in [20mm]
½in [12mm]
5¼in [134mm]
8⅛in [206mm]
1½in [37mm]
1½in [37mm]
22½in [571mm]
⅝in [15mm]
6¼in [160mm]

Side Elevation
Scale 1 : 12

47¼in [1200mm]
⅝in [17mm]
35⅝in [904mm]
3⅞in [100mm]
17½in [443mm]
3⅞in [100mm]
1⅞in [48mm]
⅝in [17mm]
⅝in [17mm]
35⅝in [904mm]
35⅜in [900mm]
1⅞in [48mm]
1⅞in [48mm]

Front Elevation
Scale 1 : 12

9⅞in [249mm]
3⅞in [100mm]
9⅝in [244mm]
3½in [88mm]
9¼in [234mm]

Drawer Details
Scale 1 : 12

1⅞in [48mm]
35⅝in [904mm]
1⅞in [48mm]
1½in [37mm]
¾in [19mm]
¾in [19mm]
1⅞in [47mm]
8⅛in [206mm]
⅝in [15mm]
8⅝in [217mm]
¾in [19mm]
9¼in [235mm]
⅝in [17mm]
1½in [37mm]
37½in [944mm]

36⅞in [938mm]
⅜in [10mm]
9¼in [234mm]
9½in [240mm]
17⅛in [433mm]
¾in [19mm]

Plan Section
Scale 1 : 12

Long Section
Scale 1 : 12

⅝in [17mm]
3⅞in [100mm]
17⅛in [433mm]
⅝in [17mm]
¾in [19mm]
9¼in [234mm]
1½in [37mm]
⅜in [10mm]
¾in [19mm]
3½in [88mm]

36⅞in [938mm]
5¼in [134mm]

Long Section
Scale 1 : 12

9½in [240mm]

Short Section
Scale 1 : 12

¾in [19mm]
⅜in [8mm]

Shelf Plan
Scale 1 : 12

37⅛in [942mm]
10⅛in [258mm]

This table was made as a companion to the 'Craftsman Style' chair on page 42

• **Very Ripley and very Arts and Crafts, with a nod to American style, too**

THE DESIGN of the table began with the vertical components in the end frame constructions and twin curved stretcher rails. The curves of the rails gradually become tighter towards the floor, working down from the straight line of the top. These are through-mortice and tenoned through the legs. The feet and spreaders are bridle-jointed to the legs. As the legs are tapered, the feet are fitted with bare-faced bridle joints while the spreaders are more sophisticated to accommodate the top rails. The legs and stretcher rails are tucked in to make leg room, and there is ample accommodation for six chairs.

TIMBER SELECTION

The table is made from boards of three different thickness: 11¼in (42mm) for the top, which is finished at 1⁵⁄₁₆in (33mm); 2½in (54mm) for the rails, feet and spreaders; and 4in (100mm) for the legs.

The 4in (100mm) will need to be of very high quality and well dried. I prefer air-dried for anything over 2½in (54mm) and free from splits or internal checking. The occasional small crack can be filled. Epoxy resin thickened with colloidal silica and oak sanding dust to match the colour is structural filler, and is all but invisible when finished.

TOP

Selecting timber for the top is always important and cannot be rushed. The planed 1⁵⁄₁₆in (33mm) boards were ripped to seven equal widths, as this gave the best balance of colour and figure. They were biscuit jointed and glued-up in two stages. The assembled top was too big to go on my pad sander, so was faced off with a portable belt sander. Beginning with 60grit, I worked down through the grits to 120 and then carried on with

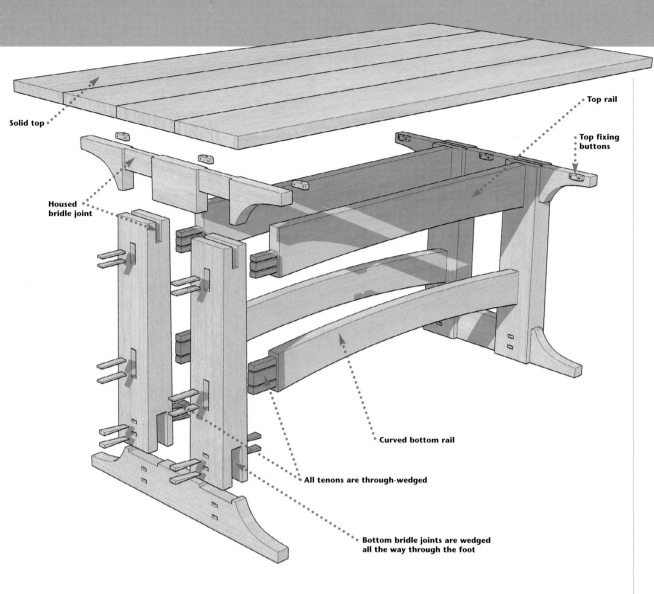

Solid top

Top rail

Top fixing buttons

Housed bridle joint

Curved bottom rail

All tenons are through-wedged

Bottom bridle joints are wedged all the way through the foot

a random orbit sander to 150grit. At this stage, it was checked with a magnifying glass for sanding marks. The underside was sanded to 100grit.

TAPERING LEGS

The parts for the frame are prepared as rectangles for marking out and jointing. The legs were tapered at this stage because the bridle joints need to accommodate the taper, and this is marked from the legs. All the joints were marked out at the same time, beginning with the legs. The positions of the tenons and bridle joints were marked all round. Angles of the bridle joints are scribed off the legs onto the feet and spreaders.

The morticing for the tenons is straightforward enough with a ¾in (20mm) chisel in the morticer, or two passes with a ½in (12mm) chisel on a small machine. It will be necessary though to chop the mortices

through from both sides to avoid breakout. In the absence of a morticer, the joints could be cut with a combination of router and drill, chopping out the middle part of the joint with a chisel by hand.

• Cutting the mortices on the legs

• The feet have the same curved shape as the top rails

• The bottom bridle joint goes over the whole thickness of the bottom rail

BRIDLE JOINTS

The bridle joints are bandsawn into the ends of the legs. A shallow recess is cut in the top of the feet to take the joint in the leg, locating it and giving a neat finish. Otherwise the feet are bare-faced bridle joints. The top bridle joints are more complex with joints cut into both sides and base of the spreaders. The shoulders are routed with the router running against a batten clamped to the spreader, carefully set to give an accurate fit.

TENONS

The tenons are bandsawn. For both bridle joints and tenons, a carefully set bandsaw is used. A false fence is clamped to the table of the machine, set in line with the 'lead' of the blade. The lead is the direction the blade wants to go, and is rarely exactly perpendicular to the front of the table and therefore is unlikely to be parallel to the fence. To gauge the lead, cut a piece of wood freehand with no fences – the direction of the cut is the angle at which the false fence must be set.

SHAPING

With the jointmaking complete and dry-fitted, the components can be shaped. The feet and spreaders are bandsawn and sanded but the rails were shaped

• The top bridle is housed into the top rail

on the spindle moulder. Plywood templates, ½in (12mm), were made for the rails – these served both to assess the positions of the stretcher rails and for shaping on the spindle. They are drawn by springing a batten between two panel pins tapped into the ply and bandsawn. The finished edge is prepared with a spokeshave. These templates were the same shape as the finished components, and were screwed to the tenons with packing strips making up the gap between the side of the rail and the tenon. The legs were chamfered fairly heavily, the rails and legs much more delicately, and the frame was sanded and sealed. Two coats of thinned polyurethane were applied and cut back after each coat.

ASSEMBLY

The first stage of assembly was rails to legs. I bolted sash cramps together to make up the length. The wedges were hammered home and when dry, both sets of leg rail assemblies were cleaned up.

• Both bridle joints ready with all the main rail mortices cut

• **Templates are used to mark out the shape of the curved rails and as guides on the spindle moulder**

• **Through-wedged tenons lock everything together**

The bearers and feet can now be glued in place. No clamps were required for these as, by the time they had been fitted with a mallet, there was clearly no need. G-clamps were used to pull the ends of the bridle joints onto the feet. PVA was used for all the glue-ups. I didn't try to fit the tapered wedges while the job was drying, but waited until after it was cleaned up, chiselled out the glue from the mortices, and fitted them at that stage. The protruding wedges and tenons were belt sanded flush, while the dry excess glue is easily peeled away from the pre-finished surfaces.

Slotted fixing blocks were made to attach the top. These were curved to echo the curves on the rest of the table.

FINISHING

Usually I seal surfaces with thinned polyurethane varnish before applying Danish Oil, but I read recently that Sam Maloof – the eminent maker best known for his chairs – uses similar products but mixes them together. I tried that here and was very pleased with the result. I have described the sanding of the top – the edges were also sanded and the edges chamfered. (Continues overleaf.)

• **Dry assembly of all the main components before shaping**

HAND FITS

The firm push-fit that you would want on a chair joint is too tight here, and the tenon needs to slide in easily without actually being loose. Easing off the mortice on the frame side, so that it is slightly tapered, is the best way of achieving this.

Bear in mind that at least four tenons have to be glued up at once and the glue will start to go off before all the joints are clamped up, possibly preventing them from being pulled home if the fit is too snug.

The mortices also need to be opened up on the outside of the legs to take the wedges which will force the tenon into a dovetail-like opening, making it impossible for the joint to come apart.

Small mortices are cut into the base of the legs and through the feet to take tapered wedges, which lock the joint.

• **I tapered the tenons to make sure there were no problems when gluing up**

• **I chose to do a dry-fit to check that it would actually go together**

• **The buttons are curved to match the curved end rails**

• **Finished table without its top**

The finishing process begins with a thinned mixture of spirit-based matt polyurethane, Danish oil and white spirit in equal amounts. This is applied with a brush and wiped off after 30 minutes or so. This is repeated three to four times at two-hourly intervals, saturating the surface but avoiding brush strokes. Oak is quite resistant and by the time this has dried after 24 hours, the surface should be sealed. I cut this back quite aggressively with 240grit aluminium oxide paper on a palm sander, which produces a silky feel.

Fill any defects in the surface such as knots, with wax (e.g. good quality wax candles). Melted wax can be dripped into the hole and when set, carefully pared flush with a chisel. The result is clear and unobtrusive.

Next, the same mix of varnish and oil is applied daily with a cloth, for three days, steadily reducing the amounts of white spirit. The final stage is to cut back by hand and apply Danish oil with a synthetic wire wool pad. Further coats of Danish oil are applied with a cotton cloth. If a shiny surface is desired, this may be enough but the surface can be burnished with a fine synthetic wire wool pad to produce a more matt finish. The oil will need to have dried for several days before this can be done. I recommend teak oil for maintenance. It does not have the strength of Danish oil, but is easier to apply. The client can then wipe the top every month or so to keep the piece looking fresh.

• **The complete suite – the chairs are a development of my earlier chairs**

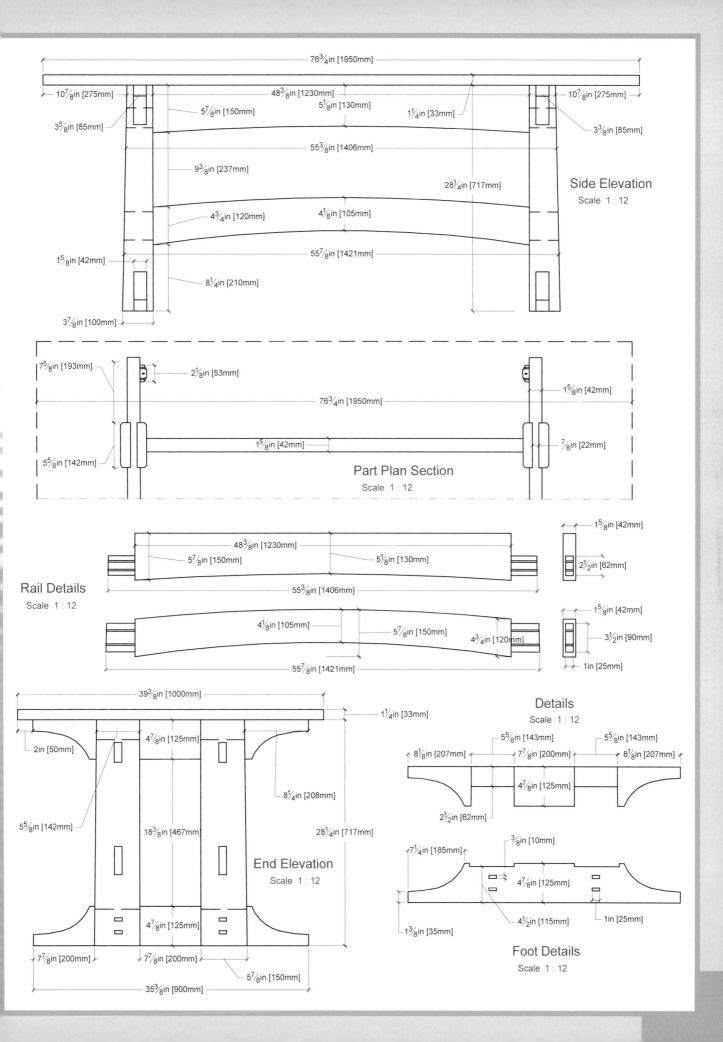

76³⁄₄in [1950mm]

10⁷⁄₈in [275mm]

48³⁄₈in [1230mm]

5⁷⁄₈in [150mm]

5¹⁄₈in [130mm]

1¹⁄₄in [33mm]

10⁷⁄₈in [275mm]

3³⁄₈in [85mm]

3³⁄₈in [85mm]

55³⁄₈in [1406mm]

9³⁄₈in [237mm]

28¹⁄₄in [717mm]

Side Elevation
Scale 1 : 12

4³⁄₄in [120mm]

4¹⁄₈in [105mm]

55⁷⁄₈in [1421mm]

1⁵⁄₈in [42mm]

8¹⁄₄in [210mm]

3⁷⁄₈in [100mm]

7⁵⁄₈in [193mm]

2¹⁄₈in [53mm]

1⁵⁄₈in [42mm]

76³⁄₄in [1950mm]

1⁵⁄₈in [42mm]

⁷⁄₈in [22mm]

5⁵⁄₈in [142mm]

Part Plan Section
Scale 1 : 12

48³⁄₈in [1230mm]

5⁷⁄₈in [150mm]

5¹⁄₈in [130mm]

1⁵⁄₈in [42mm]

2¹⁄₂in [62mm]

Rail Details
Scale 1 : 12

55³⁄₈in [1406mm]

4¹⁄₈in [105mm]

5⁷⁄₈in [150mm]

4³⁄₄in [120mm]

1⁵⁄₈in [42mm]

3¹⁄₂in [90mm]

55⁷⁄₈in [1421mm]

1in [25mm]

39³⁄₈in [1000mm]

1¹⁄₄in [33mm]

Details
Scale 1 : 12

4⁷⁄₈in [125mm]

2in [50mm]

8¹⁄₄in [208mm]

5⁵⁄₈in [143mm]

5⁵⁄₈in [143mm]

8¹⁄₈in [207mm]

7⁷⁄₈in [200mm]

8¹⁄₈in [207mm]

4⁷⁄₈in [125mm]

5⁵⁄₈in [142mm]

18³⁄₈in [467mm]

28¹⁄₄in [717mm]

End Elevation
Scale 1 : 12

2¹⁄₂in [62mm]

7¹⁄₄in [185mm]

³⁄₈in [10mm]

4⁷⁄₈in [125mm]

4⁷⁄₈in [125mm]

7⁷⁄₈in [200mm]

7⁷⁄₈in [200mm]

5⁷⁄₈in [150mm]

4¹⁄₂in [115mm]

1in [25mm]

1³⁄₈in [35mm]

35³⁄₈in [900mm]

Foot Details
Scale 1 : 12

SIDEBOARDS & CUPBOARDS

CORNER CABINET

CHESTNUT CABINET

BURR OAK CABINET

CONTEMPORARY SIDEBOARD

FOUR-DOOR CUPBOARD

This pretty piece in 'bookmatched' sweet chestnut has space-saving storage

• **The traditional fare of many a woodworker**

THIS CABINET was part of a suite in sweet chestnut (*Castanea sativa*), commissioned by a couple for a lounge in a modernized stone cottage in a rural location. (The next project – 'Chestnut Cabinet' – is part of the same suite.)

TIMBER

From the beginning I wanted to use sweet chestnut for this project as, at its best, it is a beautiful timber. It has its foibles, though: cup shakes that can wreck whole boards; violent yellow-coloured patches (to some extent these disappear on exposure to UV light, but nonetheless they are an unsightly nuisance); it is light, both in colour and weight, and the low impact-resistance makes it inappropriate for hard usage; in its unfinished state it is rather insipid, giving little impression of the colour that is revealed by a finish and the marked effect of sunlight.

Availability and quality are highly variable, but I had seen some very nice 1⅝in (40mm) air-dried stock and, although it would mean a lot of resawing to produce the jointed panels, I was keen to buy it.

DESIGN FEATURES

The construction of this piece is complicated by the return from the front frame back to the wall. It makes the design a bit more interesting than a simple flat front and gives the impression that the cabinet is smaller, without losing any useful storage space. Corner cabinets make use of otherwise dead space. The design would also work well as a display cabinet, with glass in lieu of the wood door panel.

As I had not made a corner cabinet for many years I came to it without any particular preconceptions. I wanted to invest the very simple lines with some details inside that make it worth opening the door. Because the inside back panels are so prominent when one looks inside, I was keen to use some of the best timber here. Also the top frame and panel add some interest, and will always be visible even when the cabinet is in use.

• Interior detail is important – there is a neat shadow line around the top panel

Being unsure how dry the centre of the boards were made this risky, as it could be subject to cupping and I had precious little margin to play with. It would also add a fair bit to the making time. In the event, the differential of moisture content through the boards was only about 2% and, left in stick to equalize, did not produce any ill-effects.

Due to good drying and sharp bandsaw blades, I finished the door frames and jointed end panels at $^{11}/_{16}$in (17mm) – quite pleasing from 1⅝in (40mm) boards sawn through in widths up to 8¾in (approx. 225mm). When the timber preparation was complete, I felt that both my choice of wood and the price the customer was paying were justified.

CONSTRUCTION

First, make the top frame and panel. Use a simple mortice and tenon to join the back corner. Join corner fillet blocks using biscuits to join the side rails to the front rail. Glue clamping blocks on temporarily so you can clamp up the frame for routing the groove for the panel and for gluing up. Rout a ¼ x ½ in deep (6mm x 12mm) groove into the inside edge of the frame. While the frame is clamped up (without glue) mark the top panel, scribing a line around the inside edge of the frame. Allow an additional ⅜in (10mm) all round for a rebate to be routed around the panel that will fit into the frame. Undercut this with a slotting cutter with the panel clamped face down on to the bench. Make it a dry-fit to ensure a consistent shadow line between panel and frame.

After gluing up, dimension the top frame and panel, bottom and shelves accurately. Screw the vertical panels along their back edge and to the back half of the top and bottom.

• Interior of door panel and bead moulding on the shelf add interest

To allow the boards to expand and contract, slot-screw the front halves. Finish the backs ³⁄₆₄–⅛in (2–3mm) short and rout them with a groove. This takes a tongue glued into a corresponding groove in the end panel.

Prepare the front frame and dry-fit the biscuits. Make wide plywood strips as clamping battens, with V-cuts to locate on the back corner of the cabinet. Once you have dry-fitted the front frame, you can begin the delicate task of planing the ends to size. Saw a 45° bevel, leaving a margin for accurate hand planing to align with the front frame sides.

• The bottom panel is held in using biscuits

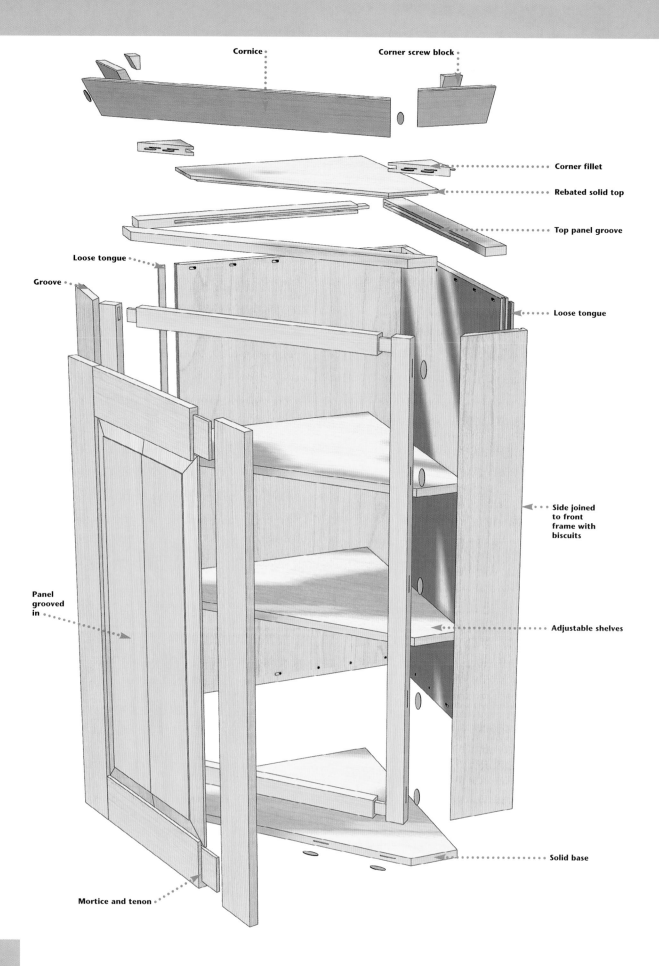

Cornice

Corner screw block

Corner fillet

Rebated solid top

Top panel groove

Loose tongue

Groove

Loose tongue

Side joined
to front
frame with
biscuits

Panel
grooved
in

Adjustable shelves

Solid base

Mortice and tenon

Use No. 10 biscuits to fit the ends to the front frame (No. 20s are too wide to be concealed within the bevel). Rout a groove corresponding with the back panel grooves and fit with a solid wood tongue. To check the fits, clamp bevelled pressure blocks onto the ends while using further G-clamps to pull the front frame end panel butt joint together. Once you have achieved a satisfactory result, dismantle the cabinet and mask off the joints in preparation for finishing the interior.

Seal and wax the interior. Apply a thinned coat of polyurethane as a sanding sealer and cut it back. I used neutral Liberon Black Bison wax for finishing, applying it quite thickly and then buffing it off.

PUT IT TOGETHER

Now reassemble the cabinet, much of which requires no glue at all. The exceptions are the front frame to base and top, and the edges of the end panels to the front frame and at the top and bottom. Remove excess glue, when it is nearly dry, using a sharp chisel, preferably one dedicated to this job.

The joint between the front frame and side panels is critical and careful clamping is necessary for a good result. Plane the two faces to a crisp arris on the point of the mitre – this is quite easy if you use a smoothing plane on the soft chestnut.

• Top of cabinet, showing the panel and screw blocks used on the cornice

True the piece up all round, keeping the top and back flush while leaving the bottom recessed by ⅟₆₄–³⁄₆₄ in (1–2mm) to give a more subtle finish. Plane a chamfer down the back edge of the cabinet, to allow for the radius that is usually present in the corner of a room.

CORNICE

The combination of a bevel and 22.5° mitre is not a problem I often come across, and it can be cut in a number of ways. A bevelled shim enables the components to be cut using the adjustable mitre guide on either a bench saw or bandsaw. The latter will require final fitting with a smoothing plane. Cut biscuit slots ready for assembly. Glue a bevelled pressure block to both ends of the central piece to make final dry-fitting and gluing up much easier. Once dry, align the cornice with the cabinet and fit with bevelled screw blocks.

MATCHED DOOR

The door is bookmatched, styles and panel alike. At ¹¹⁄₁₆in (17mm) the door frame is quite thin, so keep the panel relatively thick at ⅝in (15mm) to impart stiffness. ¼in (6mm) mortices and tenons are used to join the frame with a ¼in (6mm) wide and ½in (12mm) deep groove to take the panel. Leave an expansion gap of ⅛in (3mm) between the edge of the door panel and bottom of the groove.

How you raise the panel is a matter of personal preference. I use either a tilted bench saw to remove the waste and a rebate block plane for trimming or, as in this case, a router. A jig made some years ago still serves me well provided the proportions of the moulding are appropriate to the job. Undercut the back of the panel with a counter-rebate before routing the face side. Oil both the rebate and raised moulding before assembly; this avoids white lines appearing if the panel shrinks in service, and also prevents glue adhering to the corners of the panel.

ON THE SHELF

The value of dimensioning the shelves with the top and bottom components will now be apparent, as gaining an accurate fit at this stage would be awkward. They will need easing off slightly before bead moulding the front edge and sanding all round. Plane a small chamfer around the arrises of the shelves.

• **Shelves are removable and have been cut out underneath to take brass pins**

Turned oak (*Quercus* sp.) dowels are set into the cabinet sides, because chestnut is too soft to be strong enough. Rout corresponding notches in the shelves to locate them. I did not make the shelves adjustable, only removable.

• **Detail of the handle**

• **The hinges are recessed into door style and cabinet frame**

SETTING UP

Rout hinge recesses into the door style and cabinet frame. As the door frame is quite thin, the hinge takes the full depth of the style. Initially fit the door with posi-drive steel screws for convenience, to be replaced with 1in (25mm) slotted-head brass screws after finishing. Use a coving cutter to shape the grip of the handle. Plane the chamfers on the face side by hand and make the cutouts using a bandsaw and file. Fit a double brass ball catch to a small block screwed behind the front frame in line with the handle.

FINISHING

Remove door, shelves and handle prior to finishing. The finish is the same as the interior, but I used two coats of thinned polyurethane rather than one.

Cut each coat back by hand using 320grit silicon carbide paper, or use a palm sander with 240grit paper. The speed of the sander and quick wear of the abrasive produces a fine finish in spite of the coarser grit. The surface does not need to be particularly durable, and this is adequate preparation for a burnished wax finish. Wax inside and out with neutral Liberon Black Bison wax for a good result.

As this piece would be placed in the corner of two outside walls in an old stone cottage, I painted the back with two coats of exterior grade oil-based paint, to protect it from possible damp.

The piece was hung on four heavy-duty brass plates.

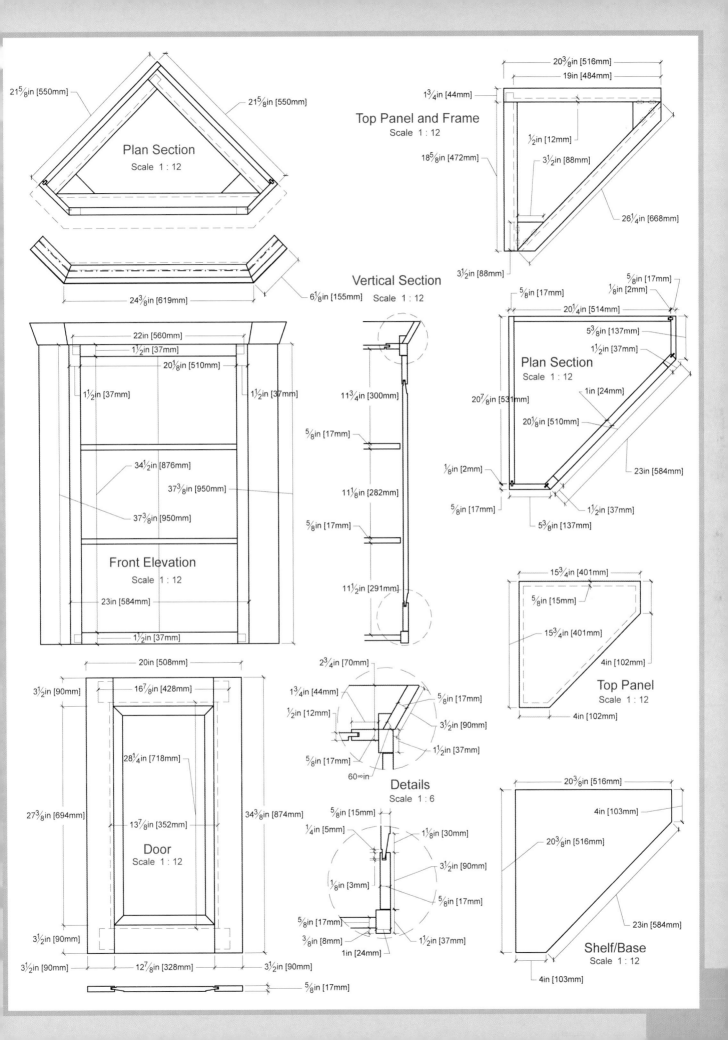

Plan Section
Scale 1 : 12

21⅝in [550mm]
21⅝in [550mm]
24⅜in [619mm]
6⅛in [155mm]

Vertical Section
Scale 1 : 12

Top Panel and Frame
Scale 1 : 12

20⅜in [516mm]
19in [484mm]
1¾in [44mm]
½in [12mm]
3½in [88mm]
18⅝in [472mm]
26¼in [668mm]
3½in [88mm]

Front Elevation
Scale 1 : 12

22in [560mm]
1½in [37mm]
20⅛in [510mm]
1½in [37mm]
1½in [37mm]
34½in [876mm]
37⅜in [950mm]
37⅜in [950mm]
23in [584mm]
1½in [37mm]

11¾in [300mm]
⅝in [17mm]
11⅛in [282mm]
⅝in [17mm]
11½in [291mm]

Plan Section
Scale 1 : 12

⅝in [17mm]
⅝in [17mm]
⅛in [2mm]
20¼in [514mm]
5⅜in [137mm]
1½in [37mm]
20⅞in [531mm]
1in [24mm]
20⅛in [510mm]
23in [584mm]
⅛in [2mm]
⅝in [17mm]
1½in [37mm]
5⅜in [137mm]

Top Panel
Scale 1 : 12

15¾in [401mm]
⅝in [15mm]
15¾in [401mm]
4in [102mm]
4in [102mm]

Door
Scale 1 : 12

20in [508mm]
3½in [90mm]
16⅞in [428mm]
28¼in [718mm]
27⅜in [694mm]
34⅜in [874mm]
13⅞in [352mm]
3½in [90mm]
3½in [90mm]
12⅞in [328mm]
3½in [90mm]
⅝in [17mm]

Details
Scale 1 : 6

2¾in [70mm]
1¾in [44mm]
½in [12mm]
⅝in [17mm]
3½in [90mm]
1½in [37mm]
⅝in [17mm]
60∞in

⅝in [15mm]
¼in [5mm]
1⅛in [30mm]
3½in [90mm]
⅛in [3mm]
⅝in [17mm]
⅝in [17mm]
⅜in [8mm]
1½in [37mm]
1in [24mm]

Shelf/Base
Scale 1 : 12

20⅜in [516mm]
4in [103mm]
20⅜in [516mm]
23in [584mm]
4in [103mm]

CHESTNUT CABINET

Bi-fold doors reveal a home entertainment system in this elegant cabinet

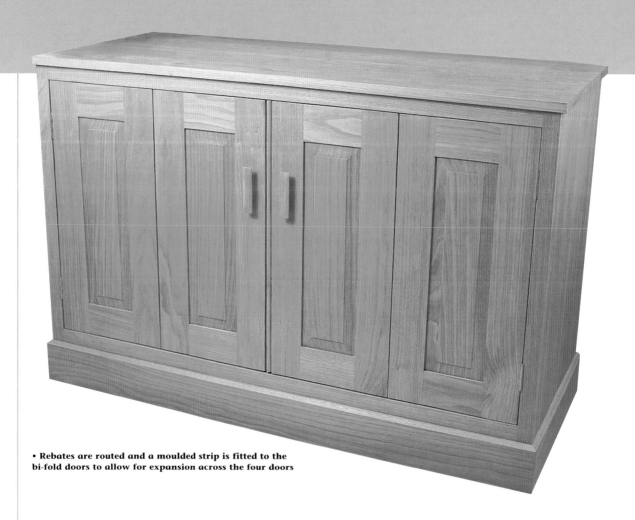

**• Rebates are routed and a moulded strip is fitted to the
bi-fold doors to allow for expansion across the four doors**

THIS CABINET was commissioned for a lounge in a modernized stone cottage, and is part of the same suite as the 'Corner Cabinet' on page 88. It sits in an interesting shallow alcove, created by a curved chimney, and provides a neat solution to housing a television. Two bi-fold doors are unobtrusive when open, but visually interesting when closed. The repeated raised-panel design and formal handle detail give it an unintended Arts and Crafts character.

TIMBER

I used solid sweet chestnut (*Castanea sativa*) throughout, resawing all but the top and shelves from 1⅝in (40mm) boards. Some shallow cup shakes were present in the top but I was able to thickness them out. I prepared the shelves from 1in (25mm) boards.

One foible of chestnut is that it splits and, after I had left the stock 'in stick' for a while to let the moisture content equalize, I had to replace some of the door frames because cracks had appeared. By this point my stock of prime quality timber was running out, so I was pleased when a complete and sound set of components was ready to go.

I made this piece open-backed for airflow and cables, with wide back rails to give stiffness. This reduces the likelihood of racking – important for strength, but also to retain the critical setting of the two pairs of bi-fold doors. The shelves have a bead detail, in keeping with the other pieces in the set. This is picked up with a wide bead on the central overlap for the doors. Movement here is a problem.

The combined width of the door frames is almost 22in (approx. 560mm) and all the shrinkage and expansion is going to be reflected in the gap between the two middle doors.

This solution produces a variable shadow line but – with a bit of luck – no ugly gaps or jammed-up doors. Because the doors are quite small, the repeated raised panel construction creates visual interest from a very simple detail. The door panels are bookmatched either side of the centre line, and a carcass plinth is slot-screwed to the solid base of the cabinet.

CONSTRUCTION

The construction is fairly straightforward, as the piece has no back. Use biscuit joints for the base to ends and also for joining the back frames to the bottom and end panels. To retain some flexibility inside, use screws to attach the divider. The measurements are determined by the size of the equipment to be housed. As these may subsequently be replaced, make it possible to alter the interior by moving the divider, plugging the screw holes and replacing or shortening the shelves.

Developing technology may produce smaller boxes of electronics in the future – but televisions just seem to get bigger. Prior to gluing up, the jointed areas are masked off and the interior faces finished.

The finish I chose was a sealing coat of polyurethane and clear wax. Chestnut darkens considerably on exposure to sunlight but, as it is rather insipid in its fresh cut state, I do not think this is a problem.

ASSEMBLY

Fit the central divider to the base and back frames first. Use masking tape to protect the finished surfaces from glue, which is applied to both surfaces of each joint, into all the biscuit slots, and the biscuits themselves (but N.B. the screwed joints are NOT glued). Use long sash clamps, or short ones bolted together, to pull the ends to the base and back frames. Remove excess glue with a chisel after it has gone off. Prepare the biscuit-joint slots in the cabinet for the front frame before carefully aligning and jointing the frame. Glue and clamp this in place and clean up the whole carcass.

• **The back is open because of all the electrical equipment, so wide rails are used to prevent racking**

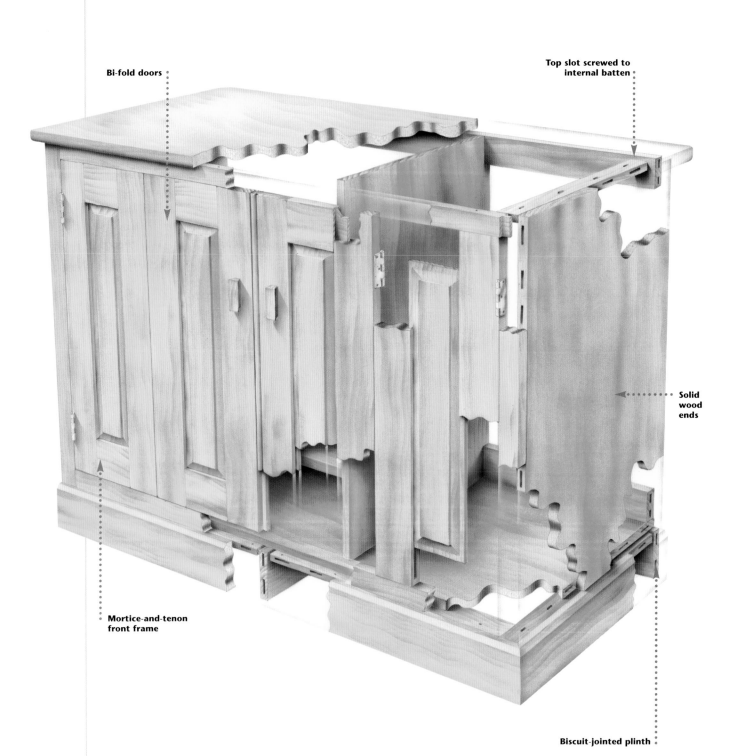

Bi-fold doors

**Top slot screwed to
internal batten**

**Solid
wood
ends**

**Mortice-and-tenon
front frame**

Biscuit-jointed plinth

TOP

Finish the top at 1in (25mm) thick and sand both sides, then seal the underside. Make slotted battens to fit the top to the ends. Use screw blocks to fit the back rail and divider and screw the front edge directly through the front rail.

PLINTH

Make this as a biscuited box, mitred at the front and butt jointed at the back, with a central spacing/support member. To provide support for the heavy television and hi-fi equipment, screw a support frame to the inside top edge of the plinth. These frames are routed with slots to take the screws that will attach them to the cabinet. After construction and a clean-up, rout a chamfer along the outside top edges. The plinth has a gratifyingly substantial appearance and is now ready to be joined to the cabinet.

SHELF SUPPORTS

Once again, you need to take into account the weight of the television when preparing the shelf supports, which are substantial blocks screwed to the cabinet sides. As they are very low down and difficult to see, their appearance is not of primary importance. The shelves for the hi-fi equipment on the left-hand side of the divider are adjustable. The supports are made in oak turned to ⁵⁄₁₆in (8mm) and glued into holes bored into the cabinet sides. All the shelves are bead-moulded along their front edges. Chamfer the smaller shelves lightly all round and seal. Make notches with a router to correspond with the shelf supports, providing positive location and a neat appearance.

DOORS

Narrow doors combined with wide styles leave elegantly proportioned panels. These are book-matched either side of the centre line. Cut mortice-and- tenon joints at ¼in (6mm) as the ¹¹⁄₁₆in (17mm) thick door frames do not permit anything much wider. ¼in (6mm) mortice bits are rather fragile and even in the soft chestnut I broke a bit, which proved remarkably difficult to get out of the mortice.

The dry-fitted frames are faced off before routing the grooves to take the panels. When dimensioning the panels, allow for a ⁵⁄₆₄in (2mm) tolerance at the bottom of the groove for expansion. While panel raising causes me to consider the benefits of a spindle moulder, a router is more than adequate for short runs.

• **Detail of the plinth**

• The substantial plinth is biscuit jointed together, and support battens are screwed to the inside edge. Note the washers on slotted holes to allow for movement

Use an inverted heavy-duty router with panel-raising cutters, or a handheld router in conjunction with a simple jig to hold the router at a 10% incline. Finish the panels flush with the door frames.

SETTING UP DOORS

This is complicated both by the bi-fold design and the expansion gap required in the centre. First trim the doors to a ¹⁄₁₆in (1.5mm) tolerance all round. Fit the hinges between the bi-folds first, then fit the doors to the cabinet frames. In all cases the hinges are let into the door styles and cabinet frames by equal amounts. Use a router to cut rebates into both styles at the centre of approximately ⁵⁄₃₂in (4mm). Fit a bead-moulded strip retrospectively and set pellets into ⁵⁄₃₂in (7mm) screw holes. Fit two pairs of double-ball catches – one to close the doors at the centre and the other to pull the middle of the bi-fold home. Fit these to blocks screwed to the inside of the top frame.

• Detail of raised panel

• Undersides of the adjustable shelves are notched for positive location

In practice, the doors initially open like a normal door before the outer half begins to fold into its partner, closing is a similar action.

HANDLES

I offered my clients a choice of three door handle designs for the suite of furniture, all made as prototypes. The one they chose was inspired by the door panel detail on this cabinet with its narrow, shallow chamfer. They are made in a long strip to make the cove routing of the grip easier. The side chamfers can also be planed at this stage before separation into individual lengths. With the end chamfers and cutaways completed by hand, you can sand and seal the handles.

FINISHING

As with the interior, seal the shelves, doors and exterior of the cabinet, but this time with two coats of thinned polyurethane rather than one. Cut it all back with 240grit silicon carbide paper on a palm sander. Finally, wax with two coats of neutral Liberon Black Bison wax.

• The hi-fi end of the cabinet has adjustable shelves while the television shelf is fixed to take the weight

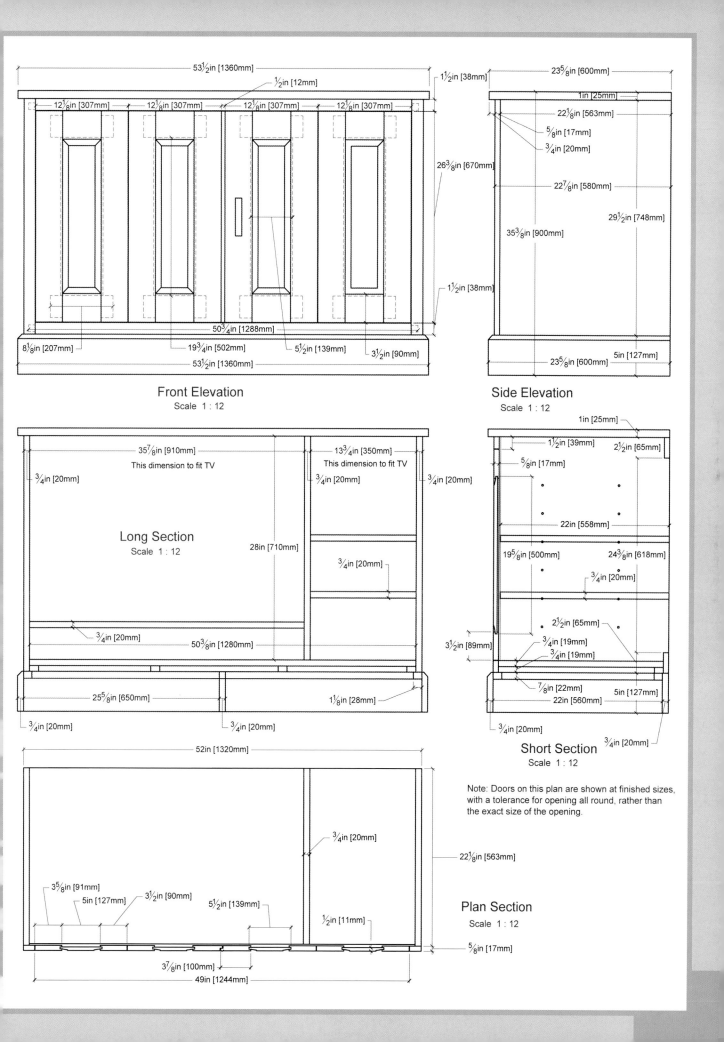

Front Elevation
Scale 1 : 12

Side Elevation
Scale 1 : 12

Long Section
Scale 1 : 12

Short Section
Scale 1 : 12

Plan Section
Scale 1 : 12

This dimension to fit TV

This dimension to fit TV

Note: Doors on this plan are shown at finished sizes, with a tolerance for opening all round, rather than the exact size of the opening.

BURR OAK CABINET

A simple cabinet and door frames surround some unusual oak panels

• **Simple and unfussy, the sideboard shows off the distinctive figure of the oak door panels**

THIS PIECE was conceived with simple lines, the drawers concealed behind a door to maintain the proportions. Although it was to be situated in a large room, the depth of the sideboard needed to be modest: it is only 16in (410mm) front to back, and recessed handles are used so that they do not get in the way of anyone passing by. The plinth is recessed so that it can tuck around some pipes on the skirting board and provide foot room for someone serving at the sideboard. The overall effect of the commission is a contemporary interpretation of traditional themes, for its home in the very modern extension of a converted coach house in West London.

TIMBER

Not realizing how many miles I would end up driving to find the right boards, I suggested decorative door panels. When eventually sourced, the 2⅛in (54mm) boards first had to be squared-up and sawn through, so that they could condition in stick, and the 14% moisture content had to be pulled down to 10%.

After sawing, the top board quickly cupped and twisted well beyond reclamation point and I began to wonder what I had been left with. I had enough to replace that panel but not many more. In stick and under heavy weights, sitting near the de-humidifier, it took two to three weeks to settle down.

• **The burr oak panels, finally found after a long search**

• **Interior drawers**

Machining was uneventful, although the blunting effect was quite pronounced.

MATCHING PANELS

The panels are bookmatched either side of the centre line, but I use the term 'bookmatched' loosely, as with such wild grain and burr, the $\frac{3}{32}$–$\frac{1}{8}$in (2–3mm) lost in sawing and planing makes a big difference; consequently arranging the panels to best effect is a time-consuming process and the matching is fairly approximate.

To fill the holes in the burr I used epoxy resin filler, mixed and then thickened with the white 'micro-balloons' that the manufacturers supply. It is further thickened with oak sanding dust to colour the mixture. I made no attempt to match the colour, as it would have been far too dark, simply obliterating the effect of the burr.

When filling knotholes or small cracks, colour matching can be done. The result is both structural and, providing it is darkened to anticipate the effect of finish and sunlight, invisible.

• **Fitted drawer components**

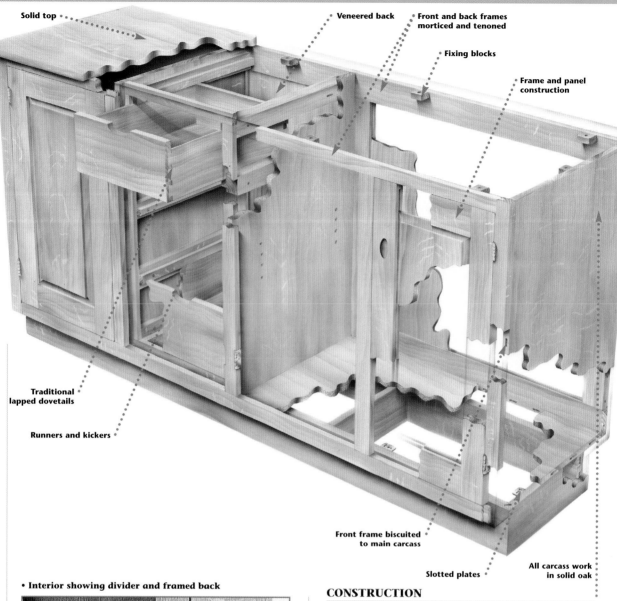

Solid top

Veneered back

Front and back frames
morticed and tenoned

Fixing blocks

Frame and panel
construction

Traditional
lapped dovetails

Runners and kickers

Front frame biscuited
to main carcass

Slotted plates

All carcass work
in solid oak

• Interior showing divider and framed back

CONSTRUCTION

Apart from the back panels and drawer bottoms
everything is in solid oak. The base, end, top, divider,
shelf and door panels are jointed up, faced off and
dimensioned, a process I mentally include in the
cutting list stage; then, when making proper starts,
I can go to a fully prepared set of components.

The epoxy-filled door panels had to be belt sanded.
This is tough stuff and sharp edges of epoxy resin can
slice up sanding belts, so it must be done carefully.
The front and back frames are mortice and tenoned
together. I use a router-tenoning jig that cuts both
cheeks and shoulders in one go with unremitting
accuracy and speed. A ¼in (6mm) x ½in (12mm) deep
groove is routed in the back frame to take
the veneered panels. It is advisable to seal and cut

back the panels before assembly, as they are quite absorbent and need two coats – easier to do before they are set in a frame.

The carcass is biscuit jointed together. All the joints are marked and cut except the front frame, which is prepared later. Holes are bored for the shelf supports at this stage, areas to be glued and sealed masked off, and all interior surfaces sealed.

I use a palm sander to cut back sealing coats of thinned polyurethane, which produces a silk-like surface – a good base for building up a Danish oil finish.

GLUING UP

A number of glue-up stages are required for the carcass:

- Firstly attach the dividers to the base, using sprung battens to ensure even pressure across the joints.

- Secondly, the back is biscuit jointed to the base and pocket-screwed to the dividers.

- Thirdly, the ends are biscuit jointed to the base and screwed to the back.

- Finally, the assembled carcass is cleaned up along the front edge and biscuited to take the front.

This is a big gluing operation so careful preparation is necessary. Remove excess glue stage by stage once it has gone off, using an old chisel. The whole cabinet is cleaned up and the screw holes plugged with pellets.

THE PLINTH

The plinth is mitred at the front and butt jointed at the back. A couple of spacers are fitted to stiffen the structure and all the joints are biscuited. Expansion plates are screwed in place before assembly, as they would be very awkward to fit once the plinth is glued up. They make necessary allowance for any expansion and contraction of the base of the cabinet. Small wood blocks are made to attach the top – no provision needs to be made for movement here.

As the blocks will be visible, all facing edges are chamfered, and the underside of the top sealed and sanded before it is fitted. At this point I turned and fitted the oak dowel shelf supports. The shelves are notched around the back frame to fit up to the back panel, and also notched to locate over the supports.

DOORS

The door frames are made in the same way as the cabinet frames. Make these $\frac{1}{16}$in (1–2mm) oversize to allow for later fitting and edge finishing. A $\frac{1}{4}$in (6mm) groove is routed for the door panels. Once dimensioned, the panels are routed to fit the groove. Working from the face side, undercut the panel with a $\frac{1}{2}$in (12mm) slotting cutter. The top panel raising is done with a cutter that has a slight relief of 45°, creating a negative chamfer. Working from the face side only means that any discrepancies in panel thickness do not affect the accuracy of the fit in the groove. Fresh burrs will be exposed by the routing, which will need additional epoxy filling. This epoxy can be routed off and the routed surfaces sanded and oiled before assembling the doors.

• **Runners and kickers being fitted – note slotting to allow for movement**

• **Plinth is attached using plates – slotted again for movement**

Chunky solid brass butt hinges are set into both the carcass frames and door stiles. My preferred tolerance around doors is ¹⁄₁₆in (1–1.5mm). This looks neat while allowing some room for movement in the door stiles. These are all set up and justified before the handles are routed. The double-ball catches were finally fitted.

DRAWERS

It is always tempting for project writers to say that drawers are made in the traditional way. I've done it often enough myself. But this time I will explain what that means and how it has developed in my own workshop.

Arriving at the correct dimensions for the cabinet is the first step. It needs to be slightly wider at the back than at the front, so that a square drawer is fitted into a space that opens up towards the back, rather than a tapered drawer entering a square space. This difference in dimension is very slight, in this case about ³⁄₆₄in (0.5mm).

This form of framed construction makes life a lot easier as it is the applied guides that are tapered rather than the sides of the solid wood carcass. It is important to get this right and a full day was spent making and fitting these, along with the rails and kickers that are screwed to them.

The drawer linings – both sides and backs – are dimensioned to fit the openings in the cabinet and marked in sets. Setting the sides in pairs, arrange them so that the grain runs from front to back. This allows for cleaning up with a plane from front to back, eliminating the possibility of breaking out on the front edge of the drawer.

The sides are planed to a sight taper so that they enter half to three-quarters of the depth of the drawer, while the backs are sawn to exactly the width of the opening. Conventionally the fronts are cut very slightly oversize and then a bevel is planed all round so that they can be pushed into the opening by about half their thickness. I no longer plane the bevel, but leave the drawer front oversize by about ³⁄₆₄in (0.5mm) all round so that, when cleaned up, the fit is exact. All the inside surfaces can be sanded or hand planed now.

The grooves for the bottoms are cut next, either with a router or table saw. I find that slips are rarely necessary as I generally use drawer thicknesses of around ½in

(12mm), which is enough to take a groove for the bottom. On particularly fine or small work I might go down to ¼in (6mm) when drawer slips – strips applied to the inside of the drawer sides specifically to take the groove for the bottoms – become essential.

Fronts are always deep enough to take the groove. The backs finish at the top of the bottom groove and the bottom runs underneath. This is so that solid wood panels can be slot-screwed to the underside of the back, allowing for movement.

Even when using veneered drawer bottoms, which I generally do, I still make drawers this way as it makes fitting easier. Also, if the drawer is a little out of square, a bottom can be used to pull it true.

Although the backs can be thinner than the sides, there is little practical point. If the sides and back are the same thickness as the length of the lap dovetails at the front, marking out is much easier as only one gauge setting is required. Setting out the front lap dovetails is largely a matter of visual discretion, creating a pleasing proportion. The joint must cover the bottom groove while leaving enough wood for a strong joint after cleaning up. I think odd numbers of dovetails usually look better, and I like to keep enough material in the pins to ensure that they have some real structural value. The ratio of the dovetail is about 1:7.

DOVETAIL PRACTICE

I have never used a dovetail jig. The older types produced pins and dovetails of equal size and the effect just looked ugly to me.

• **Fitting a bottom**

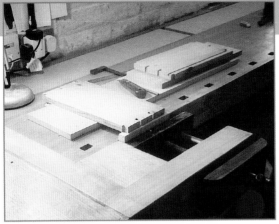

• Mark out the pins

• Use a router to take out some of the waste

Modern ones produce much prettier joints, but I suspect that it would take just as long to set one up for the short runs I need, as it takes to do them by hand.

The drawer sides are taped together and the dovetails are cut on the bandsaw. A coping saw is used to cut out the waste and a chisel to pare the joint back to the scribed line. A wood block clamped in place can be used as a guide for the chisel but with practice will probably be dispensed with.

The front is held in the vice and the sides supported so that the pins can be scribed directly off the dovetails with a Stanley knife. Pencil in the cut line for clarity and mark them back to the scribed depth line with a small square.

The back pins are marked in the same way. The pins are cut with a dovetail saw. Although the waste can be removed with a coping saw, for any but the smallest drawers I use a router fitted with a ¼in (6mm) twin-flute bit. The fence runs along the end of the front or back and produces a perfectly true finished cut, leaving only the corners to be cut in with a chisel. Although it should not be necessary, the joints may

be checked for accuracy prior to gluing up; do not clamp them up fully, as getting them apart without damaging something will be difficult.

FIXING AND FITTING DRAWERS

The insides are wax-finished before assembly, with masking tape protecting the joints. Traditionally the joints are hammered home, but I use clamps with pressure blocks, as it gives a gentler action and really pulls them up. When it has gone off, excess glue can be peeled off the inside corners with a chisel. The exterior is cleaned up with a bench plane when the glue has fully set, and gradually trued to fit and sanded. Wax polishing the sides eases the action of the drawers and reveals any high points where they may be sticking. Once a satisfactory fit has been achieved, the bottoms can be fitted and screwed in place.

FINISHING

Sideboard tops must be expected to take some punishment, so I give them as much attention as table tops. The finish is built up with six coats of thinned

• Good dovetails will always impress

• Back dovetails

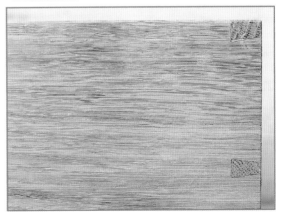

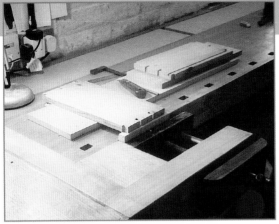

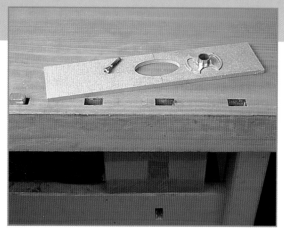

• **The router for the handle recesses – the bulk is removed with a straight-fluted cutter and then undercut with a dovetail cutter**

• **Close-up of the handle recess**

polyurethane, each one cut back with 240–320grit silicon-carbide paper on a palm sander. This gradually becomes worn, giving a finer and finer finish. Otherwise all surfaces are given two coats of polyurethane before Danish oiling.

Once everything has dried thoroughly, the piece is burnished with 00 wire wool. I have been using variations of this finish for many years and I am satisfied that it is tough, attractive and durable. I advise clients to dress the top with teak oil occasionally.

ATMOSPHERIC VARIATIONS

I am not a believer in working to microscopic tolerances just because it is possible. Most temperate solid woods simply change dimension too much with atmospheric variations for it to make sense. My own customers are not impressed by ultra-fine drawer fits if they need a hydraulic ram to open the things all summer. What is appropriate for a competition or exam is one thing, but unless you want to visit an increasingly impatient customer every few weeks to make minor adjustments, a more pragmatic approach is required. Providing the drawer runs easily without rattling around I am happy.

A good working test for checking a fit is to be able to push the drawer closed with one finger from either outside end. This works, even for very wide drawers.

DOOR AND DRAWER HANDLES

The tops of the drawer fronts are higher than the sides, leaving room for cutout handles without interfering with the contents of the drawer.

The handles are routed into the door stiles using an elliptical MDF template. By this stage the doors were very valuable so I made quite sure everything was set up properly. I had made four trial handles just to make certain that I had all the settings and the routing sequence right. The bulk of the waste is removed with a ¼in (6mm) straight-side cutter. A dovetail cutter is then fitted to undercut the inside edge of the handle and plane the bottom of the recess.

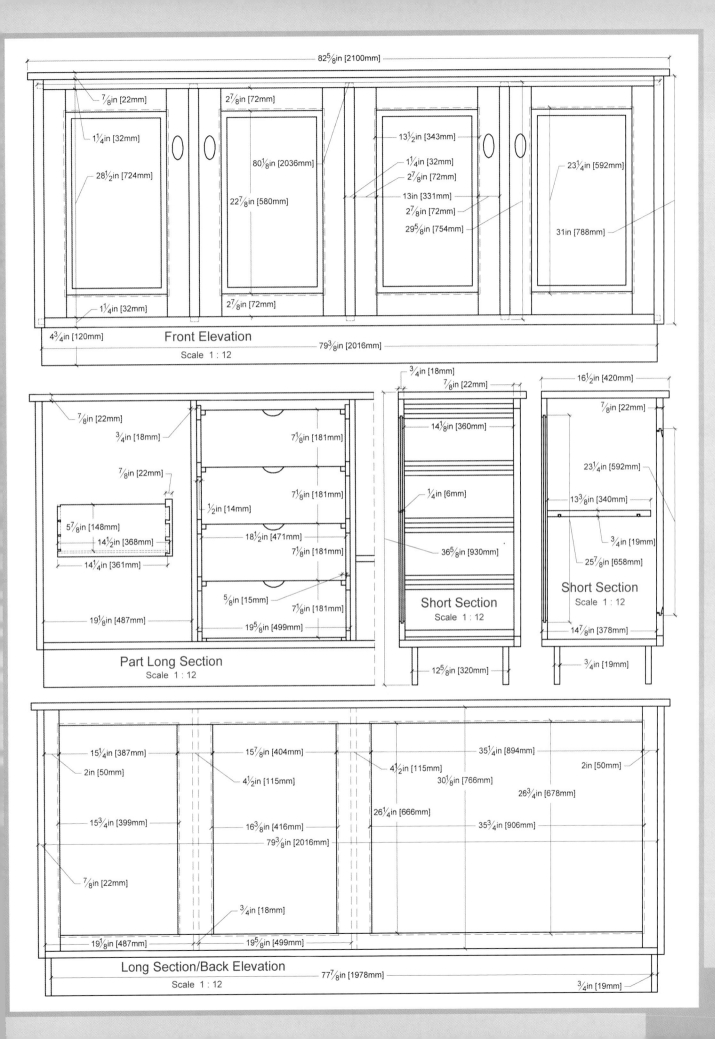

82⅝in [2100mm]

⅞in [22mm]
2⅞in [72mm]
1¼in [32mm]
80⅛in [2036mm]
28½in [724mm]
22⅞in [580mm]
13½in [343mm]
1¼in [32mm]
2⅞in [72mm]
13in [331mm]
2⅞in [72mm]
29⅝in [754mm]
23¼in [592mm]
31in [788mm]
1¼in [32mm]
2⅞in [72mm]

Front Elevation
4¾in [120mm]
79⅜in [2016mm]
Scale 1 : 12

⅞in [22mm]
¾in [18mm]
⅞in [22mm]
5⅞in [148mm]
14½in [368mm]
14¼in [361mm]
19⅛in [487mm]
7⅛in [181mm]
7⅛in [181mm]
½in [14mm]
18½in [471mm]
7⅛in [181mm]
⅝in [15mm]
7⅛in [181mm]
19⅝in [499mm]

Part Long Section
Scale 1 : 12

¾in [18mm]
⅞in [22mm]
14⅛in [360mm]
¼in [6mm]
36⅝in [930mm]

Short Section
Scale 1 : 12
12⅝in [320mm]

16½in [420mm]
⅞in [22mm]
23¼in [592mm]
13⅜in [340mm]
¾in [19mm]
25⅞in [658mm]

Short Section
Scale 1 : 12
14⅞in [378mm]
¾in [19mm]

15¼in [387mm]
2in [50mm]
15⅜in [399mm]
⅞in [22mm]
15⅞in [404mm]
4½in [115mm]
16⅜in [416mm]
¾in [18mm]
4½in [115mm]
30⅛in [766mm]
26¼in [666mm]
79⅜in [2016mm]
35¼in [894mm]
2in [50mm]
26¾in [678mm]
35¾in [906mm]
19⅛in [487mm]
19⅝in [499mm]

Long Section/Back Elevation
77⅞in [1978mm]
Scale 1 : 12
¾in [19mm]

CONTEMPORARY SIDEBOARD

A clean, uncluttered feel is achieved by using 'invisible' hinges and handles

• The completed sideboard – an interesting take on the frame and panelled door. The three central strips give a contemporary feel

THIS SIDEBOARD was commissioned for the ground floor of a town house that was being gutted and totally modernized. The soss hinges and push-action magnetic catches keep the design clean, in keeping with the uncluttered interior of the room. Four drawers are concealed behind the left-hand door.

CONSTRUCTION

Solid oak is used throughout, apart from the back panels and drawer bottoms, which are made from oak-veneered MDF.

The construction comprises a front frame, panelled back frame, solid base, ends and divider.

CARCASS

The top, ends, base, divider and shelf are all jointed from prepared oak thicknessed to ⅞in (22mm). I also prepared the three ½in (12mm) thick door panels at this stage. During the gluing process, the cutting list can be prepared for front and back frames, plinth and drawers. The panels are faced off, sanded and dimensioned and the frame members planed all round.

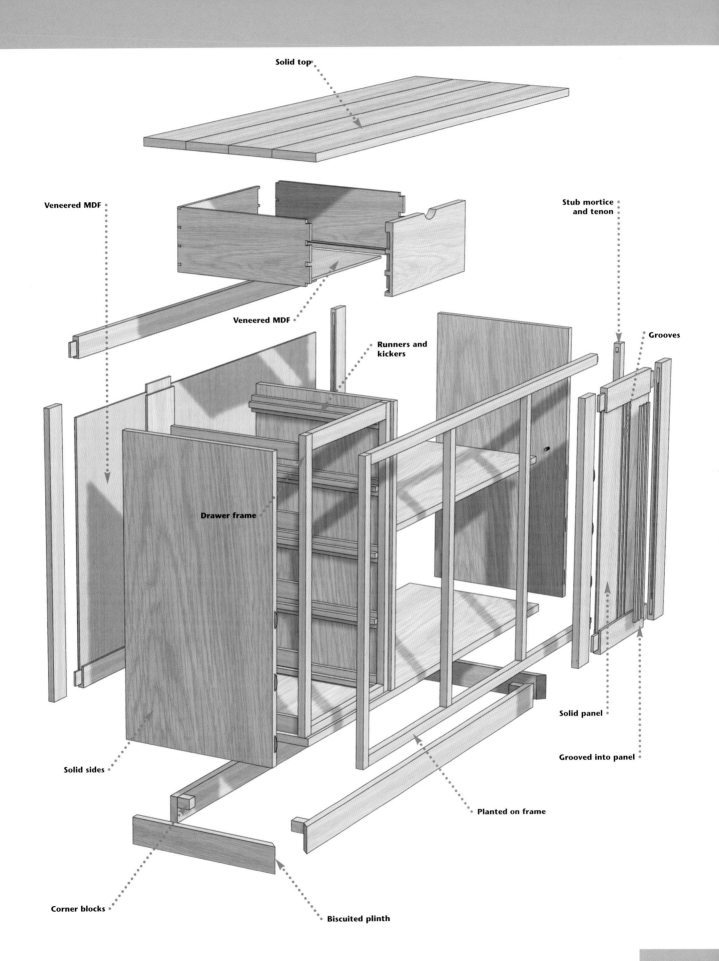

Solid top

Veneered MDF

Veneered MDF

Stub mortice
and tenon

Grooves

Runners and
kickers

Drawer frame

Solid panel

Grooved into panel

Solid sides

Planted on frame

Corner blocks

Biscuited plinth

• A close-up of the panel detail showing the three central strips, which are routed into trenches in the panels

Mortice-and-tenon joints are used to construct the front and back frames. Bear in mind that the front frame overlaps the end panels, but the end panels overlap the back, so the back is 1¾in (44mm) shorter than the front, and it is important to take this into account at the marking-out stage. The front frame construction is made first, followed by the back. The supplier I use for man-made boards now stocks French oak veneer, which makes matching veneered and solid stock much easier. The ¼in (6mm) veneered MDF didn't quite match my ¼in slot cutter. This is not particularly unusual in my experience, and required a second cut to open up the slot to the exact dimension. The panels and frame edges may be sealed prior to assembly which saves time in the long run.

Once all the components are dimensioned, the carcass joints are marked out. All areas to be glued are masked off and the internal surfaces sealed and denibbed – this includes the underside of the top.

Sequence of construction:

- Firstly, the divider is biscuited to the base.

- Secondly, the back is biscuit jointed to the base/divider assembly.

- Thirdly, the ends are biscuited in place.

- Finally, the front frame is biscuit jointed to complete the cabinet.

Excess glue can be peeled off when it's almost set. The outside of the cabinet is cleaned up, and the top edge planed true.

PLINTH

The plinth is mitred and biscuit jointed on the front corners and butt jointed at the back. Biscuits are used to reinforce the joints. The plinth is cleaned up and fitted to the cabinet with shrinkage plates. Fit the top with either slotted screw blocks or shrinkage plates.

DOORS

The door frames are morticed and tenoned. The panels are set into ¼in (6mm) grooves. Trenches are routed into the door panels into which the strips locate. The door panels, strips and inside frame edges are all finished prior to assembly.

Door frames and panels are glued up first. The strips are then accurately cut to length, before being glued into place.

DRAWERS

Fitting the drawer runners inside the cabinet needs to take into account an allowance for the thickness of the door on the left and the catch on the right. To accommodate this, an internal frame is fitted all round. The runners are fitted to slot-screwed blocks to fill the space between the frame and cabinet sides.

The drawers are traditionally constructed. The fronts stand above the sides to cover the runners and make convenient stops.

• Catches for the two right-hand drawers

• The left-hand side of the
sideboard has a set of four
drawers on runners

• The runner system for the drawers

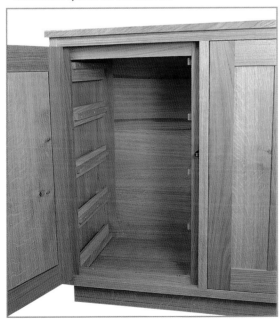

• Runners allow deeper drawer fronts and give clean
visual lines, as there are no dividers

• **Right-hand interior shelf and panel back**

In order to maximize the depth of the drawers, cutout handles in the drawer fronts are made. These are routed using a simple template and router guide bush.

SHELF

The shelf is fitted to notch around the frame of the back panel. Turned oak dowels are set into the cabinet sides to form shelf supports, and small notches are routed into the underside of the shelf to locate it.

FITTINGS

Soss hinges are concealed hinges, set into routed slots; allowing the doors to be opened to the full width – especially important for this type of drawer system. The result is very neat, the only drawback being the cost. Push-action magnetic catches are useful for making flush doors and, although a little big, look smart in black, picking up on the black features in other parts of the room. With the fittings set up, fine-tune the doors to give an equal gap all round; plane in any slight discrepancies to make the front frame and doors flush.

FINISHING

The interior of the cabinet was waxed, including drawers. Two coats of thinned polyurethane varnish were applied to the outside of the cabinet and the inside of the doors. These were cut back with 320grit silicone carbide paper and two coats of Danish oil.

• **Detail of the soss hinges**

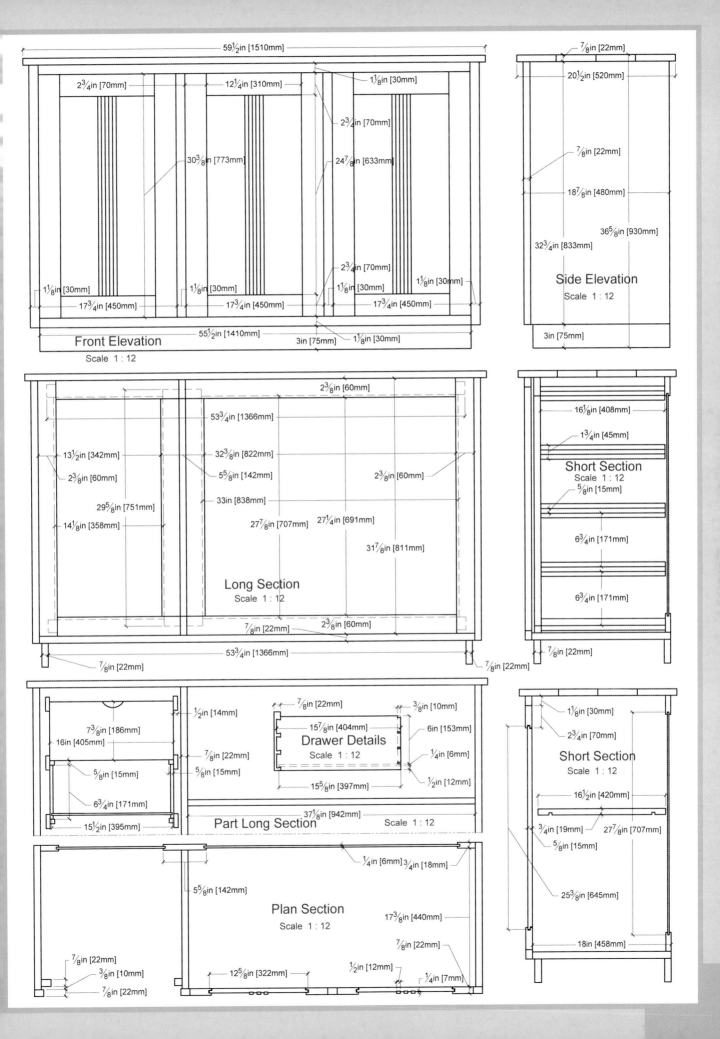

Offset handles complement the curved door frames of this large oak cabinet

• The cupboard
is made from French oak,
apart from the veneered back panel

THIS CUPBOARD was commissioned for the same chapel as the Large Occasional Table (see page 62), and continues the design theme of tapered ends and a gentle arch. I favoured recessed handles here, as they don't stick out and snag on things, and seem like they are within the piece rather than added to it. These are deliberately offset, accentuating the upward 'lift' of the piece.

TIMBER

The construction is in solid French oak (*Quercus robur*), apart from the veneered back panel. I like the pinkish tint to French oak, which gives it a warm feel, and I was gratified to find that veneered MDF boards are available in French oak, making colour matching much easier.

The top and ends are selected from the same boards as the table top. As the ends are tapered, I started with 2⅛in (54mm) boards, but selected those with only one good face. Once the waste had been planed away,

most of the rubbish had too, so the inside faces are also pretty fair.

The main part of the 1in (25mm) stock for this project was bought pre-thicknessed but still waney edged. As only the flattest boards are selected for this, they were actually straight, only requiring a final skim over with the surface planer and thicknesser to true them up. One of the advantages of buying wood like this is that selection is much easier. In this piece I wanted a curved rail to follow the curve of the tops of the doors, something also reflected in the plinth.

CUTTING LIST

The whole cutting list is prepared and the jointed panels set out for joint making. Although the door panels could have been single pieces, it is wasteful and

• The curve of the top rail is followed by the plinth rail

I felt that jointing them created a better visual balance. With the base, divider, ends, top, two shelves and four door panels there are 11 panels to glue up. The ends are tapered on the surface planer before jointing. They are ⅞in (22mm) at the top and 1⅛in (30mm)

at the bottom. This is created by planing a series of steps in the board and then turning it to plane in the opposite direction along its length. After gluing, the ends are hand planed flat and sanded. During the drying time, the frames are accurately machined.

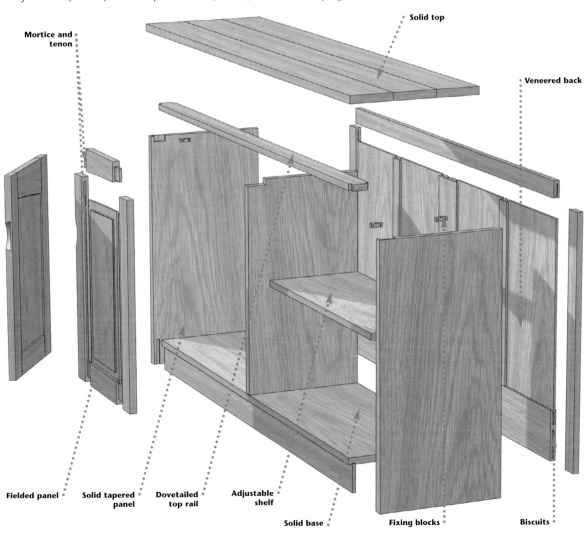

Mortice and tenon

Solid top

Veneered back

Fielded panel

Solid tapered panel

Dovetailed top rail

Adjustable shelf

Solid base

Fixing blocks

Biscuits

• The back panels have carefully placed muntins to create a symmetrical look to the cupboard's interior

BACK PANEL

The base of the back panel doubles up as a plinth and is, therefore, quite deep. A wide central muntin and two thinner muntins divide the back into four sections. The back frame is arranged in such a way that, when assembled, the width of the frame that is visible inside the cabinet is the same all around, hence the deep base rail and wide muntin.

There are a number of ways the back frame can be jointed; mortice and tenons being the strongest, but also the most time-consuming. As there is little structural demand on the panel as a whole, except to prevent racking, mortice and tenons are probably not essential. Stub tenons could fit into the same slot that the veneered panel goes into, but that can cause alignment difficulties. In the end I opted for biscuits.

MARKING OUT

With the back panel glued up and faced off, the panels can all be justified to their exact final size and the top rail and plinth dimensioned. The order of assembly is:

• Divider screwed to base

• Back screwed and plugged to divider and base

• Ends biscuit jointed to base and screwed and plugged to back

• Top rail lap dovetailed to ends and screwed to divider

• Plinth glued into groove in the base and ends.

The top is screwed to the cabinet through the top rail and with blocks to the ends, divider and back. As all the panels are solid with the grain running in the same direction, there is no need to use slotted blocks.

CARCASS JOINT MAKING

First, the positions of the drilled holes for the divider and base in the back panel are marked out – they will be counterbored to take ⅜in (10mm) pellets. The base is then marked for the screw holes for the divider, as are the positions of the holes in the back edge of the end panels.

Next, the biscuit positions are marked in the end panels and base. I fitted a lipping to the divider to make it wider at the front and more in proportion with the end panels. This lipping was 1in (25mm) wide and is biscuit jointed to the divider. A ⅜in (10mm) groove is marked in the base and cabinet ends for the plinth.

The dovetails for the top rail are marked out and cut. From these the corresponding socket is scribed onto the top of the end panels. It is easier to mark out the notch for the top rail in the divider after the front

• The frames of the back are biscuit jointed and the panels are veneered

• The inside of the door

lipping has been glued on. All the joint making is now done in the same order. The smaller diameter hole for the screw is drilled afterwards. The sides of the dovetail socket in the ends are cut with a dovetail saw and the bulk of the waste removed with a router before cleaning up with a chisel.

After fine sanding, mask off the area that will be glued and seal all the inside surfaces with thinned polyurethane. When dry, cut this back with a palm sander and 240grit silicon carbide paper.

ASSEMBLY SEQUENCE

First, the divider is lipped and cleaned up. The notch for the top rail can then be marked and cut, before fitting the divider to the base. The back edges of the base and divider must be perfectly aligned or planed true before fitting the back. The ends are clamped to the base with curved battens. These pull straight when the clamps are tightened up and exert even pressure along the biscuited joints.

With the clamps in place, pilot drill and screw the ends to the back. Each stage needs to be trued up, as necessary, in preparation for the next.

• Wooden pegs are used to support the adjustable shelves

• Fixing blocks on the top

The top rail dovetails are glued and tapped home with a mallet and block of scrap wood, and the centre is screwed to the divider. Finally, the plinth is thicknessed and sanded to push fit into the groove. The excess glue can be removed with a chisel (a crank-handled paring chisel is particularly useful for this).

The front, top and base are now planed flush and the corners chamfered. I use a tapered plug cutter to make pellets which gives more or less foolproof results, providing the plugs are cut from matching material. The top is sealed on its underside, edge-sanded and chamfered before fitting.

DOOR MAKING

The carefully selected top rail is cut to the length of the inside measurement between the ends. In order to keep the grain running true, the top rails are marked so that, when fitted, each will be in the same relative position as before it was cut. It is set out like a rod, with the divider, door stiles and length of tenons all marked out before cutting, and clearly marking which is which.

The bottom rails being straight grained are less of an issue. The stiles are cut slightly, about ³⁄₆₄in (1mm), over length to allow for fitting.

As the width of the top rails varies, so do the corresponding mortices and tenons, which are graduated in proportion. All the tenons are cut with a router on a tenoning jig before cutting the curves on the top rails. After the frames have been dry-fitted to check that the frames are flush, a ¼in (6.5mm) groove is routed for the door panels using a bearing-guided slot cutter.

FITTING THE DOORS

Begin with planing in one corner, bottom and hinged edge, then the opposing side and top are planed to fit. The tolerance round the edge of doors is a matter of preference: some very good makers, capable of producing very close fits if they want, often fit doors with a tolerance of ³⁄₆₄–¹⁄₁₆in (1–1.5mm), while others have closer fits of half that amount.

I tend to begin with doors almost push-fitting into their openings and then fit the hinges (in this case 2½in [63mm] drawn brass butt hinges), knowing the doors will bind and then ease them off.

By the time the edges are sanded the tolerance is ³⁄₆₄–¹⁄₁₆in (1–1.5mm) all round. It is certainly prudent to allow some room for movement on the closing edge of doors and I think it is neater if that gap is consistent. The edges are slightly rounded over.

• **The recessed handles are undercut with a dovetail cutter**

The panels are dimensioned, including the curve, to ⅜in (10mm) bigger all round than the inside of the edge of the door frame. Routing the panels to fit the grooves begins with undercutting the panels with the slot cutter.

The top panel raising is done with a twin-flute flat bottom bit with a 45° angle on the corner. I like the effect of what is a reverse chamfer that complements the chamfered corners on many of my pieces.

Because all the routing is done from the front of the door panel, the groove is of consistent thickness, even if the panel is not, and any small discrepancy is in the back. The routed mouldings are sanded and sealed prior to assembly.

The shelves are dimensioned and sanded. My usual practice is to fit turned oak dowels for shelf supports with notches routed into the underside of the shelves to locate on them.

The shelves are notched around the back frames. Again, a sealing coat is applied as a base for an oil finish.

HANDLES

The handles are recessed into the edges of the door in a shallow arc. As the handles overlap at the closing edges, the handle recesses can be quite shallow.

A simple curved template is clamped to the door frame and the handle routed with a dovetail cutter. To provide a better grip, the handle undercut is cut deeper with carving gouges and sanded smooth. The catches are double-ball types.

FINISHING

With the top and fittings removed, a sealing coat of polyurethane is applied to the cabinet and doors. The top is built up with two further coats of polyurethane, cut back between coats, and the outside of the cabinet given a second coat.

Two coats of Danish oil are applied to the whole cabinet with further coats to the top at 24-hour intervals.

After several days the piece is burnished and a final dressing of oil applied before delivery.

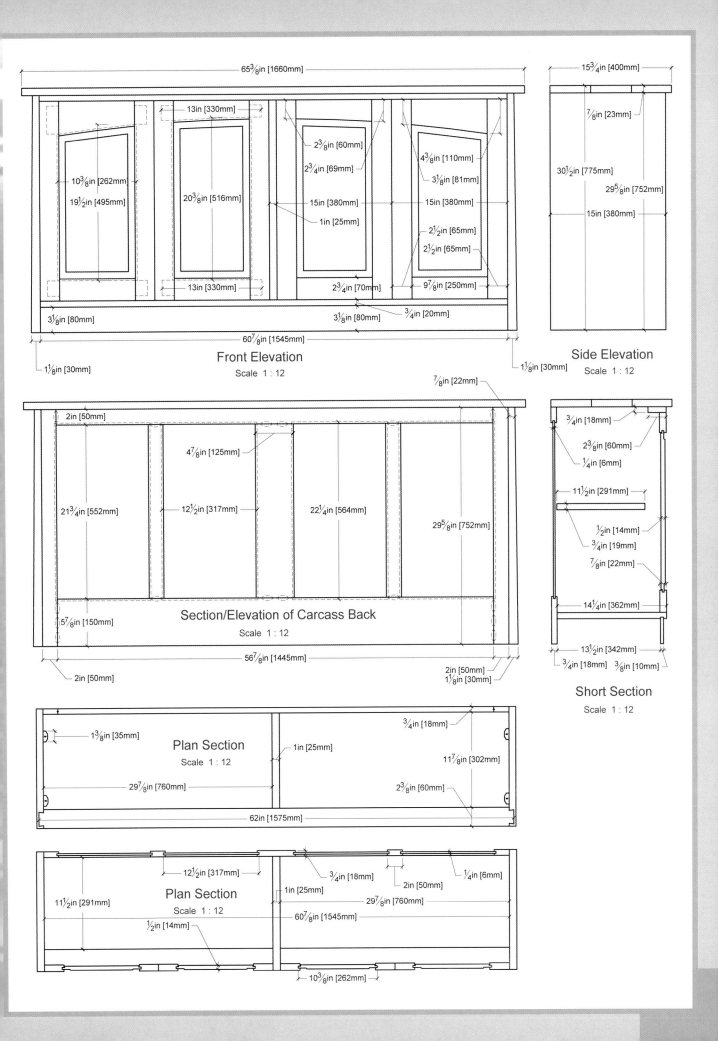

Front Elevation
Scale 1 : 12

Side Elevation
Scale 1 : 12

Section/Elevation of Carcass Back
Scale 1 : 12

Short Section
Scale 1 : 12

Plan Section
Scale 1 : 12

Plan Section
Scale 1 : 12

CHESTNUT DRESSER

One of a series for an 'unfitted' kitchen in sweet chestnut

THE DRESSER IS an interesting furniture type for a number of reasons: it offers versatile storage and display options, provides the focal point of a room and, for a cabinetmaker, it presents an opportunity to practise a wide range of techniques in a single piece of work, which makes up for the hard labour involved.

This example is the last in a series of nine individual pieces, mostly freestanding and sharing common design themes. They now live in the kitchen of a Victorian town house where some original pine (*Pinus* sp.) joinery still exists, and the designs take their cue from this.

To allow the dresser to fit into the space available it is deeper than it might otherwise be. At 4ft (1200mm) wide it is also quite narrow for a three-door format. This helps to create a chunky feel, but the same design, carefully reproportioned, could be longer and shallower and consequently more elegant.

TIMBER CHOICE

The selection of wood for this project is down to personal preference. I chose sweet chestnut (*Castanea sativa*) for this project, as its light colour which is reminiscent of stripped pine, suits the Victorian kitchen setting. Given the origin of the dresser, I think they work best in native hardwoods. Of these, coarser-grained timbers such as oak (*Quercus robur*), ash (*Fraxinus* sp.) or elm (*Ulmus* sp.) are most appropriate, although a good quality softwood like Parana pine (*Araucaria angustifolia*) could work well.

PREPARATION

Before embarking on the project I mentally divided the job into three sections of more or less equal amounts of work: preparation of the cutting list; joinery and construction; then fitting up and finishing. Preparing the timber for a complex cutting list can be

• Dresser in sweet chestnut

a daunting prospect, and I sometimes sub-contract out some of the initial machining. This doesn't, however, include the critical jointing up, facing off and dimensioning of the wider boards. To face-plane wide boards I use a No. 7 jointer plane working at 45° to the direction of cut, the iron being ground straight; it is tempting to grind a curve on the blade to remove stock more quickly, but this creates more work later on. The drawer linings should be prepared as early as possible, then put into stick in a dry place.

CONSTRUCTION SEQUENCE

The illustrations show the construction of a dresser without base shelves and with only one shelf in each of the top cupboards; these details can easily be altered. The sequence of construction is as follows: base carcass and plinth; top carcass; backs and bottoms; doors; drawers.

The base carcass is made from a front frame dowelled to four vertical panels, with two horizontal rails forming the main structure of the back.

The front frame is a mortice and tenon structure with cross-halvings at the intersections. A bead is cut into the end stiles of the frame on their outer edge.

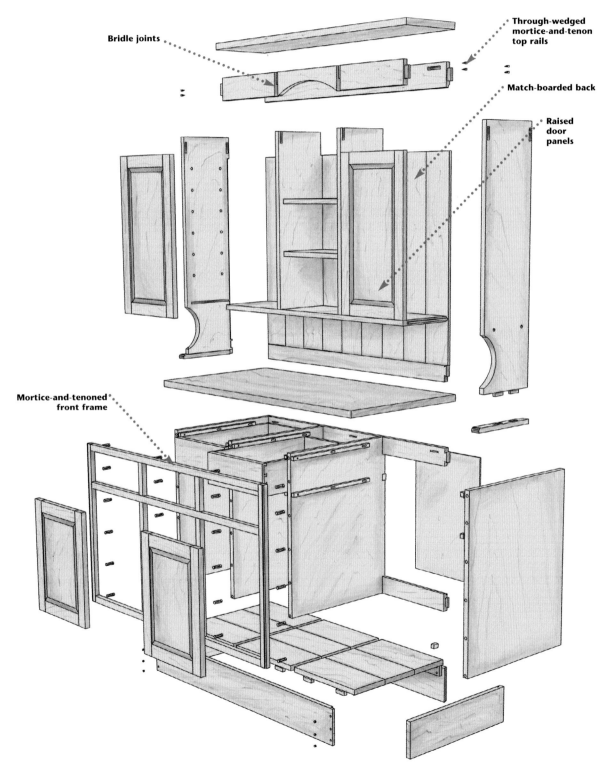

Bridle joints

Through-wedged mortice-and-tenon top rails

Match-boarded back

Raised door panels

Mortice-and-tenoned front frame

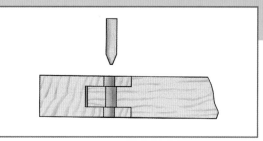

• **Draw-boring mortice and tenon – ¾₄in (1mm) offset between holes**

DRAW-PEGGED TENONS

To fit pegs to the mortice and tenons the same approach may be used as in the loose-tenon edge joint (see 'Joint Action' panel, right). Draw pegs, which pull the tenon into the mortice rather than merely restraining it, are a stronger solution.

The diagram above shows the relative position of the holes, and the modified peg cut almost to a point to ease it through the staggered holes and out the other side without damaging the wood. This is worth practising as the positioning of the holes is vital to the success of the joint. The pegs can be made on the lathe, or whittled with a knife.

The construction of the base demands a step between the drawer aperture in the front frame and the cabinet sides. This is overcome by fitting ply spacers against which the drawer sides will run.

The hardwood top and bottom runners are slot-screwed to the cabinet sides.

BASE CARCASS

The construction of the rest of the base carcass is relatively straightforward. The sides and dividers are dowelled to the front frame at approximately 4in (100mm) intervals.

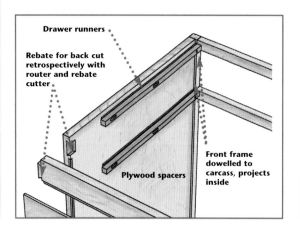

Drawer runners

Rebate for back cut retrospectively with router and rebate cutter

Plywood spacers

Front frame dowelled to carcass, projects inside

JOINT ACTION

There are various schools of thought about improving on the basic glued edge joint. Most of the time a straight and square joint that is glued under pressure is adequate, but, being a little cautious, I like to reinforce it.

Ply tongues increase the gluing area and help to align the pieces in gluing up; however, they are fiddly and time-consuming, and still totally dependent on glue.

Here I used a variation of the mortice and loose tenon joint. Mortices are routed into the end of each board – on longer work in the middle as well – and birch ply loose tenons are fitted. These are usually about 1¾ x ¾ x ¼in (45 x 19 x 6mm). They provide extra gluing area where it is needed, and can be pegged.

Holes for pegs are drilled before assembly; after assembly and planing the hole is rebored to clear out glue and the tenon drilled through.

If the peg is to be visible it can be turned on the lathe in the same material as the rest of the work, cut to a slight taper, glued and hammered home. If there is a face side where the joint is not to be seen, the hole for the peg can be stopped and a fluted dowel fitted from the 'in' side of the panel.

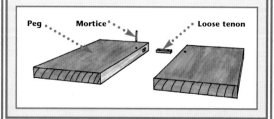

Peg   Mortice   Loose tenon

The back rails are joined to the sides with lap dovetails, and notched and screwed to the central dividers. The small rail to take the dust board above the kneehole is half-lapped and screwed. The groove for the dust board must be cut before assembly, along with the mortices for the buttons onto which the top is fitted.

The rebates for the back are cut at this stage, though some of them can be finished off with a rebate cutter and router after assembly.

Ash-veneered ply was used for the cupboard backs and dust board, with solid wood match-boarding for the kneehole back.

SAND, SCRAPE OR PLANE?

A fine and sensitive finish is produced by the use of a sharp smoothing plane and cabinet scraper, but there is a lot of surface area here. An alternative is a portable belt sander – a difficult tool to use with a consistent degree of accuracy, but useful as part of the process of developing a finished surface.

I use mine as the basis for either a hand-sanded or scraped surface where the grain is wild and does not plane easily.

Once assembled and cleaned up, the plinth is fitted and the bottoms prepared. Keep these loose for now to make finishing less awkward.

TOP CARCASS

The top carcass appears complex but, with careful planning, it can be made in a series of fairly simple follow-through operations. Mark out all the joints in the order in which they will be cut, as follows:

- Housing joints – bottom shelf to sides; dividers to bottom shelf; small central shelves

- Rails – front top rail bridle joints to dividers; back top rail, notched and screwed to dividers

- Both top rails – mortice and tenons to sides

- Bottom rail – lap dovetails into sides

- Sides/feet – mortice and tenons.

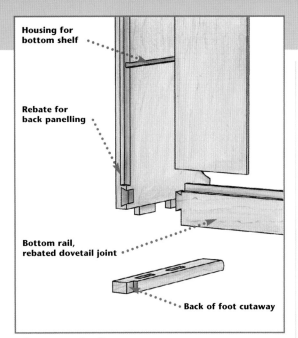

Housing for bottom shelf

Rebate for back panelling

Bottom rail, rebated dovetail joint

Back of foot cutaway

• Top carcass detail

When marking out the joints note the arrangement of the feet and bottom rail (see diagram above). The housing joints in the bottom shelf are screwed, counterbored and plugged. Once all the joints are marked and double-checked they may be cut.

Cut the rebates for the back before assembly. The bottom shelf and dividers are set forward of the ends to allow the back to lie on them, so that rebates need only to be cut in the sides and top/ bottom rails.

The curves in the top rail and sides are cut after the joints, but before assembly.

TOP ASSEMBLY

The top may be assembled in a number of stages: dividers and central shelves; top rails and bottom shelf to divider assembly; feet to sides; sides and bottom rail to shelf assembly.

To help with cleaning up, fit the housing joints dry and apply masking tape around them, peeling it off when the glue has gone off.

Lastly, make and fit the match-boarded back.

DOORS, DRAWERS, HANDLES

The door construction is in keeping with the rest of the piece, with fielded panels and drawbored mortice and tenons.

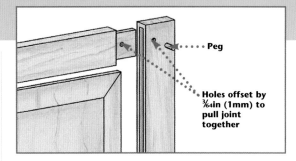

Peg

Holes offset by ¾in (1mm) to pull joint together

• Drawers are fitted through a front frame

Drawers are of an entirely conventional dovetailed construction; the sides are thick enough at ¾in (18mm), to be grooved for the drawer bottoms; drawer slips aren't necessary. Ash-veneered ply is used for the bottoms, and the drawer stops are small blocks screwed to the cabinet sides at the backs of the drawers.

The design of the handles picks up the moulded detail from the front frame. A disc is turned to make the profile, the pieces then being sawn, sanded and reassembled.

The pegs are fitted after assembly – I used elm offcuts to make the handles as the grain is very similar to chestnut, with a complementary colour.

BASE TOP AND FINISHING

The top of the base is finished to 1⅛in (30mm). The stock is darker than the rest of the piece and matched the elm handles perfectly – a happy accident. The hinges are 2⅜in (60mm) solid brass butts, and the catches are double ball, again in brass.

Thinned polyurethane varnish was used to build up the finish. The main top is also finished in polyurethane, burnished and dressed with Danish oil.

To set up the dresser, screw the top section to the base, then fit the base top to the base unit.

MECHANICAL CONSTRUCTIONS

The simplicity and efficiency of traditional joinery fascinates me and I am more and more drawn to mechanical constructions, i.e. structures that work without glue. Glue is used in this design but the piece could work well without it.

A piece of furniture is never really finished, even when it leaves the workshop: humidity changes that cause wood to move, sunlight and the marks of everyday use will all affect the piece.

• Doors have drawbored mortice and tenons, back made up as match-boarding

• Conventional hand-dovetailed construction

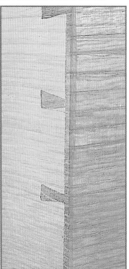

• Part section of turned disc showing profile of handle

• Handles are sawn from a turned disc

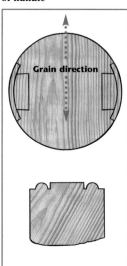

Grain direction

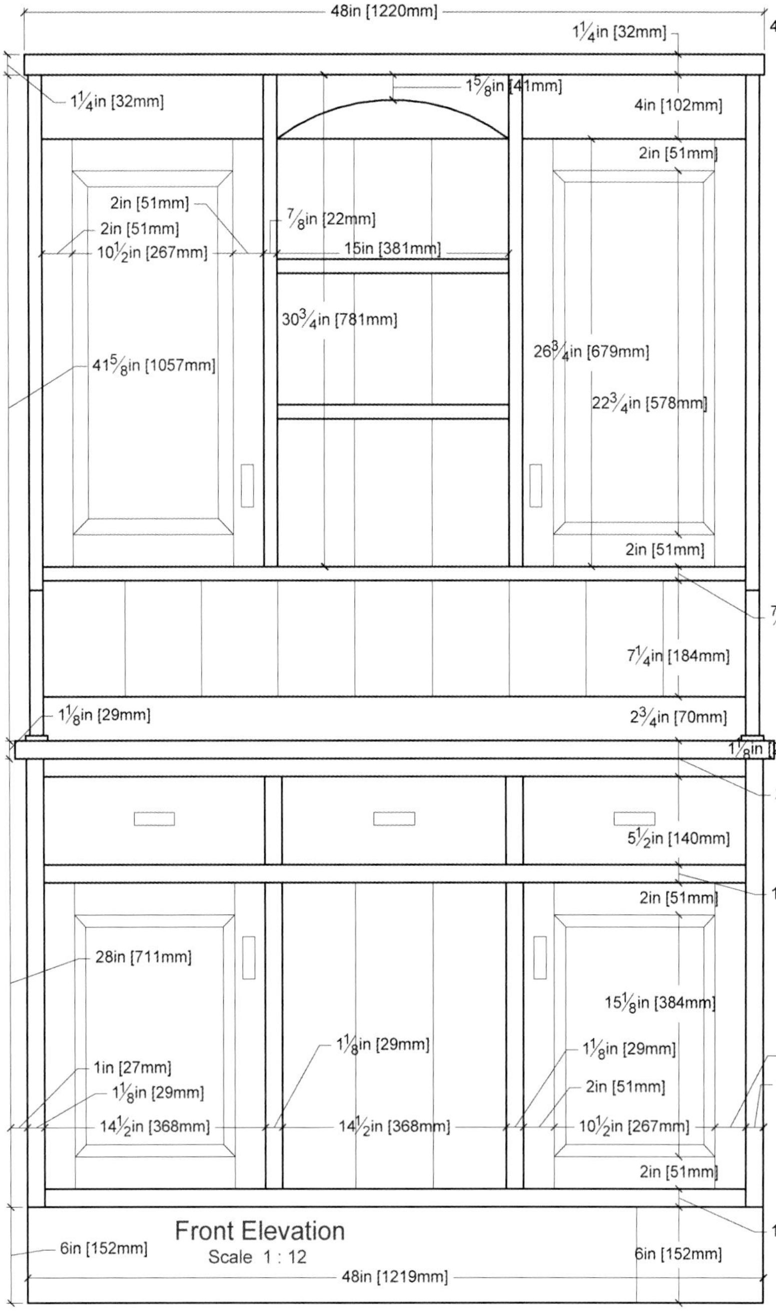

48in [1220mm]
1¼in [32mm]
4in [102mm]
1¼in [32mm]
1⅝in [41mm]
4in [102mm]
2in [51mm]
2in [51mm]
2in [51mm]
⅞in [22mm]
10½in [267mm]
15in [381mm]
30¾in [781mm]
26¾in [679mm]
41⅝in [1057mm]
22¾in [578mm]
2in [51mm]
⅞in [22mm]
7¼in [184mm]
1⅛in [29mm]
2¾in [70mm]
1⅛in [29mm]
2¼in [57mm]
5½in [140mm]
2in [51mm]
1⅛in [29mm]
28in [711mm]
15⅛in [384mm]
1⅛in [29mm]
1⅛in [29mm]
2in [51mm]
1in [27mm]
1⅛in [29mm]
2in [51mm]
1⅛in [29mm]
14½in [368mm]
14½in [368mm]
10½in [267mm]
2in [51mm]
1⅛in [29mm]
6in [152mm]
6in [152mm]
48in [1219mm]

Front Elevation
Scale 1 : 12

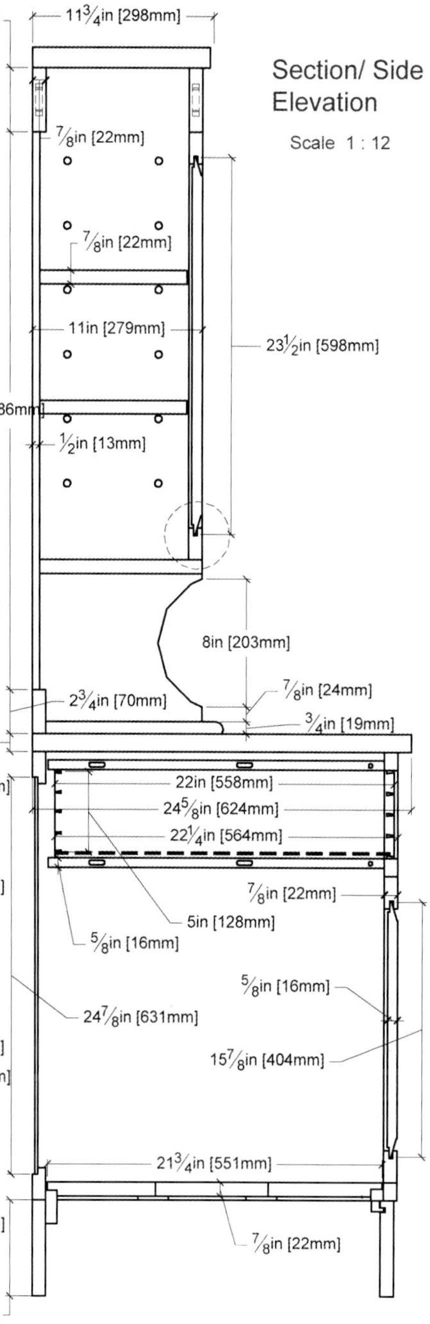

11¾in [298mm]
⅞in [22mm]
⅞in [22mm]
11in [279mm]
23½in [598mm]
34⅞in [886mm]
½in [13mm]
8in [203mm]
2¾in [70mm]
⅞in [24mm]
¾in [19mm]
22in [558mm]
24⅝in [624mm]
22¼in [564mm]
⅞in [22mm]
5in [128mm]
⅝in [16mm]
⅝in [16mm]
24⅞in [631mm]
15⅞in [404mm]
21¾in [551mm]
⅞in [22mm]
6in [152mm]

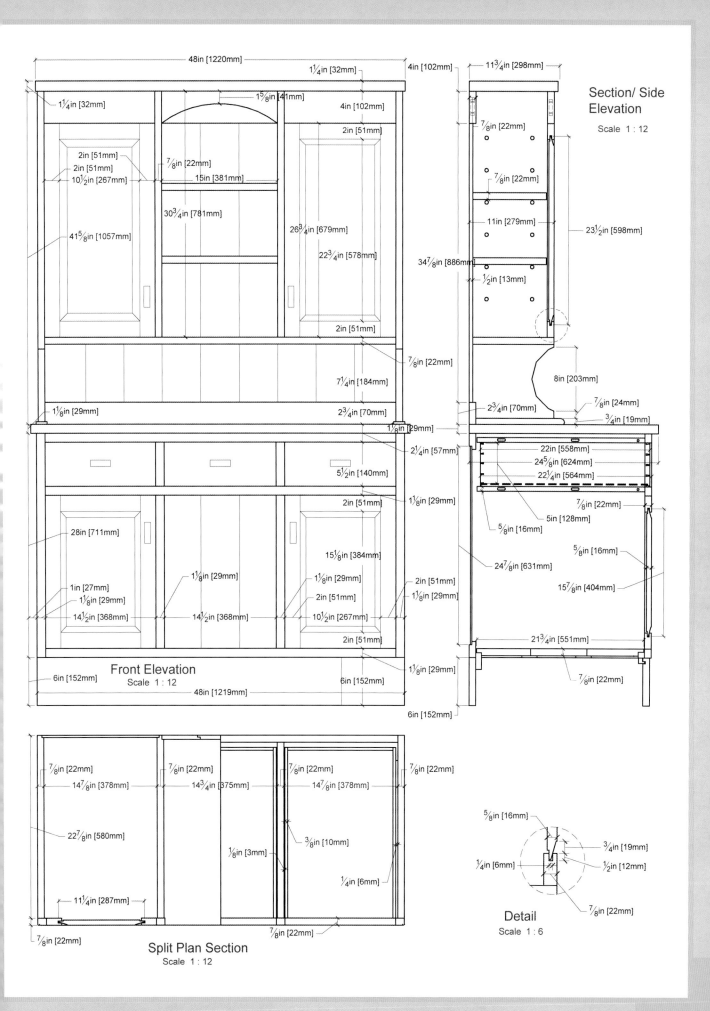

Section/ Side Elevation
Scale 1 : 12

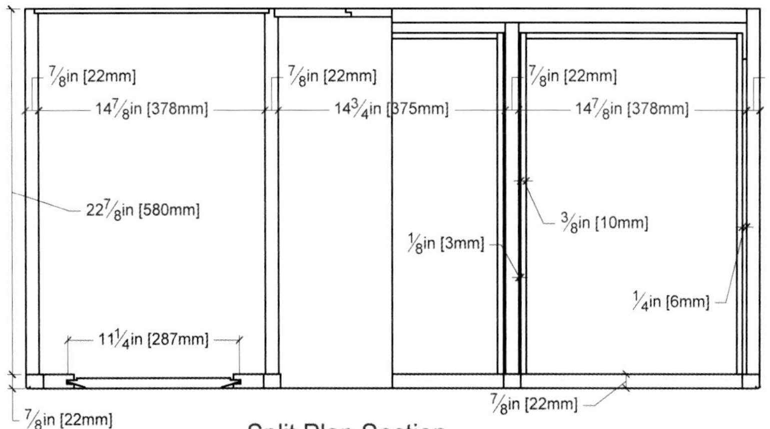

⅞in [22mm]
⅞in [22mm]
⅞in [22mm]
⅞in [22mm]
14⅞in [378mm]
14¾in [375mm]
14⅞in [378mm]
22⅞in [580mm]
⅜in [10mm]
⅛in [3mm]
¼in [6mm]
11¼in [287mm]
⅞in [22mm]
⅞in [22mm]

Split Plan Section
Scale 1 : 12

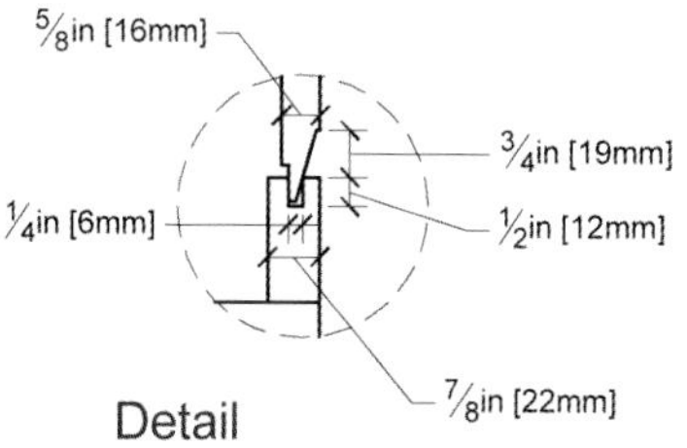

⅝in [16mm]
¾in [19mm]
¼in [6mm]
½in [12mm]
⅞in [22mm]

Detail
Scale 1 : 6

CHARACTER OAK DRESSER

Wild English oak is used in this piece for an old English manor house

• **Minimal decoration allows the figure of the wood to speak for itself**

THIS PIECE is the final stage of a study that was installed in a rambling manor house. The building seems to have grown organically over hundreds of years and recent improvements have been sympathetic to the original oak timber framing. Consequently, the timber was never in doubt – it just had to be English oak (*Quercus robur*). The client had a good idea of what the furniture was to achieve and the bulk of the job was built in. This comprised a large kneehole desk and wall-to-wall shelf fittings. Prior to redesign, the study also had a row of two-drawer steel filing cabinets. While practical, they were ugly and we decided to make a cabinet that would accommodate them. So, this dresser is designed so that the filing cabinets can be inserted through a removable back.

Making wooden filing drawers would have been an alternative but would have limited future uses of the piece. The top shelves are also adjustable.

DESIGNING THE DRESSER

I have used solid oak for the frames, doors, plinth and cornice. While I often use veneered boards for the interior dividers, shelves and backs of cabinets, and for the carcasses of fitted work, I rarely use them in the exterior of a piece. In this case I was swayed by a good stock of particularly attractive oak-veneered MDF, lipped with substantial solid wood edging.

This design is typical of my approach, which is to accommodate the client's requirements within a carefully proportioned cabinet. The proportions are delineated with simple recurring mouldings that also soften the piece visually and often reduce wear. I aim to harmonize the many factors that comprise a piece of furniture and provide a canvas for the wood to speak for itself. The handles are a repeat of the flush handles on the desk.

ATTRACTIVE CATSPAWS

All the stock I bought for the room was subtly infused with character. I cut the door panels on the bandsaw from 1⅛in (30mm) boards and finished them at ⅜in (10mm). Clusters of catspaws were arranged in the centre of each panel, the middle one higher than the others to create an arrow configuration that gives a visual lift to the base of the cabinet.

The stock had been conditioning in the workshop for several weeks after planing and thicknessing, having originally been air and then kiln dried. Wood that has been properly air dried and finished in a kiln is more stable than wood that has been superficially aired and then aggressively dried out in a kiln.

The construction of the base cabinet comprises a front frame biscuit jointed to the veneered end and divider panels. Wide top and bottom rails at the back are again biscuit jointed. A close-fitted veneered ply back is screwed in place and prevents racking in the rear of the cabinet. The bottom panels are fitted onto rabbets screwed to the end and divider panels. Using veneered panels greatly simplifies the construction, as you needn't take account of timber movement. The top section of the dresser is removable, as is customary, because the whole piece would be immovable otherwise. The construction is very simple but it is a big cabinet in its own right and requires some careful planning to make single-handed.

DAY OF THE DUST MASK

Preparing the MDF panels is relatively simple and considerably less pleasant. When using this stuff I am in the habit of doing all the machining in one day. Initially I cut up boards using a portable circular saw run against battens clamped along their length. I do the cross-cutting and sizing on the dimension saw. It is a day that the dust mask does not come off until after the whole shop has been vacuumed and all extractor filters thoroughly cleaned.

There are a lot of lippings to glue up, especially for the top section and they are fairly long, needing five to six clamps at a time. I made the shelves in three full-length pieces and cut them to length later. To avoid a clamping logjam later, it is worth preparing the biscuit joints first and gluing up three or four a day while constructing the base cabinet. I have a couple of old ½in (12mm) chisels with plastic handles that I use just for scraping off congealed excess glue – the easiest way of cleaning up.

• Interior of cupboard

LEAP OF FAITH

In preparing timber it is not really possible to see what the wood will look like until it is planed and, even then, the type of finish will affect not only the initial appearance but also the degree to which ultraviolet light will change the colour of the wood over the first year of exposure to sunlight. Synthetic finishes tend to inhibit this effect more than natural ones. For this reason I consider how and where the piece will be used and the effects this will have, then work back from how I want the piece to be in 12 months' time.

In cutting out material, I cut pieces as far as possible into common denominator widths and as long as the board will allow. By common denominator I mean that if the top is, for argument's sake, 23½in (600mm) wide and rails are required of 2⅜in (60mm) and 1⅜in (35mm) widths, then preparing 8in (200mm) wide boards is an economical width that can be sawn down or jointed up to make the necessary components. It is also comfortably accommodated by my 10in (255mm) planer thicknesser. Once the timber is faced off, you can decide what goes where.

IN THE FRAME

The first stage in construction is the front frame of the base unit. This is mortice and tenoned except for two cross-halvings, where the vertical centre rails intersect the bottom rail. Once glued up it is faced off and sanded. The biscuit joints between the centre panels and dividers are marked and cut. The outside panels are finished flush with the frame. Although it is theoretically possible to cut both parts of the joint from the same fence setting, in practice it is safer to reset the jointer to allow a ⁶⁴⁄₆₄in (1mm) projection of the solid wood from the veneered panel.

• **Doors are solid in construction with flat panels and a beaded groove**

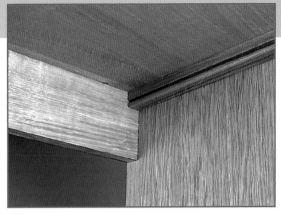

• **Batten supporting back of the top carcass**

In the interests of sanity, do not try to glue up the whole base assembly in one hit. The centre panels come first, followed by the back rails, then the ends.

Planing off the protruding frame flush to the ends is done with the cabinet up-ended and secured against the bench. I use a sharp, finely set smoothing plane to bring the frame to within a hair's breadth of the veneer. A cabinet scraper and sanding block will finish the job.

The plinth is mitred at the front. The front of the plinth is fitted first and the ends trimmed to fit afterwards. The front is screwed from the back of the front frames and the ends screwed from the insides of the end panels. The mitre joints are glued and cramped. Rabbets are fitted to take both the back and the bottom panels, which are planed to a close fit before being screwed in place.

FITTING THE TOP

The top is fitted with metal stretcher plates – although these are not as elegant as slotted wooden blocks, they are considerably stronger. Once the top section lippings have been cleaned up and cut to length, a couple of

• **Substantial solid lippings were biscuit jointed to all the carcass edges**

jobs remain before biscuit jointing and assembly can commence. Firstly, shims have to be fitted to the top and bottom of the insides of the end panels. These are finished flush with the inside edge of the front frame, and bead-moulded to create an attractive detail inside the cabinet. Secondly, notches are cut in the dividing panels to take the top and bottom back rails. The rails are screwed from the back into the vertical panels.

All the biscuit joints are marked out and cut before the joints are masked ready for finishing. I apply two coats of thinned polyurethane and cut them back with 240grit silicon carbide paper, providing a base for later oiling. I glue the dividers to the top and bottom panels first. They are clamped up with curved battens, which apply constant pressure across the whole length of the joint. The ends are glued in the same way and the back rails fitted retrospectively when the carcass is dry and cleaned up.

TOUGHER MITRE

Compound mitres are quite straightforward if you have a tilting-arbor bench saw with a sliding table; if not, mark out and cut by hand before planing to an accurate fit.

• **The simple, clean cornice**

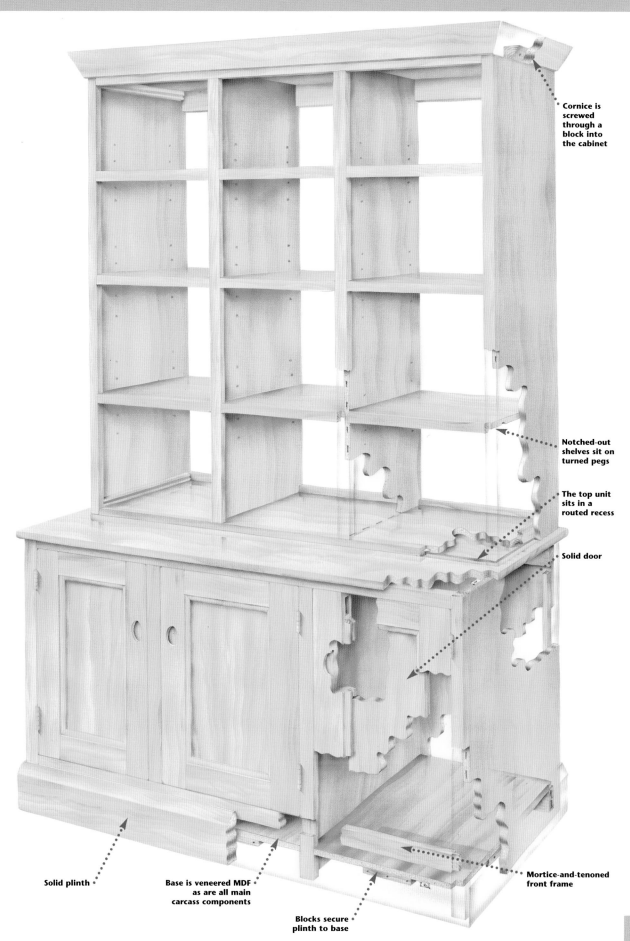

Cornice is screwed through a block into the cabinet

Notched-out shelves sit on turned pegs

The top unit sits in a routed recess

Solid door

Solid plinth

Base is veneered MDF as are all main carcass components

Blocks secure plinth to base

Mortice-and-tenoned front frame

• Detail of notched-out shelf

• Drilling the holes for the adjustable shelving

This does not take long, as there are only two compound mitres. Offcuts from the mitre joints are glued onto the outside of the rails to act as clamping blocks. Biscuits provide structural integrity and align the joint, which is glued and pulled home with a G-clamp. Dry-fit and clamp the joints before gluing and check that everything is square and true. Prime the faces of the joint with thinned glue before gluing up as the end grain soaks up glue, which can compromise the strength of the joint. This is important, as mitre joints are not that strong at the best of times.

Small wood blocks, bevelled to the angle of the cornice, are made to screw it to the cabinet. The top of the base cabinet is recessed to take the top unit by approximately ¼in (6mm). The top cabinet is placed in position and its perimeter scribed onto the base top. A dado is cut with a router and a small rebate plane is used to trim back to the scribed line. Joining the top to the bottom really is a two-person job, as the top has to be lifted up and down several times to check and trim to fit.

SOLID SUPPORT

I use ⁵⁄₁₆in (8mm) dowels turned from oak as shelf supports. I find that any form of removable shelf support eventually either falls out or gets lost, so I glue them in. It is fiddly and time-consuming, but a neat row of stub dowels is no more visually intrusive than the

holes they go into. The bead moulding from the inside corners of the top cabinet are repeated on the underside of the shelves. Small notches are routed into the ends of the shelves to locate them on their support dowels.

The door constructions are simpler than the normal raised panel design. The only complication is that the bead moulding is mitred at the corners. The top and bottom rails have to be made correspondingly wider to allow for the required cutout in the vertical rails.

A rebate on the back of the panel reduces it to the requisite thickness to enter the groove in the door frame. The door panels should be finished prior to assembly as, if subsequently they shrink slightly, ugly white lines will appear at their edges as unfinished wood is revealed.

The finish is as for the interior of the top cabinet, plus three coats of Danish oil, the final one burnished with 000 wire wool.

HANDLES AND FITTINGS

A template for the the door handles is made from ⁵⁄₁₆in (8mm) MDF. This is clamped to the door frame and used in conjunction with a template guide. The bulk of the waste is removed, using a ¼in (6mm) straight-fluted bit, before undercutting with a dovetail cutter. Dovetail cutters do not allow for a plunge action.

• Finished handle

• Template and guide bush for cutting the handle

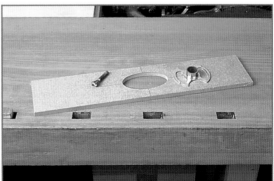

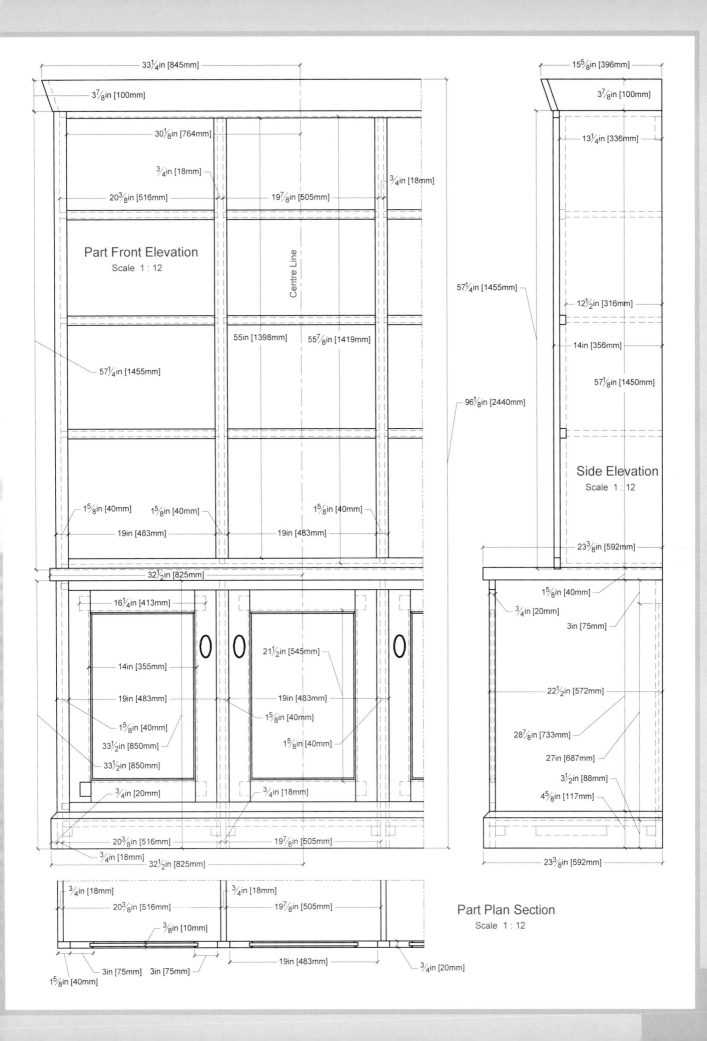

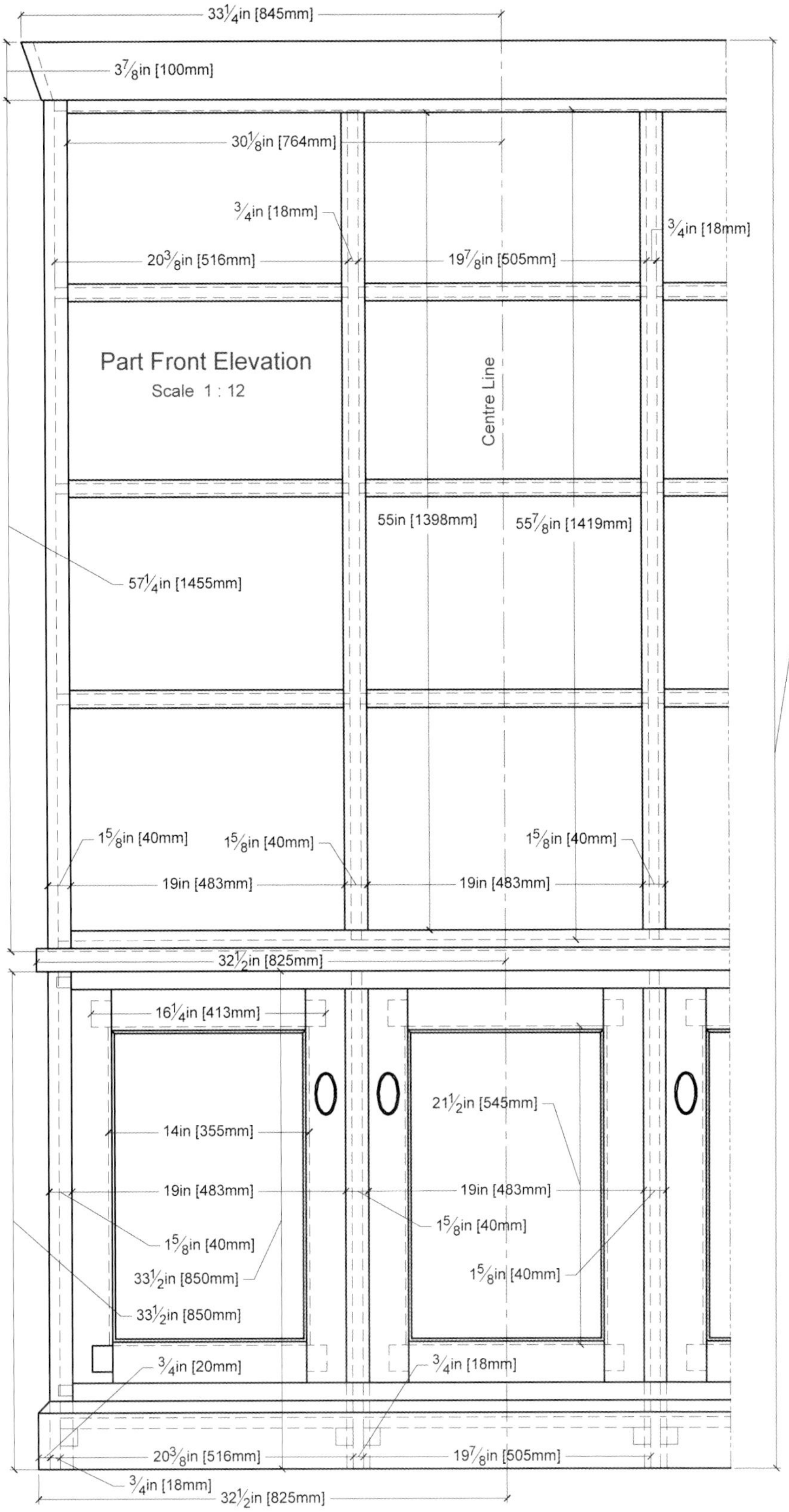
33 1/4in [845mm]
3 7/8in [100mm]
30 1/8in [764mm]
3/4in [18mm]
3/4in [18mm]
20 3/8in [516mm]
19 7/8in [505mm]
Part Front Elevation
Scale 1 : 12
Centre Line
55in [1398mm]
55 7/8in [1419mm]
57 1/4in [1455mm]
96 1/8in [2440mm]
1 5/8in [40mm]
1 5/8in [40mm]
1 5/8in [40mm]
19in [483mm]
19in [483mm]
32 1/2in [825mm]
16 1/4in [413mm]
21 1/2in [545mm]
14in [355mm]
19in [483mm]
19in [483mm]
1 5/8in [40mm]
1 5/8in [40mm]
1 5/8in [40mm]
33 1/2in [850mm]
33 1/2in [850mm]
3/4in [20mm]
3/4in [18mm]
20 3/8in [516mm]
19 7/8in [505mm]
3/4in [18mm]
32 1/2in [825mm]

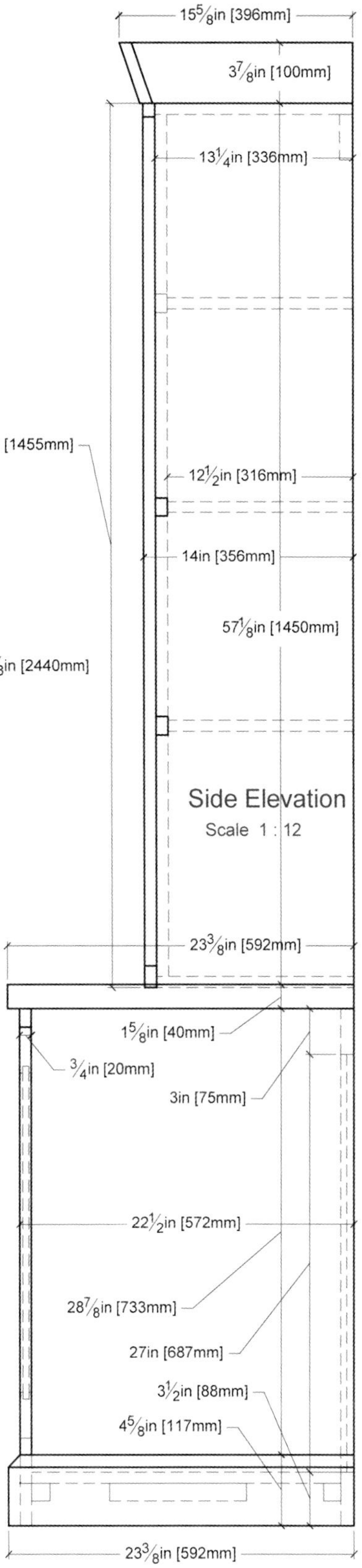
15 5/8in [396mm]
3 7/8in [100mm]
13 1/4in [336mm]
57 1/4in [1455mm]
12 1/2in [316mm]
14in [356mm]
57 1/8in [1450mm]
Side Elevation
Scale 1 : 12
23 3/8in [592mm]
1 5/8in [40mm]
3/4in [20mm]
3in [75mm]
22 1/2in [572mm]
28 7/8in [733mm]
27in [687mm]
3 1/2in [88mm]
4 5/8in [117mm]
23 3/8in [592mm]

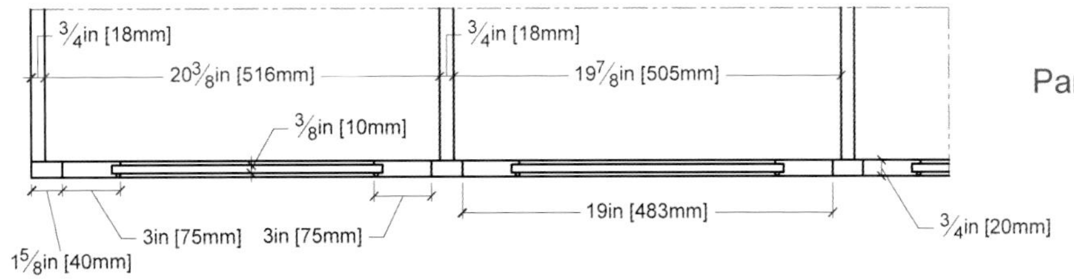
3/4in [18mm]
3/4in [18mm]
20 3/8in [516mm]
19 7/8in [505mm]
3/8in [10mm]
19in [483mm]
3in [75mm]
3in [75mm]
1 5/8in [40mm]
3/4in [20mm]

Part Plan Section
Scale 1 : 12

BREAKFRONT BOOKCASE

This simple, but imposing, piece in fine quarter-sawn oak would suit many homes

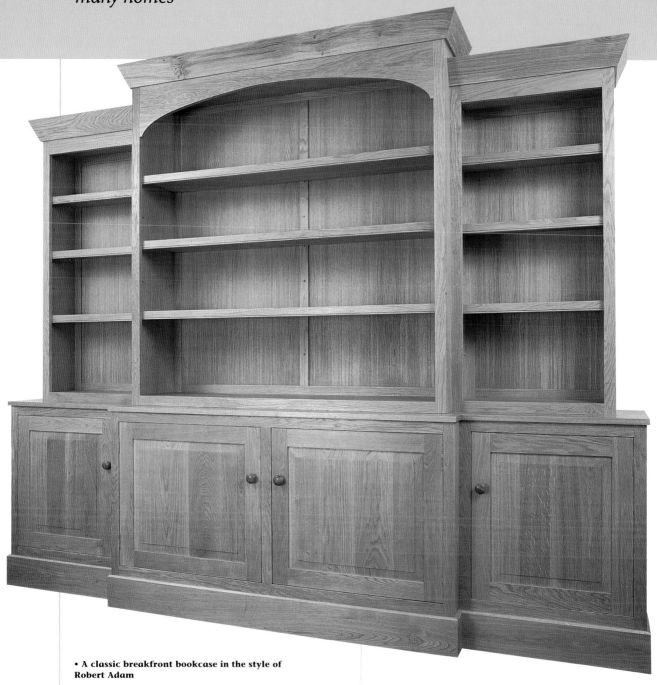

• A classic breakfront bookcase in the style of Robert Adam

THIS PIECE was commissioned to occupy a space in a big reception room. The open-minded approach of the client and my long-standing desire to make a big breakfront bookcase combined to generate this design.

The breakfront bookcase was first developed from the library bookcases found in grand country houses, some examples being 12ft (3.6m) long. George Hepplewhite & Co. mentioned the style in 1794 in the third edition of *The Cabinetmaker and Upholsterer's Guide*.

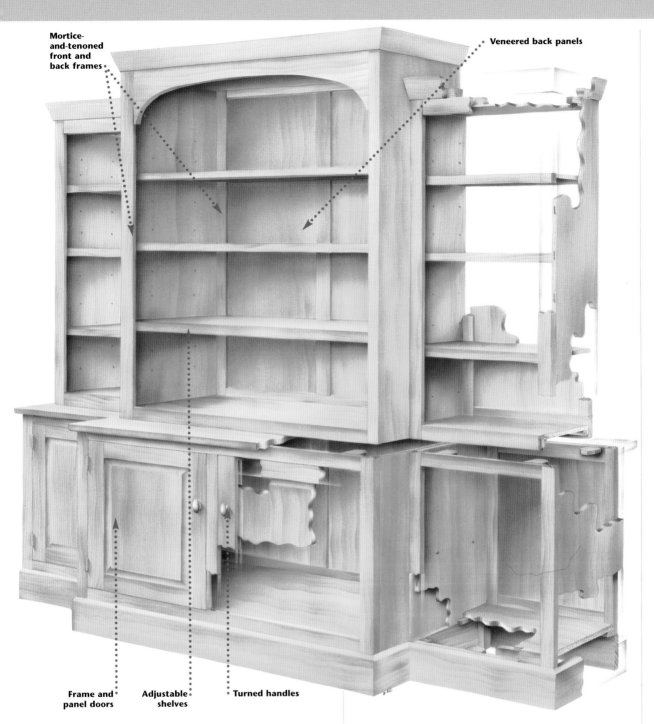

Mortice-and-tenoned front and back frames

Veneered back panels

Frame and panel doors

Adjustable shelves

Turned handles

He said the design was 'largely after the manner of Robert Adam', the legendary architect and furniture-designer who lived from 1728–92. Chippendale executed many of Adam's designs.

A pair of smaller pieces I had made for an adjacent room a few months earlier served as the basis for the detailing – when making a series of pieces for a house, even in different rooms, I like to create a strong visual link between them. European oak (*Quercus robur*) was specified and I bought it from a source I had used before.

CONSTRUCTION

The piece is made from six cabinets on a plinth, screwed together with brass screws. If it were ever necessary to move the bookcase, it would need to come apart. Rather than risking damage, I have made the means of assembly subtle, yet easy for someone else to find. Each cabinet is formed from a front frame, panelled back frame and ends. The bottoms are fitted to rabbets after assembly. Likewise the tops of the upper sections are fitted to rabbets.

VENEERED MDF BOARDS

Good quality veneered MDF boards are a
cost-effective alternative to solid wood for
interior dividers, shelves and back panels
and I specified them in this instance.
I also suggested them for the vertical end
panels in this piece.

There is a happy correlation between
European oak and crown-cut American
oak (*Quercus alba*) veneered boards – once
finished they are indistinguishable.

One positive side effect of this construction
is weight. Although this piece comes apart
for transportation, the top middle section
is still pretty heavy. Had I made it in solid
oak throughout it would have been more
difficult to manage.

I made the plinth so that it too would break down into
three sections, but on delivery it went into the room
in one piece. All the corners are mitred and the backs
are butt jointed.

European oak comes straight-edged, something of a
luxury for those like me used to waney-edged English
oak. Initially I thought the colour was a bit dull but,
by the time we took the pictures four weeks after
delivery, it had coloured up a bit and I was happier
with the result. Machining was a delight thanks to
the easy-to-handle sizes of the boards, combined
with good drying.

Plane and stack the various sections for the front
frames, back frames, door frames, plinths and cornices,
shelf-lippings, door and top panels. Apart from the
base top, which is finished at around 1in (25mm),
everything is finished at ⅞in (22mm). Reduce the
door panels to ²³⁄₃₂in (18mm) before butt jointing and
sanding. Dimension and label all the MDF panels so
that the grain runs through from top to bottom in
the vertical panels.

BASE TOP

This is made in solid oak. As most of it will never
be seen, selection for the central area is not critical.
Glue it up in two operations so that it can be machine
thicknessed. Finally, plane the central butt joint by
hand and sand on both sides.

FRONT FRAMES AND BACK PANELS

First, make the front frames and panelled back frames.
All have straightforward mortice-and-tenon joints.
At 10in (approx. 250mm) wide, the top arch in the
centre is at the upper limit for a glued joint without
allowing for movement across the grain. PVA adhesive
allows for some flexibility, and the wood was very dry
so I felt confident in using biscuits.

Set the veneered backs into routed grooves. Once the
front and back frames and vertical panels have been
accurately dimensioned, prepare biscuit joints for the
fronts and corresponding screwed back joints. Before
assembly, mask the joints off and seal all the internal
surfaces with two coats of thinned polyurethane,
then cut back ready for oiling. Given the large areas
involved in this project, a palm sander fitted with
320grit silicon carbide paper is a great time-saver.

CABINET ASSEMBLIES

Use biscuits to fit the front frames to the sides. Set
the sides in from the front frames by a small margin
so that you can carefully plane the edges of the

• Plinth detail

• There is an overhang on the end

solid wood frames flush with the ends. The bottoms of the cabinets are fitted onto rabbets and screwed from the underside.

PLINTH

Given the size of the project – and the need for the corners of the cabinets to meet the mitres all the way round the breakfront plinth – you need a high degree of accuracy. A mason's mitre in the reverse angle helps to simplify things and makes it easier to reduce the piece to manageable sizes for transportation. I like to think ahead in such situations, considering what will make the piece easier to move, use or, if necessary, repair, in the future. These are the small things that could make the difference between a piece lasting for

one generation, or several generations. The backs of the plinth carcasses have butt biscuit joints, while all the outside corners are mitred. 45° clamping blocks are glued to the outside ends of the joints and allowed to dry. The joints can then be clamped up dry and planed to a perfect fit, before cutting the biscuit slots and gluing up. After sawing off the clamping blocks and cleaning up the assembly, a chamfer is routed along the front top edge.

CORNICES

The compound mitres in the cornices are individually marked out, and sawn slightly off the line on the bandsaw after the bevels are planed top and bottom. Because of the forward tilt of the cornice, the angles are some way off 45° to the faces of the components and are complex to set up on a bench saw. Bandsawing to a marked line, and planing in by hand, is quick enough since there are so few of them. Once again clamping blocks are fitted to aid assembly. The cornices are fitted with bevelled blocks screwed to the tops of the carcasses.

SETTING UP

Set up the three base sections upside down and screw them together from the insides of the end cabinets. Plane any minor discrepancies flat before fitting the plinth with small screw blocks. Once turned over, the assembly can be planed flush on the top surface and set up perfectly level.

• View from the ground, showing cornices and curved arch on main carcass

• Interior of main cabinet with doors open

• **Cabinets are screwed together – note the wooden dowels to support the shelves**

Use slotted screw blocks to fit the solid wood top. Apply two coats of sanding sealer before fitting the top cabinets. The centre top section is next, followed by the ends. Again these are screwed together from inside the end cabinets. Having carefully aligned the top assembly, screw through the underside of the top.

SHELVES

The shelves are lipped along their front edges with heavy solid oak strips. Apply a bead moulding to the top shelves. Turn ⅜in (8mm) diameter oak dowels and glue into holes bored into the cabinet sides.

• **Traditional fielded panels on the doors**

You can make a template to do this. The shelf positions are graduated, getting closer together towards the top, creating a more visually satisfying arrangement than equal increments. How the shelves are spaced, however, is determined to a large extent by the intended use.

DOORS

These doors are quite big in cabinetmaking terms and are proportioned appropriately. I cut the raised panel mouldings on the bench saw. To do this, remove the crown guard and replace with a long L-section shop-made guard clamped along the length of the table, making physical contact with the blade impossible. Finish the cut with a skew-angle block plane and seal prior to assembly.

Undercut a rebate with the router to fit an ⅜in (8mm) wide by ½in (12.5mm) deep groove in the door frames. The only fittings I bought were 2½in (65mm) butt hinges and double-ball catches, both in solid brass.

FINISHING

Give all the shelves, doors and exterior surfaces two coats of thinned polyurethane and cut back in preparation for building the finish with Danish oil. Having allowed a few days for the final oil coat to harden, burnish and wax the whole piece.

• **Fielded doors are flat on the interior side**

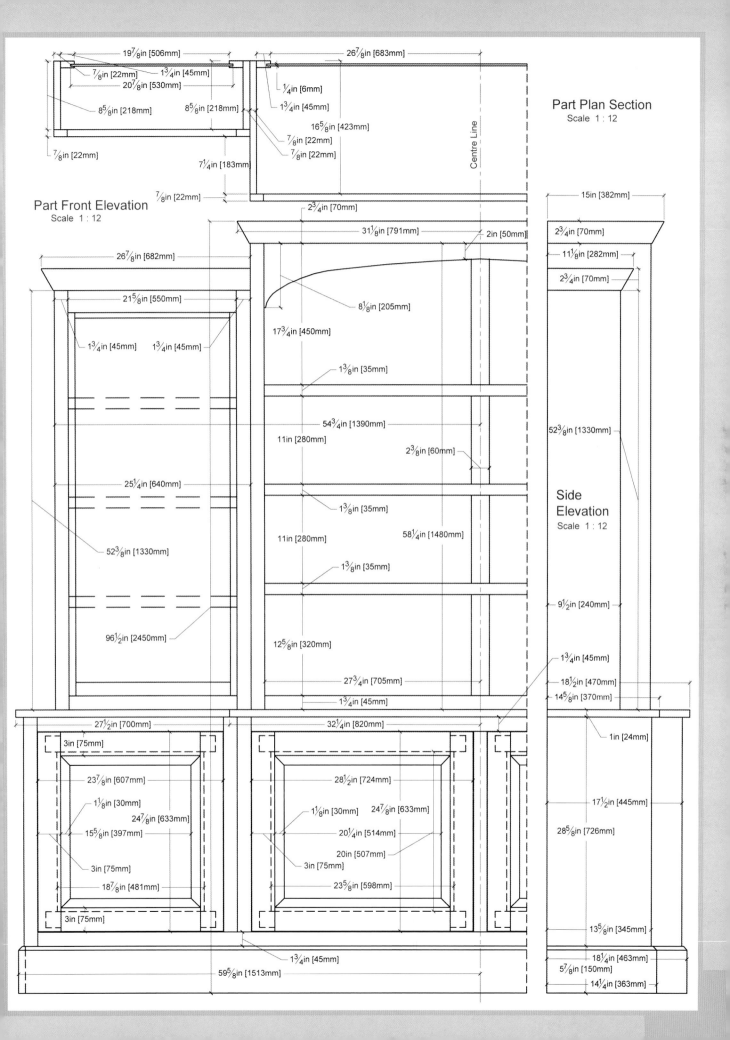

Part Plan Section
Scale 1 : 12

Part Front Elevation
Scale 1 : 12

Side Elevation
Scale 1 : 12

19⅞in [506mm]
26⅞in [683mm]
⅞in [22mm]
1¾in [45mm]
20⅞in [530mm]
¼in [6mm]
8⅝in [218mm]
8⅝in [218mm]
1¾in [45mm]
16⅝in [423mm]
⅞in [22mm]
⅞in [22mm]
⅞in [22mm]
7¼in [183mm]
⅞in [22mm]
Centre Line

15in [382mm]
2¾in [70mm]
2¾in [70mm]
31⅛in [791mm]
2in [50mm]
11⅛in [282mm]
26⅞in [682mm]
2¾in [70mm]
21⅝in [550mm]
8⅛in [205mm]
1¾in [45mm]
1¾in [45mm]
17¾in [450mm]
1⅜in [35mm]
52⅜in [1330mm]
54¾in [1390mm]
11in [280mm]
2⅜in [60mm]
25¼in [640mm]
1⅜in [35mm]
58¼in [1480mm]
52⅜in [1330mm]
11in [280mm]
1⅜in [35mm]
9½in [240mm]
96½in [2450mm]
12⅝in [320mm]
1¾in [45mm]
27¾in [705mm]
18½in [470mm]
1¾in [45mm]
14⅝in [370mm]
27½in [700mm]
32¼in [820mm]
1in [24mm]
3in [75mm]
23⅞in [607mm]
28½in [724mm]
1⅛in [30mm]
1⅛in [30mm]
24⅞in [633mm]
17½in [445mm]
24⅞in [633mm]
15⅝in [397mm]
20¼in [514mm]
28⅝in [726mm]
20in [507mm]
3in [75mm]
3in [75mm]
18⅞in [481mm]
23⅝in [598mm]
13⅝in [345mm]
3in [75mm]
1¾in [45mm]
18¼in [463mm]
59⅝in [1513mm]
5⅞in [150mm]
14¼in [363mm]

SPECULATIVE PIECES & 'ONE-OFFS'

Stunning olive ash and asymmetric drawers make this cabinet unique

• **Contemporary feel in design and timber,
but traditional in construction**

THIS CHEST of drawers – and the two bedside tables on page 150 – were designed for the master bedroom of a spacious apartment. The clients knew what they wanted the pieces to do, but were open-minded about the design. One proviso was that they should be clearly a one-off, without being wacky – not a problem, as my work is quite traditional.

DESIGN AND TIMBER

The design was composed of traditional elements with a slightly unusual configuration, aimed at creating a pleasing asymmetry while retaining practicality.

Luckily, my first proposal was accepted and we quickly proceeded to viewing samples of the proposed materials.

I would never suggest a wood like olive ash (*Fraxinus* sp.) unless I had already found a supply. Nonetheless, a lot of wastage must be accounted for in order to ensure consistent colour. I also used English white ash (*Fraxinus americana*) with English oak (*Quercus robur*) for the drawer linings. I usually use American white ash for its consistent colour, but was assured this really was white, and ordered enough for the whole project on the basis of a small sample. The oak was bought as ¾in (19mm) but was actually slightly under.

DRAWERS

The drawer fronts are prepared from three boards 9¾in (250mm) wide and 59in (1500mm) long, finished at ⅞in (22mm). The selection of the drawer fronts is particularly important here, because of the contrasting colour. Having the grain running through from one side of the piece to the other, ties the whole thing together visually. The linings – drawer sides and backs – are finished at ⁷⁄₁₆in (11mm). Given the size of the bigger drawers this is too narrow to fit the bottoms into grooves, so drawer slips are used.

Veneered ply is used for the bottoms. This is strong, stable and economical and I generally use it for drawer bottoms in preference to solid wood. Olive ash is used for the slips to create visual interest inside the drawer.

The individual drawer components are fitted into the main carcass before the joints are marked out.

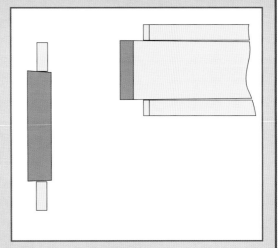

• Nuances of drawer fitting

The fronts are cut marginally over size and then very slightly bevelled all round by hand, until they push into their opening by about half their thickness. Recesses are routed into the underside of the drawer fronts to correspond with the recesses on the cabinet frame. A simple template is made for this, which is screwed to a batten enabling the template to be clamped to the drawer front.

As with the fronts, the sides are cut about ³⁄₆₄in (1mm) over width and then slightly tapered until they enter by about half their length. If possible, the grain should run from front to back of the drawer so when cleaning up and fitting later you are planing away from the front, and not towards it. The backs are scribed off the fronts for length.

• Inside the carcass, showing the drawer runner strips

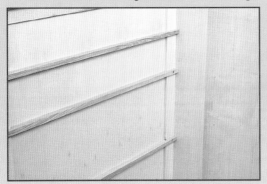

• The template for the slots

• Routing the finger slots in the drawer front bottom

• The completed finger slot and scallop

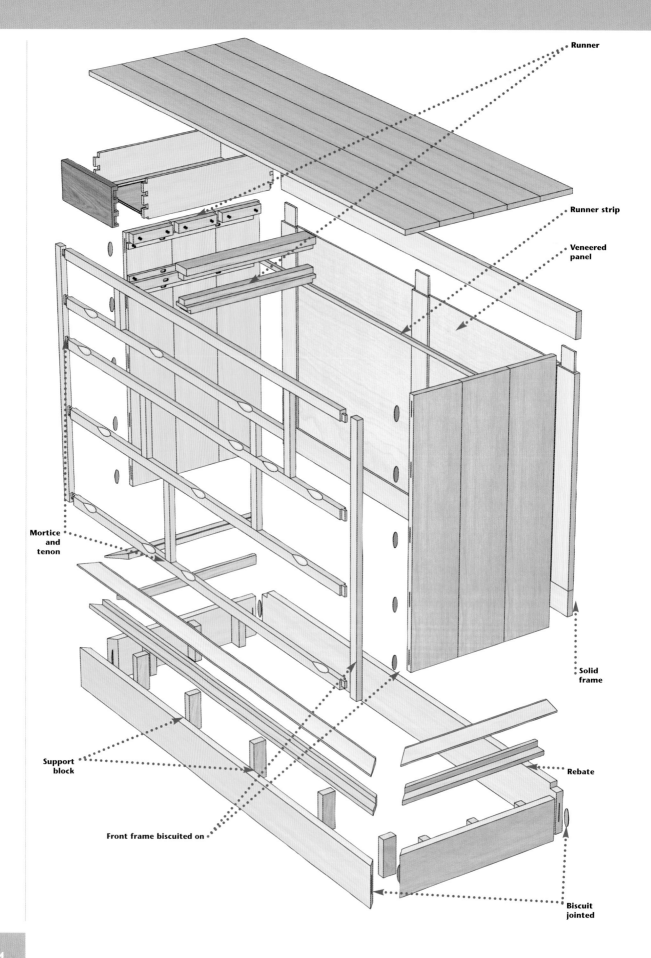

CHEST OF DRAWERS

Runner

Runner strip

Veneered panel

Mortice and tenon

Solid frame

Support block

Rebate

Front frame biscuited on

Biscuit jointed

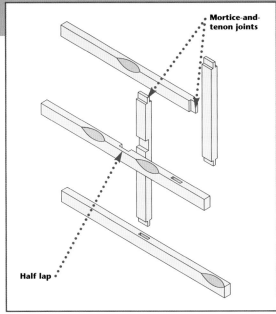

Mortice-and-tenon joints

Half lap

• **Front frame construction**

However, it was so flat and clean it machined up beautifully and, despite some worrying moments with stick marks, I was very happy with the prepared cutting list.

The selection of components from rough-sawn stock through to planing and dimensioning can be a nerve-racking process, as well as a physically tiring one, but once accomplished I could settle down and enjoy making the piece.

Customers visiting my workshop for the first time are often surprised to see their furniture starts out as large slices of tree, often with the bark still on. I like them to visit at least once, if possible, to get an idea of the work that goes into a one-off commission. The timber for all three of this client's pieces was prepared at the same time, though the stock for the small cabinets and drawers for the chest were put into stick for later use.

CONSTRUCTION

The jointed-up boards for the top and ends are prepared, and then faced off with a bench plane. This was a pure delight and boded well for workability in the joint making. This stage is, I reckon, to be about a third of the way through a project and is a good time to work on finishes, jigs and fittings if these have not been finalized already.

The construction consists of a frame and veneered plywood panel back screwed to the solid wood ends (see diagram on facing page). The front frame is biscuit jointed to the end panels. The plinth is a

separate carcass and the top is screwed to the main cabinet after assembly. Because the drawer runners are so complex they are fitted after the assembly of the cabinet. To incorporate them in the main construction would have resulted in an impossible glue-up.

Mortice and tenons are used for all but one of the front frame joints, the exception being a single cross-halving. Apart from the corners, the tenons are all the width of the rails. This saves time and, because the inner faces of the frame will eventually be covered by the drawers, any marginal discrepancy will not show. It goes without saying that marking out the joints for the front frame is critical.

At this point the recesses for the handles are cut. I had visions of a clever routing jig to do this but a mock-up of the handle detail made on the bandsaw revealed a jig would be difficult to make, and that the bandsaw was an efficient alternative. The curve is marked on the frame and the bandsaw table set to 45°. With a careful touch and a sharp ¼in (6mm) blade, the cut is quite straightforward. The job is finished on the end of the linisher.

A full dry assembly is required before gluing up, to check for fits and overall accuracy. It is necessary to glue and clamp the frame in a number of operations.

BACK FRAME

This is a reasonably straightforward procedure, but remember the back frame is shorter than the front frame by the combined thickness of the end panels.

• **Front frame is biscuited on to the main carcass**

For simplicity the three vertical components are all tenoned and the mortices are in the corresponding top and bottom rails. Dry assemble and face off the frame before dismantling to rout the grooves for the back panels. It is important to check the router cutter against the thickness of the ply. A ¼in (6mm) router cutter will be just that, but ¼in (6mm ply) may be anything from ³⁄₁₆–⁹⁄₃₂in (5–7mm). Fortunately for me this time it all matched, but it doesn't always!

The end panels, back frame and front frame now need to be justified so they are exactly the same height and the correct widths. Once trued up the battens can be fitted, which will take the drawer runners. These are ³⁄₈in (10mm) square except where additional depth is required to enter the recess formed by the back panels. They are screwed in place from the back, on the ply back panels.

Assembly begins with the end panels and back, which are glued screwed and plugged. The front frame is biscuit jointed to the end panels.

PLINTH

This is a complicated construction when made from 1in (25mm) ex-stock. From 2in (50mm) material it would be quick and simple, but may run the risk of the mitres opening up over the wider joint. So, for ⁷⁄₈in (22mm) finished stock, the process is as follows:

- A simple carcass is constructed using biscuits for butt joints at the back, and mitres at the front.

- The back piece of the plinth is ⁵⁄₈in (15mm) higher than the rest to allow for the addition of the bevelled lipping.

- Rebated strips are biscuit jointed around the inside top of the front and ends of the plinth, and trued up to provide an even face for the lipping.

- Reinforcing blocks are glued into the corners of the plinth and at intervals to the front and ends. This is to strengthen the joints and create a load-bearing structure.

- The outside corners of the mitres are routed and lipped to give protection to this exposed area.

- A bandsaw is used to cut the bevels for the lippings, which are cut over size and planed back after being glued in place.

SETTING UP

The plinth and top are fixed to the main carcass with small, screwed blocks. At the top and bottom of the end panels these double as drawer runners.

• **Interior, showing the veneered back panel**

• **Plinth support blocks**

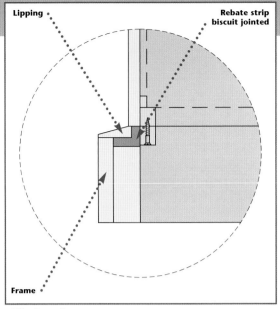

Lipping

Rebate strip
biscuit jointed

Frame

• **Plinth section**

At the front and back, screw blocks are used again. At the front these need to be rebated to fit onto the plinth. I spent a whole day on this job, setting up, planing in the top and bottom chamfers, checking for square and fine sanding, but this effort certainly pays off when it comes to fitting the drawers. The whole job can now be sealed – to retain the lightness of the ash I used a clear water-based lacquer.

DRAWER RUNNERS

As indicated earlier, the solution to this problem is driven by pragmatism rather than elegance. The runners at the ends of the cabinet are slot-screwed.

• **Plinth with bevelled lipping located on rebated fillet**

These are planed to the width of the frame members. Additional strips are prepared to fit above and below these to guide the sides of the drawers. Again, these are slot-screwed to allow for movement in the solid carcass sides.

The internal runners are cut to length and notched to fit onto the battens fitted earlier. These are screwed in place using 2 x ¾in (19mm) No. 6 screws at each end. Battens planed to the width of the front frame are screwed to the runners to guide the drawer sides. This is a full day's work and then some!

Supporting the cabinet on its end gave the best access, but final checking must be done when the piece is set up level and true on its base.

DOVETAILS

A marking gauge is used to mark the length and width of the dovetails. These are marginally less than the thickness of the linings – except on the ends of the drawer fronts – to allow for planing in after assembly. The setting out of the dovetails on the front is largely an aesthetic decision but here, where the drawer sizes vary, the dovetails gradually get bigger towards the bottom of the piece while the pins remain the same size.

Grooves are cut in the fronts to take the bottoms. These run straight through and will be covered by the lap dovetails.

• **Traditionally lapped dovetails on fronts**

• Runners and kickers

• Central runners and kickers

The drawer backs are cut to their finished height which will allow the bottom to run underneath. Dovetails can be cut effectively with a bandsaw, and the waste cleaned out with coping saw and chisel down to the scribed mark made by the gauge. The pins are scribed off the dovetails with a marking knife and are cut with a dovetail saw. Much of the waste between the pins can be removed with a router which produces a perfectly flat face, the remaining corners being cleaned up with a chisel.

The joints are masked off and the insides of the drawers waxed prior to assembly. I pull the joints in with sash cramps – this is gentler than the traditional hammer and seems to make a tighter joint.

Finally, the drawers are cleaned up and fitted with a constantly sharpened bench plane, before sanding and waxing. The runners are also waxed to ease running. The slips are prepared, glued and clamped in place and the drawer bottoms fitted. The bottom can distort a drawer so care is required.

The method outlined above differs in some respects from traditional practice and other makers will have developed their own variations, but such developments keep both our craft and its traditions alive.

FINISHING

The lacquer is cut back and two further coats applied; then cut back with 320grit silicon carbide paper, and given three coats of clear finishing wax before finally burnishing with 0000 wire wool. The drawer fronts – in order to maximize the colour contrast – are finished with Danish oil.

The slightly grey tones of the sanded olive ash burst into life with the first coat of thinned Danish oil. The marble-like figure flows through the front and I was pleased that we had decided not to plant handles on it, as this would have disturbed the effect.

Pure oil finishes lie in the wood, rather than on it, so preparation is particularly important as minor abrasives marks will not be 'filled' with the finish. Ash is coarse-grained and planing by hand will tend to leave it open.

My preference is to fine sand to 180grit with a palm sander, and sand by hand to 240 or 320grit. The resulting surface more than justifies the effort. To check that all abrasive marks have been removed, use a magnifying glass and low-angle light, preferably sunlight.

Thinning the Danish oil 50/50 with white spirit for the initial coat, and 80/20 for subsequent ones, prevents a thick build up of finish and really drives it into the wood.

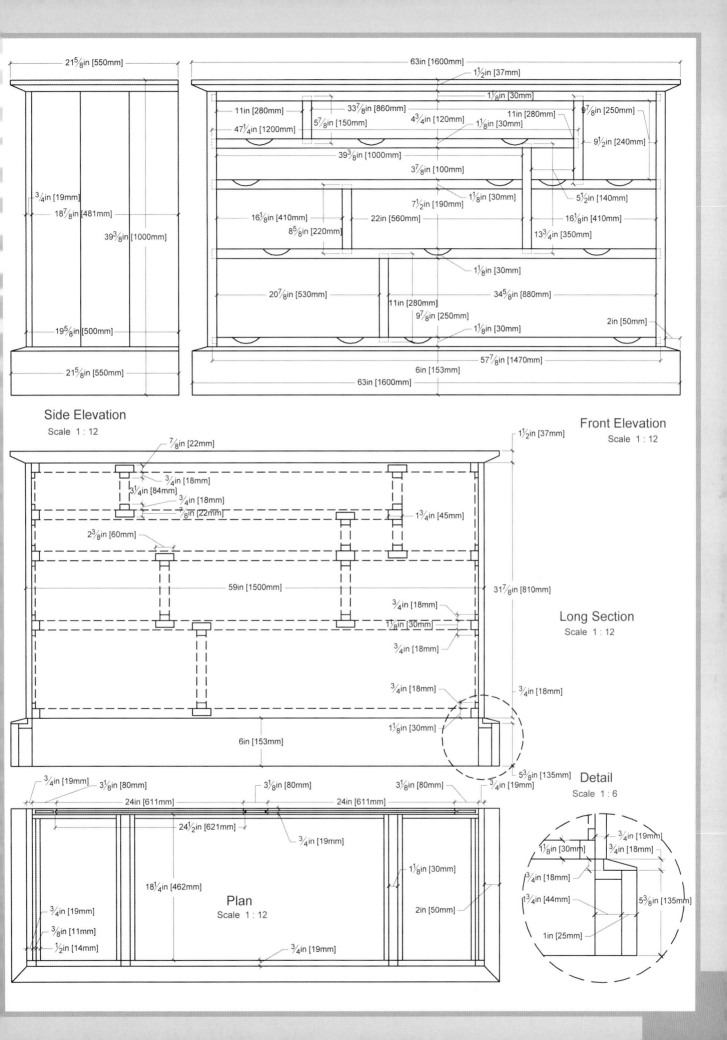

21 5/8 in [550mm]

63in [1600mm]
1 1/2 in [37mm]
1 1/8 in [30mm]
11in [280mm]
33 7/8 in [860mm]
11in [280mm]
9 7/8 in [250mm]
47 1/4 in [1200mm]
5 7/8 in [150mm]
4 3/4 in [120mm]
1 1/8 in [30mm]
9 1/2 in [240mm]
39 3/8 in [1000mm]
3 7/8 in [100mm]
3/4 in [19mm]
18 7/8 in [481mm]
1 1/8 in [30mm]
5 1/2 in [140mm]
16 1/8 in [410mm]
22in [560mm]
7 1/2 in [190mm]
16 1/8 in [410mm]
39 3/8 in [1000mm]
8 5/8 in [220mm]
13 3/4 in [350mm]
1 1/8 in [30mm]
20 7/8 in [530mm]
34 5/8 in [880mm]
11in [280mm]
9 7/8 in [250mm]
2in [50mm]
19 5/8 in [500mm]
1 1/8 in [30mm]
57 7/8 in [1470mm]
6in [153mm]
21 5/8 in [550mm]
63in [1600mm]

Side Elevation
Scale 1 : 12

Front Elevation
Scale 1 : 12

7/8 in [22mm]
1 1/2 in [37mm]
3/4 in [18mm]
3 1/4 in [84mm]
3/4 in [18mm]
7/8 in [22mm]
1 3/4 in [45mm]
2 3/8 in [60mm]
59in [1500mm]
31 7/8 in [810mm]
3/4 in [18mm]
1 1/8 in [30mm]
3/4 in [18mm]
3/4 in [18mm]
3/4 in [18mm]
1 1/8 in [30mm]
6in [153mm]
5 3/8 in [135mm]

Long Section
Scale 1 : 12

Detail
Scale 1 : 6

3/4 in [19mm]
3 1/8 in [80mm]
3 1/8 in [80mm]
3 1/8 in [80mm]
3/4 in [19mm]
24 [611mm]
24 [611mm]
24 1/2 in [621mm]
3/4 in [19mm]
1 1/8 in [30mm]
18 1/4 in [462mm]

Plan
Scale 1 : 12

3/4 in [19mm]
3/8 in [11mm]
1/2 in [14mm]
2in [50mm]
3/4 in [19mm]

3/4 in [19mm]
1 1/8 in [30mm]
3/4 in [18mm]
3/4 in [18mm]
1 3/4 in [44mm]
5 3/8 in [135mm]
1in [25mm]

'UNMATCHED' SIDE TABLES

A pair of small cabinets with 'bookmatched' door panels

• **Although these cabinets have a 'feel' of William Morris about them, they are still contemporary**

THESE TABLES were designed to complement the large chest of drawers on page 142. English white (*Fraxinus americana*) and olive ash (*Fraxinus* sp.) were used, with ash-veneered ply for the backs and bottoms. The underside of the tops are heavily chamfered and complemented by tapered legs.

CONSTRUCTION

The door panels and end panels are 'bookmatched', a process of deep-ripping a solid panel to create mirror-image grain. The board, once sawn, is opened like a book, hence the name of the technique. The less stock removed in the cut, the more accurately the pieces will match. A finely tuned bandsaw is much better than a circular saw for this, because it will cut far deeper and has a much thinner kerf, thus removing less material.

The cutting list comprises small components and so poses few problems. Otherwise useless boards can be used to good effect by working around defects, stick marks and so on. The tops are butt jointed using biscuits for alignment and added strength. The end panels and door panels are bookmatched and glued up.

PANELS

The plywood panels can now be dimensioned and checked for fit, then the end panels cut to size. To ensure a perfect fit in their respective grooves, a grooving cutter can be used in the router: working from the face side, set the cutter so the distance between the router base and the cutter is the same as the width of the groove. A shallow rebate is left on the inside of the panel.

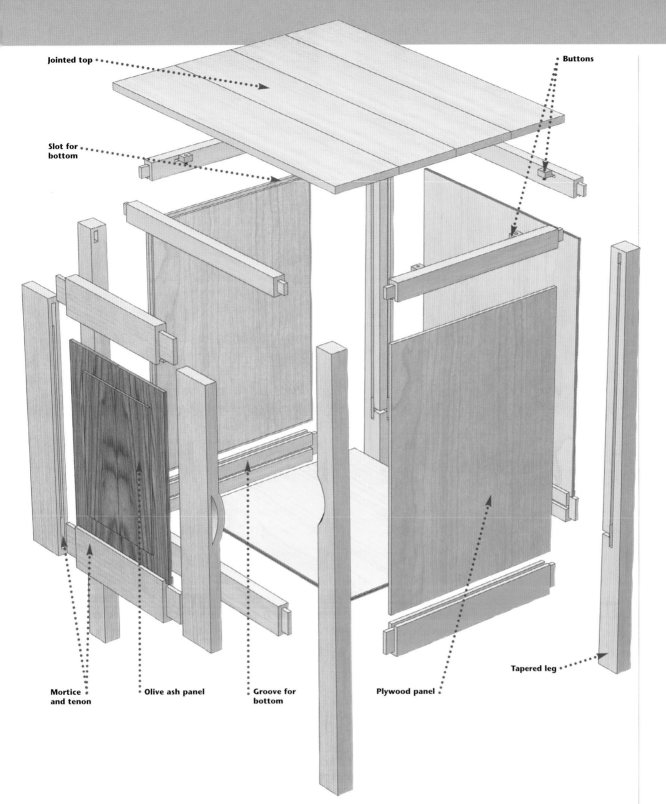

Jointed top

Buttons

Slot for bottom

Mortice and tenon

Olive ash panel

Groove for bottom

Plywood panel

Tapered leg

MORTICE AND TENONS

Mortice and tenons are used in the construction of the frames. These are tricky if done all at once, but less so if done sequentially. Beginning with the front and back frames, the joints are prepared. The mortices may be cut either with a router or morticer, if available.

Tenon cheeks can be bandsawn, but a bench saw will make a cleaner job of the shoulders. Once dry assembled and faced off, cut the end mortice-and-tenon joints; these are not finished flush, so the mortices must be cut on two different fence settings.

• **The ply bottom is grooved in**

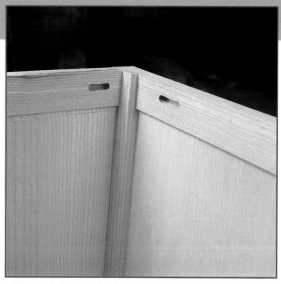

• **The top is held on in the traditional fashion, with buttons**

Grooves for end, back and bottom panels are routed next. Although the solid wood panels will be thicker than the ¼in (6mm) ply, all the grooves are cut to the thickness of the ply for the sake of simplicity – about ⁵⁄₁₆–³⁄₈in (8–10mm) deep. This allows a tolerance of ⅛in

(3mm) either side for the solid wood panels to expand and contract. The bottom panels have to negotiate the inside corner of the legs, so a notch is cut to let the panel in. This can be done either by hand, or by marking out carefully the waste to be removed and clamping the pieces together, with a router running against a fence clamped to the pack of components.

TAPERS

When satisfied everything fits, the tapers on the legs can be cut approximately on the bandsaw, before being planed in. Slots are routed into the top rails to take the buttons that will hold the tops in place. The handle recesses are cut on the bandsaw: the diameter of the curve is 5¼in (135mm) and the bandsaw table is set to 45° to make the cut. This is then sanded, and the whole job is fine sanded prior to assembly.

ADJUSTING FOR LEAD

An important factor in setting up a bandsaw is to adjust for lead, the tendency for the cut to veer from parallel to a fence fitted at right angles to the front of the table. It is different for each blade, and will vary from non-existent to quite marked, and can be corrected by simply clamping an auxiliary wooden fence parallel to the direction the blade is actually cutting in.

This, assuming that the blade is sharp, properly tensioned and is tracking correctly, will transform a decent bandsaw into a highly versatile and accurate machine, capable of cutting veneers, tenons and other deep-ripping cuts.

A good bandsaw was – and would still be – my first choice of machine in a workshop specializing in one-off solid wood furniture.

• **Trimming the panels**

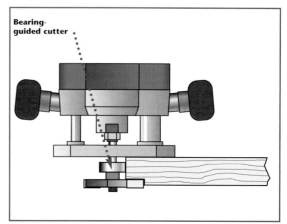

Bearing-guided cutter

• Interior showing the buttons

END ASSEMBLIES

The end assemblies are glued up first. After cleaning up, check the panels can move slightly and have not become glued in. A sharp tap with a mallet should release any spot-gluing to the panel. The front and back frames, with their corresponding panels, are glued up next. At this stage the whole job can be cleaned up, sanded and sealed. I used clear water-based lacquer to preserve the light colour of the ash.

DOORS

These are mortice and tenoned, assembled, faced off and grooved as per the cabinet construction. The section of the door frame is much greater, but otherwise the procedure is the same. The olive ash door panels are raised, the simpler the moulding the better. I used the tilting fence on my bench saw to set the required angle and after that a light sanding was all that was needed. The door panels are finished with Danish oil before assembly. This accentuates colour contrast. Finishing at this stage means the door panel will not reveal ugly light stripes if it shrinks slightly in service.

HANDLES

Recessed handles give a contemporary feel to a fairly traditional door. Their practical advantages include reduced obstruction and likelihood of damage – to the user or handle!

A curved block is glued behind the handle position, as the door itself is not thick enough to take the handle recess.

The door is offered up and the position of the handle drawn off the recess in the cabinet frame. To cut the side of the handle, use a biscuit jointer set to maximum depth of cut and ⁵⁄₃₂in (4mm) in from the outside face of the door. The scalloped part of the handle is hand carved using a fishtail gouge, followed by assiduous sanding.

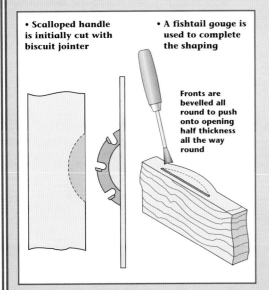

• Scalloped handle is initially cut with biscuit jointer

• A fishtail gouge is used to complete the shaping

Fronts are bevelled all round to push onto opening half thickness all the way round

• Finished scalloped handle

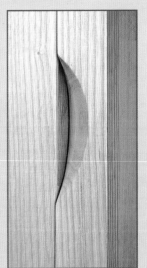

• Handle recess

• **Ready for hinge fitting**

The hinges are solid brass butts, burnished and recessed into the door frames. The hinges are also recessed on the inside of the cabinet frame.

The shallow chamfers on the underside of the tops are hand planed and sanded. Buttons are used to fit the tops to the cabinets.

FINISHING

The white ash is finished with two coats of clear water-based lacquer, cut back with 320grit silicon carbide paper between coats. The top is given a third coat. The piece is finally given three coats of clear finishing wax before a 0000 grade wire wool burnish.

• **Planing the chamfer on the underside of the top**

• **Catch and chamfered top detail**

• **Close-up of panel**

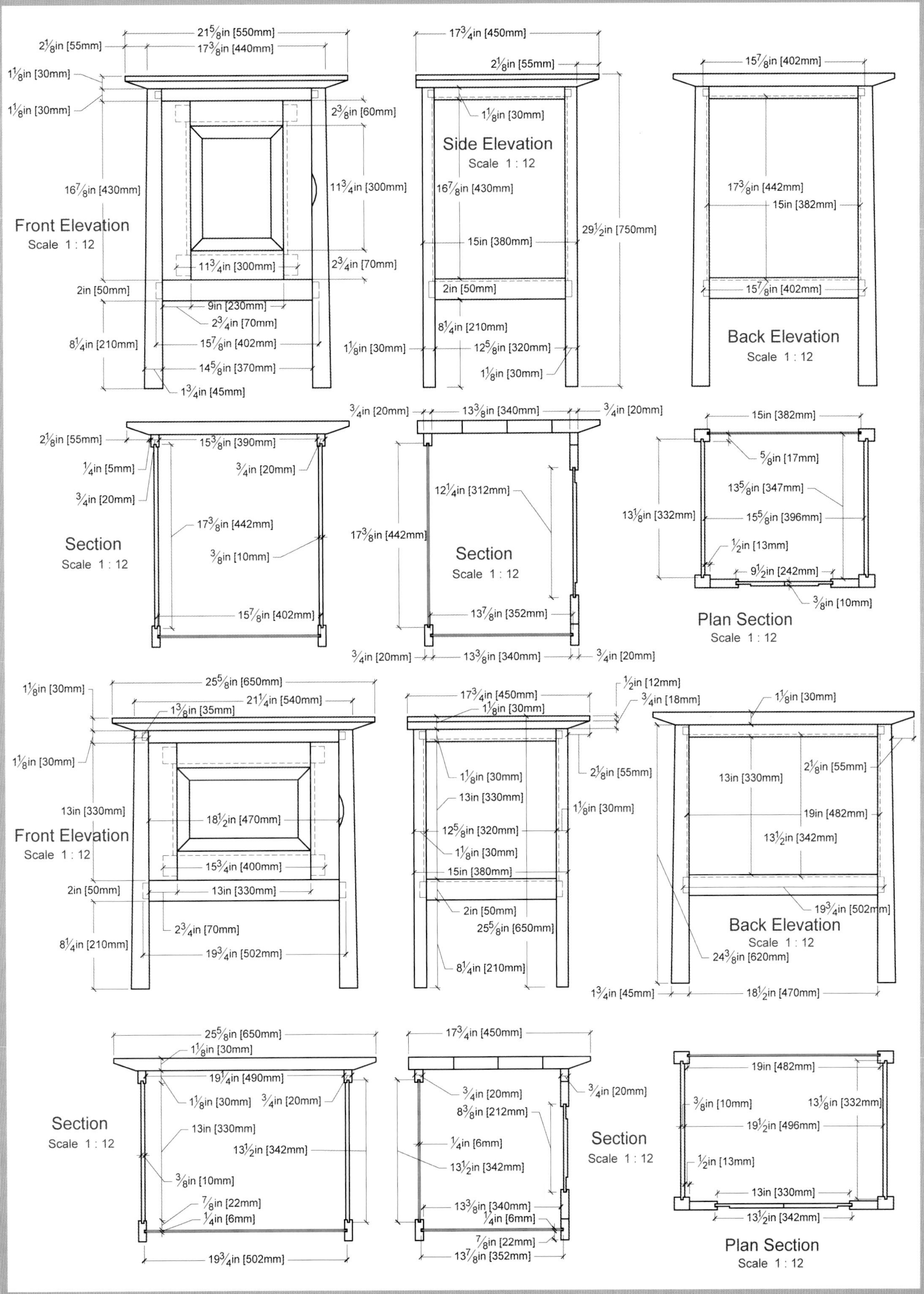

Front Elevation
Scale 1 : 12
21⅝in [550mm]
2⅛in [55mm]
17⅜in [440mm]
1⅛in [30mm]
1⅛in [30mm]
2⅜in [60mm]
16⅞in [430mm]
11¾in [300mm]
11¾in [300mm]
2¾in [70mm]
2in [50mm]
9in [230mm]
2¾in [70mm]
8¼in [210mm]
15⅞in [402mm]
14⅝in [370mm]
1¾in [45mm]
Side Elevation
Scale 1 : 12
17¾in [450mm]
2⅛in [55mm]
1⅛in [30mm]
16⅞in [430mm]
15in [380mm]
29½in [750mm]
2in [50mm]
8¼in [210mm]
1⅛in [30mm]
12⅝in [320mm]
1⅛in [30mm]
Back Elevation
Scale 1 : 12
15⅞in [402mm]
17⅜in [442mm]
15in [382mm]
15⅞in [402mm]
Section
Scale 1 : 12
2⅛in [55mm]
15⅜in [390mm]
¼in [5mm]
¾in [20mm]
¾in [20mm]
17⅜in [442mm]
⅜in [10mm]
15⅞in [402mm]
Section
Scale 1 : 12
¾in [20mm]
13⅜in [340mm]
¾in [20mm]
12¼in [312mm]
17⅜in [442mm]
13⅞in [352mm]
¾in [20mm]
13⅜in [340mm]
¾in [20mm]
Plan Section
Scale 1 : 12
15in [382mm]
⅝in [17mm]
13⅝in [347mm]
13⅛in [332mm]
15⅝in [396mm]
½in [13mm]
9½in [242mm]
⅜in [10mm]
Front Elevation
Scale 1 : 12
1⅛in [30mm]
25⅝in [650mm]
21¼in [540mm]
1⅜in [35mm]
1⅛in [30mm]
13in [330mm]
18½in [470mm]
15¾in [400mm]
2in [50mm]
13in [330mm]
2¾in [70mm]
8¼in [210mm]
19¾in [502mm]
17¾in [450mm]
1⅛in [30mm]
½in [12mm]
¾in [18mm]
1⅛in [30mm]
2⅛in [55mm]
13in [330mm]
1⅛in [30mm]
12⅝in [320mm]
1⅛in [30mm]
15in [380mm]
2in [50mm]
25⅝in [650mm]
8¼in [210mm]
Back Elevation
Scale 1 : 12
1⅛in [30mm]
13in [330mm]
2⅛in [55mm]
19in [482mm]
13½in [342mm]
19¾in [502mm]
24⅜in [620mm]
1¾in [45mm]
18½in [470mm]
Section
Scale 1 : 12
25⅝in [650mm]
1⅛in [30mm]
19¼in [490mm]
1⅛in [30mm]
¾in [20mm]
13in [330mm]
13½in [342mm]
⅜in [10mm]
⅞in [22mm]
¼in [6mm]
19¾in [502mm]
Section
Scale 1 : 12
17¾in [450mm]
¾in [20mm]
¾in [20mm]
8⅜in [212mm]
¼in [6mm]
13½in [342mm]
13⅜in [340mm]
¼in [6mm]
⅞in [22mm]
13⅞in [352mm]
Plan Section
Scale 1 : 12
19in [482mm]
⅜in [10mm]
13⅛in [332mm]
19½in [496mm]
½in [13mm]
13in [330mm]
13½in [342mm]

INLAID CHEST

A low chest in sycamore, with walnut inlay for graphic effect

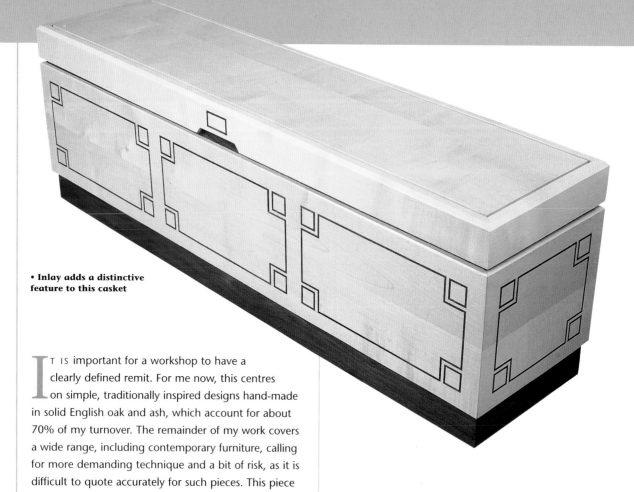

• **Inlay adds a distinctive feature to this casket**

I T IS important for a workshop to have a clearly defined remit. For me now, this centres on simple, traditionally inspired designs hand-made in solid English oak and ash, which account for about 70% of my turnover. The remainder of my work covers a wide range, including contemporary furniture, calling for more demanding technique and a bit of risk, as it is difficult to quote accurately for such pieces. This piece was suggested by an architect for his own use, though I was able to influence the design and develop it.

TIMBER

The main timber was sycamore. The final colour is to be a mellow lightish honey and, with time, sycamore will darken from its initial white to the required tone. The contrasting plinth and inlay was to be either English or American walnut. The latter is the darker of the two, though both – contrary to most woods – lighten in colour on exposure to sunlight. The contrasts in this piece will become less pronounced within a few months. It can be argued that the use of starkly contrasting woods in contemporary furniture has become a little hackneyed;

however, it can work if the idea and the timbers justify it. Sycamore can suffer more than most timbers from stick marks, but this wood was air dried, standing on end to avoid this.

PREPARATION

The preparation of the cutting list was straightforward. I decided to put a butt joint along the centre of the panels for the carcass. The boards were wide enough without jointing, but were not quarter sawn and I wanted to minimize the risk of cupping.

The whole cutting list was belt sanded to 120grit before marking out for the inlays.

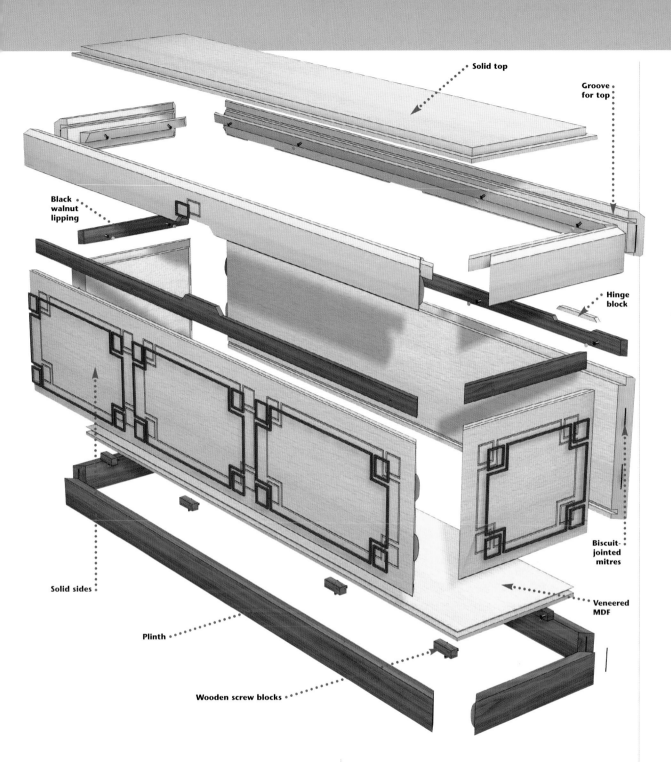

Solid top

Groove for top

Black walnut lipping

Hinge block

Solid sides

Biscuit-jointed mitres

Plinth

Veneered MDF

Wooden screw blocks

CONSTRUCTION

The construction consists of separate mitred carcasses for the chest, lid and plinth. The bottom is veneered MDF, but a solid piece of cedar of Lebanon would be a nice alternative. The top is solid sycamore with a rebate set into a groove in the lid carcass. This has a tolerance of about ⅛in (3mm) all round, to allow for expansion and contraction across the width of the top. The shadow line created echoes the inlay detail.

How the mitres are cut depends on the technology available and the way in which they will be joined. If time is not critical, a secret hidden dovetail is the strongest solution. There are router cutters available for cutting locking mitres. However, someone working with me used the technique on a long mitre joint, but it took him two days to set it up and I consequently have some doubts about their cost-effectiveness.

INLAYS

I used a ⅛in (3mm) router bit to cut ³⁄₁₆in (5mm) deep grooves to take the inlay. While the majority of these are simple to cut, running the standard fence along the edges of the work, you do need steely concentration to avoid over-running a marked line; at such times I am grateful for recent developments in router technology, that have given us quieter machines with reasonably efficient dust extraction.

An auxiliary fence had to be clamped to the work for the central grooves in the front panel. All the corners were squared off with a chisel and the grooves cleaned out with a vacuum cleaner.

The inlays themselves were cut from ⁹⁄₃₂in (7mm) thick stock on the bench saw. Fourteen lengths 48in (1200mm) long disappear surprisingly quickly once you get going on fitting them. They need to be cut to give a firm push-fit. Mark and cut to length on a fine bandsaw or by hand.

I cut the mitres on a linisher set up in 'waterfall' mode. This produces a fine and accurate result with no fear of breakout, and it is also easy to trim off a fraction if the piece is too long. Apply glue along the bottom with a brush,

• **Routing the inlay grooves**

and hammer the inlay home – preferably with a leather hammer. Cut, mitre, glue and fit each piece sequentially. I kept the bandsaw running continuously and the linisher set up on the work bench for convenience. If you do it the same way, just wash out the glue brush occasionally.

The protruding ⁵⁄₆₄in (2mm) is squashed to about ³⁄₆₄in (1mm) by hammering, but this is removed with a portable belt sander. All your hard work should be revealed in a most satisfying way.

• **Squaring up the corners of the inlay grooves after routing**

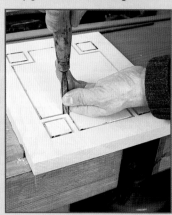

• **Fitting the inlay**

• **A sander, accurately set up can make the task of cutting a lot of mitres less frustrating and time-consuming**

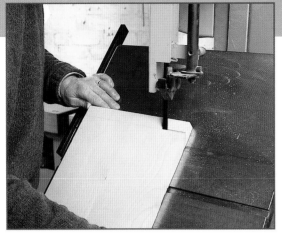

• Initially the mitres are cut on the bandsaw

So we are back to good old biscuits. I did some gluing tests with epoxy resin and PVA to see which had the better properties for endgrain. Two short pieces of sycamore, 1 x ⅝in (25 x 15mm), were glued end to end and kept under pressure for 24 hours, and both required a decent clout with a hammer to break them. Predictably, they broke on the glue line, but the PVA was considerably, and reassuringly, stronger than I had expected. It should be said that different timbers have varying gluing properties, and sycamore does glue well. The point of all this is that a mitred joint is structurally weak and depends, effectively, on gluing end-grain. The biscuits add considerable strength as they expand into their slots. An advantage of the MDF bottom here is that it can be closely fitted, adding stiffness to the structure.

My bench saw, heavy, accurate and reliable, has a sliding crosscut table, but no tilting arbor. My choices for long mitres (which, frankly, is a technique I do not use very often) are either the tilting table on the bandsaw or a portable circular saw set at 45°. Neither is accurate, so the joints have to be sawn clear of the line and hand planed in.

The biscuit slots are cut and 45° clamping blocks are glued to the outside of each joint. The blocks should be of softer wood than the work, to make removing them easier later and, in this instance, I used cedar. There are other ways of gluing up mitres but this one is probably the safest, if not the fastest. The greatest advantage of this method is that the joints can be glued and clamped one at a time. It also allows for a full dry assembly, and any minor adjustments to be made easily. All inside surfaces are sealed and cut back prior to gluing up.

• Blocks are glued on to assist with the sometimes tricky operation of assembly

SETTING UP

The clamping blocks are sawn off and sanded away and the assemblies cleaned up. Top and main carcass constructions are checked for alignment and can be hand planed and sanded true if they are slightly out, bearing in mind that the mitres always have to come to a point.

A rebate is routed on the inside bottom edge of the top, to take the raised walnut fillet that separates the top from the chest. A deeper cut is made where the handle will be cut out.

• Corner detail – the chamfer on the lid and the bottom carcass allow light to play

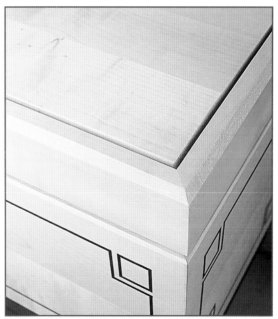

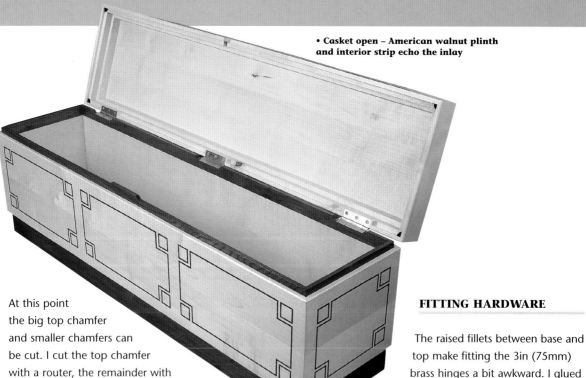

• Casket open – American walnut plinth and interior strip echo the inlay

At this point the big top chamfer and smaller chamfers can be cut. I cut the top chamfer with a router, the remainder with a block plane, then I sanded them. Bevelled strips are screwed and glued into the top. These add strength to the top panel rebates, which would be strained if someone sat on the chest – which is inevitable.

I mitred, glued and screwed the walnut strips around the inside of the chest, then I plugged all the screw holes with ⁹⁄₃₂in (7mm) pellets and sealed all the outside surfaces with thinned polyurethane varnish.

FITTING HARDWARE

The raised fillets between base and top make fitting the 3in (75mm) brass hinges a bit awkward. I glued small sycamore pieces to provide a flat base for the hinges. All one-off work is a prototype and we do not always hit on the best solution immediately. I cannot help feeling there must be a neater way of solving this problem. Nevertheless, it works well. I gave the solid brass butt hinges a brushed finish on the linisher.

A second coat of polyurethane was cut back and burnished before applying an oil dressing, while the interior was waxed. Small blocks were used to screw the plinth to the chest.

The lid was quite heavy and to prevent it closing with a bang, I fitted self-adhesive felt pads to soften the action.

• Inside of box lid hinge position

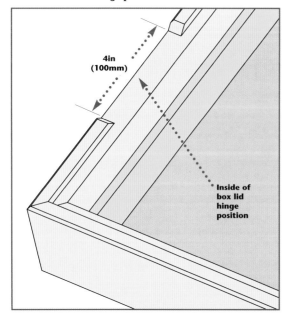

4in (100mm)

Inside of box lid hinge position

• Sycamore hinge support block

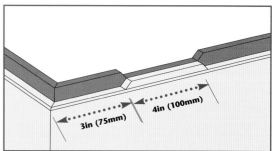

3in (75mm) 4in (100mm)

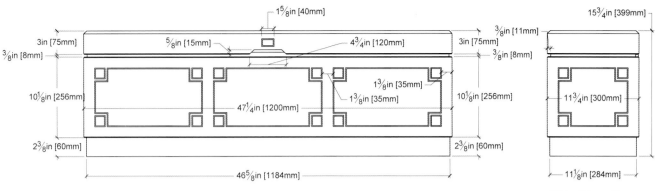

Front Elevation
Scale 1 : 12

Side Elevation
Scale 1 : 12

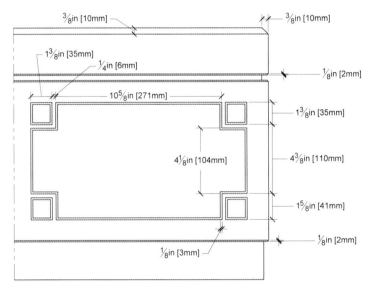

Front Elevation/Inlay Details
Scale 1 : 6

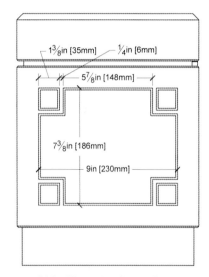

Side Elevation/Inlay Details
Scale 1 : 6

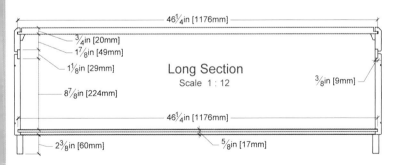

Long Section
Scale 1 : 12

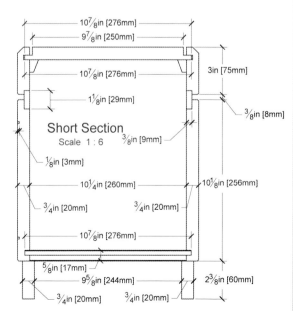

Short Section
Scale 1 : 6

An exhibition piece in ash, with light oak panels

THIS PROJECT came about as part of a rare opportunity to develop some new speculative work. Speculative pieces are a way to try new ideas without the constraint of a brief – they can then become part of the portfolio, informing the clients' choices. Evolution through commissioned work certainly happens; in fact it was observing the way my commissioned work was evolving that inspired me to take five weeks out to create a suite of linked pieces for an exhibition. Financial investment or reckless risk? That depends on how positive one is feeling. Other than knowing I wanted this piece to be a cabinet, that it had to fit in my car and be big enough to take CDs and DVDs, I had no particular sense of direction. This article is as much about the way the piece evolved as it is about how to make it.

• **The interior with framed panels in the back**

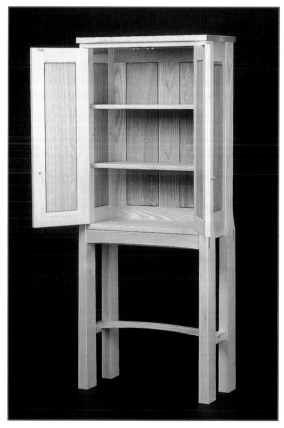

• **A chance to create a speculative piece resulted in this CD/DVD cabinet in ash, with French oak quarter panels**

Originally I saw it in white oak with ash panels. I had plenty of ash, but it wasn't really interesting enough for panels, so I reversed the effect and used a lovely board of quartered French oak (*Quercus petraea*) for the panels. The legs were made as long as the 2in (50mm) ash would allow, avoiding defects, and the cutting list for the base, top, shelves and rails were all prepared. The width was constrained by the maximum width of door panels I could cut from well-matched pieces without jointing. As the oak was a thicknessed 1in (25mm) board, it was too thin to bookmatch. Laying out the pieces and adjusting them, I gradually resolved the proportions and marked out the joints.

CONSTRUCTION

The frame is mortice and tenoned, with stopped tenons in the end frames and through-wedged joints in the front and back base rails. The top rails are dovetailed into the top of the legs. A frame-and-panel back is set into a groove in the frame. A through-morticed stretcher assembly is fitted in the lower part of the frame.

TIMBER CHOICE

An advantage of speculative pieces is that they can, to some extent, be designed around the wood. General principles apply, such as arranging grain to follow curves and line. In this case the grain in the legs and doors is arranged like an arrow, converging on the centre line and lifting the eye, accentuating the effect of the tapers.

The grain in the stretcher and base rails curves slightly upwards. Quarter-sawn oak is sometimes just too much of a good thing, but here its decorative effect can be used without restraint. Each pair of panels, doors, end and back are matched for balance.

MORTICE AND TENONS

All the joints are marked out at the same time. The mortices are cut before the taper and the joint is cut from both sides to prevent breakout. Stopped mortices are cut for the end rails. The inside faces of the top and lower rails are flush with the inside of the legs and, together with the panel, produce a flat inside surface for the cabinet. Cutting tenons on the short end rails is difficult as there is so little work to hold onto, so I cut the joints on the bandsaw and finished the shoulders by hand. The front and back rail tenon cheeks were also bandsawn, but the shoulders were cut on the bench saw.

GROOVES

With the end frame assemblies dry-fitted and faced off, grooves can be cut for the panels. This was done with a ¼in wide x ½in deep (6 x 12mm) slot cutter with guidebush. The back of the legs and the top and bottom rails, also need to be grooved to take the back panel. These are cut with a twin-flute straight bit – they only need to be ¼in (6mm) deep.

DOVETAILS

The dovetails are marked out and bandsawn. They are held in position and the sockets are scribed onto the ends of the legs with a marking knife. With two legs clamped together between bench dogs on the bench, the sides of the joint are sawn with a dovetail saw.

• **The base of the carcass is biscuited to the front rail**

• **Wedged through-tenons on the bottom carcass rails**

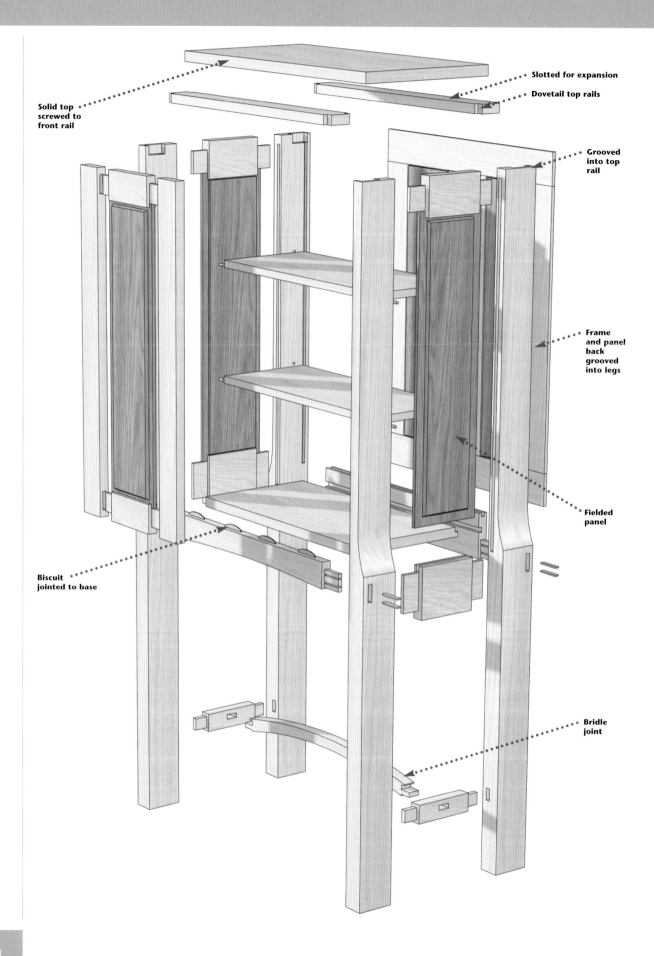

Slotted for expansion

Dovetail top rails

Solid top screwed to front rail

Grooved into top rail

Frame and panel back grooved into legs

Fielded panel

Biscuit jointed to base

Bridle joint

• The back is grooved into the back rail and vertical side rails

Most of the waste is removed with a router, running the fence against the top of the legs. A chisel is used to finish off the joint.

STRETCHER ASSEMBLY

The joints in the stretcher are made before any shaping is done. This joint consists of a single through-wedged tenon but with part of the rail lapping the top of the frame – an arrangement like one-and-a-half tenons.

The through-mortice is cut like the leg mortices, but thinner at ⁵⁄₁₆in (8mm). The tenon cheeks are cut with the bandsaw and the shoulders finished by hand.

• Everything is locked together by the two dovetailed top rails

Cutting the slits for the wedges is very awkward, as there is only about ⁹⁄₃₂in (7mm) between the two parts of the joint for the saw to move in. Only the lower tenon is slit, as the other one is on top of the rail.

BACK AND DOORS

The back panel is a repeat of the doors. The frame is about ⁹⁄₁₆in (14mm) thick with ¼in (6mm) mortice and tenons. A wide muntin echoes the width of the door frames. All six panels are the same height and the frame in the back continues the line of the side frames.

A small rebate in the panels allows for movement and provides a shadow line. The same detail is repeated on the outside of the back.

Once the joints are cut and hand fitted the frame is planed flush and ¼in (6mm) grooves routed to take the back panels.

The doors are finished marginally thicker than the back at ⅝in (16mm). The construction is the same.

PANEL PREPARATION

The panels are thicknessed and dimensioned to the internal frame sizes, plus ⅜in (10mm) all round, and sanded. The inside rebate is undercut with a slot cutter from the face side.

• The finished doors

• **Adjusting the fit of a panel**

• **Dry-fitting one of the side panels**

A ¾in (19mm) flat-bottom bit with a 45° degree corner produces a subtle inverted chamfer effect, which I like for panel raising. Although this technique should theoretically produce a perfectly consistent tongue, in practice a few tight spots usually need relieving with a rebate plane. The fit is checked with a mullet – a short length of wood with a groove routed into it.

All router marks are sanded off and the arrises slightly rounded. As the grooves cut with the slot cutter leave rounded corners, the panel corners also need to be rounded. After fine sanding, seal and oil the panels.

The assembled back panel is prepared for fit in much the same way, though here the corners should not be rounded. The doors can also be glued and cleaned up at this stage.

BASE AND TOP

The base is biscuit jointed to the front frame and let into a groove in the back frame to allow for movement. It is cut to fit between the end assemblies.

The top will be screwed to the cabinet. At the front, holes are bored and countersunk. Slots are routed into the top back rail to take screws, allowing for expansion and contraction. Two small blocks are also fitted to the end of the cabinet; these need not be slotted.

Problem ...
A dry assembly of the frame was set up, then the legs were tapered from 1⅜in (35mm) at the base to ⅞in (22mm) at the top, before dry assembling again.

So far it seemed to be going well and I spent some time preparing the raised panels for the ends, doors and back. The doors and back panel were glued up and faced off.

The second full dry assembly with the panels fitted was more worrying. The combination of tapered legs and vertical panels made it look as though the end panels sloped inwards towards the bottom – horrible!

My first thought was to make tapered panels but that would have created a very awkward detail at the lower end and anyway I didn't have the wood for it.

• **Detail of the interior**

My second was to plane the taper out of the legs, making them vertical but probably too thin. The position of the through-tenons made cutting the legs off and making a separate stand difficult, but not impossible.

... solved

My solution was to make a visual break at the bottom of the doors, bandsawing the top half of the legs back to the vertical and leaving the taper in the base. The effect of the taper is continued to the top by working a tapered chamfer from the foot to the top, following the curve that takes the vertical top half into the tapered base. When I did it I wasn't at all sure it would work but, in the event, it does seem to, and creates some interesting – if accidental – visual detail.

CHAMFERS

Small chamfers are cut on the arrises of all the frames. Both stretcher rail and the underside of the front base rail are chamfered with a spokeshave and the base rail is scalloped to a depth of about ⁵⁄₁₆in (8mm).

Chamfers are planed on all outside corners of the legs and on the insides of the legs up to the level of the base. The outside corners of the legs are chamfered to about ⁵⁄₃₂in (4mm). Only the front legs have tapered chamfers. These are hand-cut with a block plane and spokeshave.

• **The through-tenon before wedging**

ASSEMBLY

All surfaces are sealed and cut back in preparation for assembly, taking care not to coat areas to be glued. The outside of the legs need not be sealed at this stage. As usual, I used thinned polyurethane cut back with 240grit silicon carbide paper on a palm sander.

Before gluing up, the wedges need to be prepared and I bandsawed them from stock planed to the same thickness as the tenons, slightly longer than the tenon and 0–⅛in (3mm) in thickness. The end frame and panel assemblies are glued up first, followed by the stretcher rail and base rails.

After sanding off the protruding through-tenons and wedges, the back can be dropped into place and the top dovetailed rails glued in place and clamped. The base is fitted into the groove at the back, glued to the front base rail and clamped.

FITTING DOORS

After cleaning up the cabinet, all bare areas of wood are sealed and cut back. The doors can now be trimmed to size, allowing ³⁄₆₄in (1mm) tolerance in height. They should be slightly wider than necessary to allow for fine-tuning after the hinges have been fitted. Set 2½in (63mm) solid brass butt hinges into the door frames by almost their whole depth, then rout out most of the waste before finishing the job with a chisel.

I find the top-of-the-range butt hinges from Hafele don't need any attention before use, but most do, and before screwing them to the doors these were wire wool burnished on the inside and sanded on the linisher to give a brushed finish on the barrel.

The hinges are planted onto the legs, the centre line of the screw holes is scribed with a marking gauge, and the hole positions marked with a bradawl to give a positive location for the pilot drill.

One screw in each hinge is enough for setting up. Once the top and bottom are aligned the centre line can be planed true.

To produce a close fit, a bevel needs to be planed on the closing edge of the doors, otherwise the inside corner will hit the opposing door. Not much needs to be allowed in terms of expansion gap, as the total width of the door frames is not very great. When the closing gap, top and bottom are fitted, plane the hinge side to give a consistent gap all round.

Obviously, small door frames expand and contract less than wide ones, so the size of the gap around the doors will vary according to the size of the door frame. In this instance it is about ⁴⁄₆₄in (1mm), but in a sideboard ¹⁄₁₆in (1.5mm) is probably more appropriate.

When a good fit is achieved, scribe around the hinges on the cabinet and remove the doors, then cut an angled recess up to the scribed line to take the hinge. Fit the remaining screws.

FINISHING

Anything that has not yet been sealed should be sealed now (the oak panels were sealed and oiled before assembly).

As it will get a lot of wear, the top needs to be given two coats of thinned polyurethane, applied with a rubber.

Finally, I gave the whole piece two coats of Liberon neutral wax applied with a fine ScotchBrite pad, and removed any wax that had collected in the corners.

SHELVES, HANDLES AND CATCHES

The shelves are ½in (12mm) thick and supported on turned ⁵⁄₃₂in (4mm) dowels. Routed recesses in the undersides of the shelves locate on the supports, keeping the shelves in place.

From the outset I wanted to use a recessed handle, but the fine section of the doors meant that some form of projection would be needed to provide a finger pull. I liked the idea of a shallow oval relief between the doors, with a thin vertical wafer split horizontally. But, while it would look fine if the doors were perfectly aligned, any shrinkage of the door stiles would pull them out of alignment.

Also, on this small scale it would be difficult not to pull both doors open at once. Since I had already risked failure on the legs I played safe with applied handles. These are turned white oak, with spigots that protrude through the door, and wedged on the inside.

I used brass double-ball catches. Single-ball catches set into the side of the door are visually neater, but almost impossible to adjust after fitting. However, these are fitted at the top of the cabinet and are beneath the eyeline.

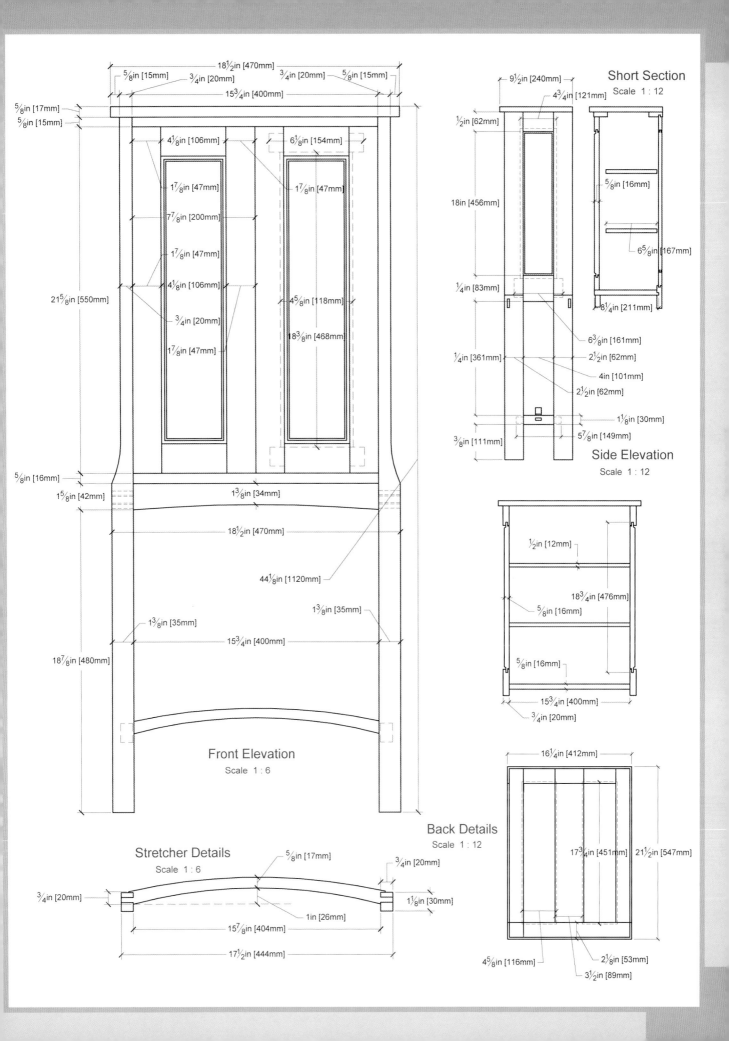

Short Section
Scale 1 : 12

9½in [240mm]
4¾in [121mm]
½in [62mm]
18in [456mm]
¼in [83mm]
⅝in [16mm]
6⅝in [167mm]
8¼in [211mm]
6⅜in [161mm]
¼in [361mm]
2½in [62mm]
4in [101mm]
2½in [62mm]
1⅛in [30mm]
⅜in [111mm]
5⅞in [149mm]

Side Elevation
Scale 1 : 12

18½in [470mm]
⅝in [15mm]
¾in [20mm]
¾in [20mm]
⅝in [15mm]
15¾in [400mm]
⅝in [17mm]
⅝in [15mm]
4⅛in [106mm]
6⅛in [154mm]
1⅞in [47mm]
1⅞in [47mm]
7⅞in [200mm]
1⅞in [47mm]
4⅛in [106mm]
4⅝in [118mm]
¾in [20mm]
18⅜in [468mm]
1⅞in [47mm]
21⅝in [550mm]
⅝in [16mm]
1⅝in [42mm]
1⅜in [34mm]
18½in [470mm]
44⅛in [1120mm]
1⅜in [35mm]
1⅜in [35mm]
15¾in [400mm]
18⅞in [480mm]

½in [12mm]
18¾in [476mm]
⅝in [16mm]
⅝in [16mm]
15¾in [400mm]
¾in [20mm]

Front Elevation
Scale 1 : 6

Stretcher Details
Scale 1 : 6

⅝in [17mm]
¾in [20mm]
¾in [20mm]
1⅛in [30mm]
1in [26mm]
15⅞in [404mm]
17½in [444mm]

Back Details
Scale 1 : 12

16¼in [412mm]
17¾in [451mm]
21½in [547mm]
4⅝in [116mm]
2⅛in [53mm]
3½in [89mm]

ROUND PEDESTAL TABLE

A table worthy of exhibiting at shows, which would also look impressive in your home surroundings

• **The finished table**

THIS TABLE is part of a suite – together with four breakfast chairs (see page 36) – which I made to exhibit at a show. It followed a specific brief that had emerged over several months, in response to comments made by clients and exhibition visitors.

Choosing speculative projects is not that easy – they need to be a creative development, but also fit into a well-thought-out marketing plan. They must be good enough to exhibit, i.e. acceptable to exhibition promoters, gallery owners and, from a practical point of view, portable. They need to be a clear statement about the direction of the workshop.

Finally, they need to be cost-effective, meaning that the transportation, making and material costs will be covered by the eventual sale of the piece and/or subsequent commissions based on it.

The chair design came first and the table had to complement it. Like the chair, the table needed to be simple and economical, but still sophisticated. Again, a series of discussions about tables informed the choice of shape, while the diameter was dictated by the size of the back door in my estate car! The base had to be a simple and sculptural pedestal, to allow all-round access.

• A soft edge is given to the brown oak top

• Chamfer detail on the top section follows through on the foot

TIMBER

I had enough French ash left from a previous project to make the chair frames and bought some more from the same source for the table base. French ash is nice – I have had no trouble with stick marks and it is often rippled. The colour isn't all that consistent, but that can be a problem with ash anyway. The option is whether to agonize over perfect selection, or go for a more random look. I opted for the second option – this is supposed to be kitchen furniture, after all. I had previously been persuaded to buy a board of 3in (75mm) brown oak, which became the table top and chair seats. Although I had spent more than I had intended on that trip, the oak was sumptuous, and lovely to work and finish. The chair frames and table frame are all made from 2⅛in (54mm) boards.

TABLE CONSTRUCTION

The 3in (75mm) thick brown oak was cut to manageable sizes with a portable circular saw, and planed to 7½ x 3in (190 x 75mm) sections, after which it could be resawn on the bandsaw. The 7½in (190mm) width was chosen as the most economical to make the most of this valuable wood. Slowly sawing through the sections presented no problem and, when the wood had been thicknessed to 1⁵⁄₁₆in (33mm), it was allowed to settle for a while.

Selecting the layout of a table top is always enjoyable and nerve-wracking in equal measure. Fluctuating between hope and despair, a layout finally emerges after many trials in every configuration. As this wood is quarter sawn, allowance for cupping was not required,

making the job easier. I was happy with the light stripes, as they echo the ash, but I wanted to avoid abrupt changes of colour between boards. Somehow, unexpectedly, it clicks and the layout that feels right suddenly appears. Eventually seven pieces were used with six joints. It was fun watching people playing 'spot the joins' at the exhibition and the wood itself proved to be a useful talking point, starting many conversations with people.

TOP ASSEMBLY

The carefully selected top is glued up with biscuits between the butt joints, in two stages, then the two 'halves' – one wider than the other, due to the odd number of pieces – glued up and sanded off. This made them easier to manage before the whole top was glued, and left only the central joint to be cleaned up.

A router bolted to an MDF trammel was used to cut the circle, the trammel screwed to the centre of the underside of the table top. A number of passes were made, with particular care on the final one, to avoid the waste ripping the grain on the table top. Finally, the edge was belt sanded.

THE FRAME

The base is made from 2⅛in (54mm) ash with the feet laminated into 4in (100mm) square sections. Although the joint is visible on the side after shaping, the join lines up with the chamfered detail on the end of the foot. To have the join visible on the top of the curved foot would be most unfortunate.

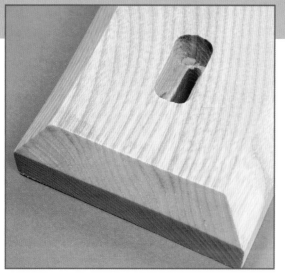

• Close-up of the fixing slotted hole on the chamfered ends

The top frame is constructed from 4 x 2in (100 x 50mm) sections, and both feet and spreaders are jointed with a simple cross-halving. The legs are joined with loose tenons, making joinery easier – particularly at the base – than making the tenons as part of the legs.

LEGS AND FEET

Although big, the cross-halvings are quite simple – those in the feet are cut before shaping, as doing it afterwards would be very difficult. The joints can be cut in various ways, the safest being on a radial arm saw.

With the cross-halvings cut, the feet can be shaped. These were marked out on one of the feet by tapping a couple of moulding pins into the feet at the ends of the curves, ⁵⁄₆₄in (2mm) in from the edge. A thin batten is pushed against these, up to a point marked on a centre line, and the curve scribed off with a soft pencil (the small holes left by the pins are lost when the feet are chamfered). The curves are sawn on the bandsaw and sanded in with a portable belt sander, or large linisher if one is available. The second foot is scribed off the curve of the first. A flat is left on the underside of the feet where the cross-halving is.

• The main frame upside down – note the slotted fixing holes to allow for movement of the top

• Close-up of the cross-halving joint on the foot

The top curves are finally faired in after assembly. With the feet dry assembled and shaped, the legs can be scribed off. Again, these start from rectangular blocks which are cut to length from the floor to the underside of the spreader frame. The foot assembly was placed on the bench saw table and the positions of the legs marked across the feet. Each leg-foot joint is labelled and scribed off with the leg standing on the saw table – or any other big, flat surface – and clamped against the foot in the right position. The joints are bandsawn to the scribed line.

The curves of the legs are drawn, in the same way as those on the feet, onto one component which acts as a template for the rest. The positions of the mortices are marked onto all the legs – top and bottom – and the feet and spreaders.

• The same joint but on the top braces

USING A BANDSAW

If you are unsure of your bandsawing skills, spending a few hours practising cutting curves to a line using offcuts, would be time well spent. It requires a slow and steady feed speed and a sureness of touch that only comes with practice.

Obviously there are situations where jigs and templates are cost-effective and necessary for producing a series of identical components, but often in pieces such as this table – which will never be repeated in quite the same way – well-honed hand skills are quicker and more economical.

• A good bandsaw is indispensable in a small workshop

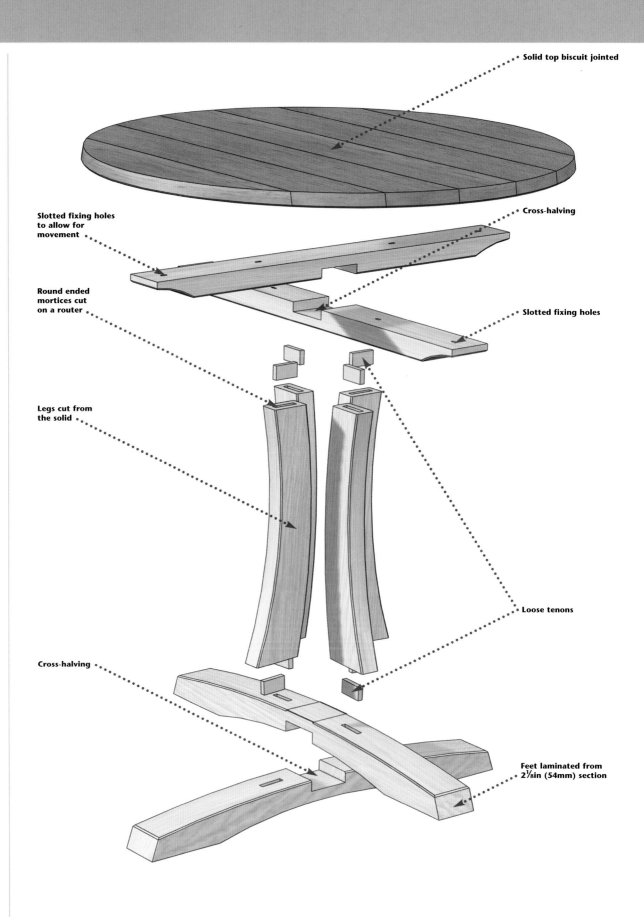

Solid top biscuit jointed

Slotted fixing holes
to allow for
movement

Cross-halving

Round ended
mortices cut
on a router

Slotted fixing holes

Legs cut from
the solid

Loose tenons

Cross-halving

Feet laminated from
2⅛in (54mm) section

CHAMFERING

A full dry set-up with the top *in situ* is a good time to reflect on the piece. In a job of this nature, I rarely work out every detail in advance. There are no client expectations to accommodate and, with the bulk of the work done, it is time to have some fun with the detailing.

Aware of my self-imposed budget, I resisted the temptation to start spokeshaving tapered chamfers onto the legs, and limited myself to a router with a chamfering cutter and a block plane. The spreaders and feet are heavily chamfered, and the 'toes' chamfered neatly down to the glue line. A much smaller chamfer is cut into the legs, and the top is more heavily chamfered on the underside than the top.

All of this reduces the visual weight of the piece, but still leaves it looking very solid and creates a lot of added interest to what is, essentially, a very simple design.

• Chamfer detail on the foot section. Chamfers can add an effect of lightness and take the sharp edges from a piece

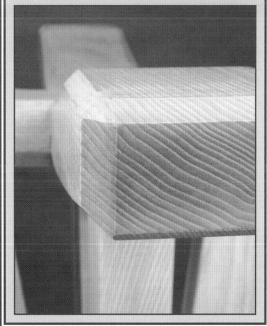

MORTICES

Mortices are routed into the ends of the legs and the feet/spreaders. These joints need to be robust, so a substantial ½in (12mm) width and 1⅝in (40mm) depth are cut. The length of the joint needs to be as long as possible whilst ensuring that a comfortable margin is allowed for the curves in the legs. Strips of wood are prepared and chamfered to fit into the round-ended mortices and cut to length. A dry assembly can be set up at this point, to check that everything is working.

The legs can now be shaped and sanded – again on the bandsaw – but all this bandsawing does require a certain level of competence on the machine. An alternative would be to make MDF patterns that act as spindle-moulder templates; however, this approach would require a 4in (100mm) high moulding block for the feet, take appreciably longer, and would still necessitate the making of accurate templates in the first place and the finishing of spindle-moulded components afterwards.

TOP

The top is wide and plenty of allowance has to be made for movement. Slots are routed into the spreaders to take screws and washers to fit the top. These are routed from the underside first with a ¹¹⁄₁₆in (17mm) wide slot, and from the top with a ¼in (6mm) slot. Scallops are marked and sawn on the ends of the spreaders, making the spreader all but invisible at a normal viewing angle, and creating an interesting detail of the end slots.

ASSEMBLY

All the components are individually sanded and sealed with the joints masked off. The cross-halvings are glued first. I used epoxy resin for the glue-up as I didn't want to take any chances with the loose tenons. I have found that epoxy doesn't work as well on oak as some other woods – I wouldn't feel confident about laminating oak with epoxy, for example. With ash there are no problems and the thickening silica used in epoxy resin has the advantage of drying to the same colour as ash.

First, the epoxy resin – a two-pack adhesive – is brushed onto all mating surfaces, 'wetting out' the joint to ensure a good bond (it's very runny at this stage).

Next, thickening micro-fibres are added to make it more like the consistency of PVA, and this is brushed on. Removing dried epoxy from a sealed surface takes a bit more care than PVA as, when dry, it is harder than the wood.

Before gluing the legs, the corners of the chamfers need to be cut in by hand to form a 'mason's mitre' (so-called because stone carvers use the same technique to cut mitres, rather than construct them, as we tend to). These are marked and then cut in with a bevel-edged chisel: first cut the mitre at the centre of the joint with a chisel and mallet, then pare the chamfer flush into the centre, removing a little at a time.

With the mitres cut in and the cross-halvings cleaned up, the spreaders and feet will need a further coat of sealer. The relatively long open time of epoxy means that the whole leg, feet and spreader assembly can be glued up in one go. A dry run is advisable to ensure that all the loose tenons fit, and that the legs pull up true when under pressure.

Although expensive and time-consuming, epoxy is a remarkable adhesive and, in the right circumstances, more than justifies itself.

FINISHING

With the frame and top complete, the finish can be built up. I waxed the base and Danish-oiled the top, the latter bringing the brown oak up beautifully. The top is screwed to the spreaders with No. 8 screws and washers.

If the table is to be positioned on a stone or wood floor, felt pads could be fitted to the feet, but these would be a nuisance on a carpet.

As the table had no immediate home to go to, I continued to add a light coat of Danish oil every few days.

The suite sold in an exhibition 12 months after completion having generated two or three commissions on the way.

• **The finished suite**

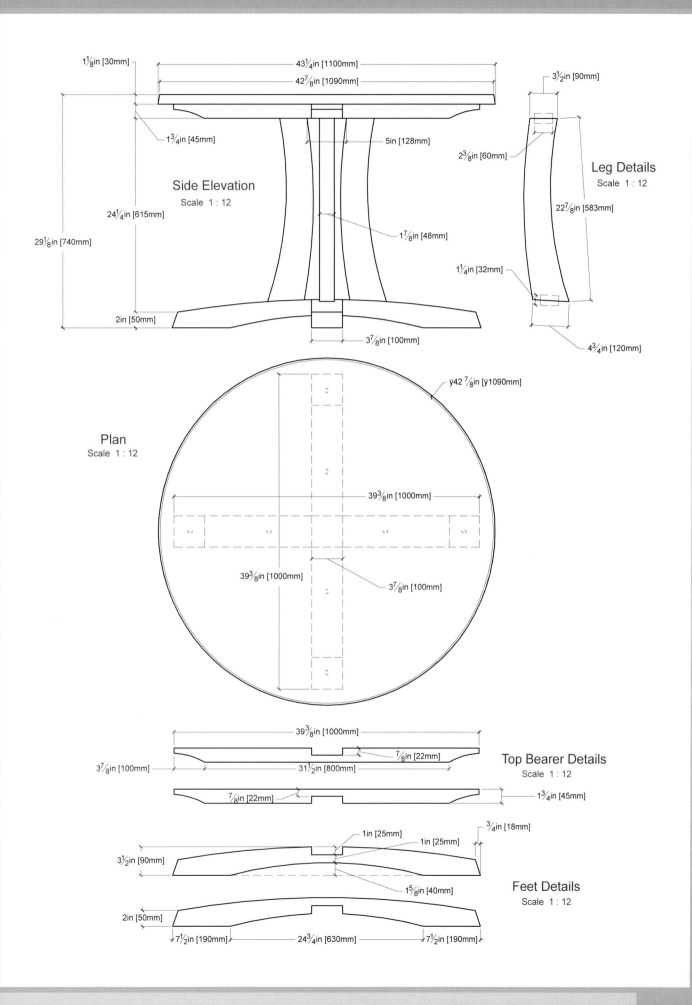

$1\frac{1}{8}$in [30mm]

$43\frac{1}{4}$in [1100mm]

$42\frac{7}{8}$in [1090mm]

$3\frac{1}{2}$in [90mm]

$1\frac{3}{4}$in [45mm]

5in [128mm]

$2\frac{3}{8}$in [60mm]

Leg Details
Scale 1 : 12

Side Elevation
Scale 1 : 12

$22\frac{7}{8}$in [583mm]

$24\frac{1}{4}$in [615mm]

$1\frac{7}{8}$in [48mm]

$1\frac{1}{4}$in [32mm]

$29\frac{1}{8}$in [740mm]

2in [50mm]

$3\frac{7}{8}$in [100mm]

$4\frac{3}{4}$in [120mm]

ÿ$42\frac{7}{8}$in [ÿ1090mm]

Plan
Scale 1 : 12

$39\frac{3}{8}$in [1000mm]

$39\frac{3}{8}$in [1000mm]

$3\frac{7}{8}$in [100mm]

$39\frac{3}{8}$in [1000mm]

$\frac{7}{8}$in [22mm]

Top Bearer Details
Scale 1 : 12

$3\frac{7}{8}$in [100mm]

$31\frac{1}{2}$in [800mm]

$\frac{7}{8}$in [22mm]

$1\frac{3}{4}$in [45mm]

1in [25mm]

1in [25mm]

$\frac{3}{4}$in [18mm]

$3\frac{1}{2}$in [90mm]

$1\frac{5}{8}$in [40mm]

Feet Details
Scale 1 : 12

2in [50mm]

$7\frac{1}{2}$in [190mm]

$24\frac{3}{4}$in [630mm]

$7\frac{1}{2}$in [190mm]

KNEEHOLE DESK

A contemporary treatment of a traditional theme in ash and light oak

• **One advantage of this type of desk is that it can be broken down into components, for access through small doorways. A laminated chair to the same design as that on page 30 is part of the same suite**

SHOWING PIECES at exhibitions can generate a lot of work, and this project – part of a suite for a small study – was the result of one such exhibition. One of the benefits of work gained in this way is that people are inspired by the work they see, rather than having preconceived ideas which must then be gently steered in a direction that satisfies both maker and buyer. I was pleased with this commission, as it completes a body of work with a more contemporary design approach than much of my previous work, which I have been developing over a period of time.

DESIGN

I kept the design of the desk simple and spare. I wanted to avoid a break in the ends where the whole top section traditionally lifts off the pedestals, but the desk still had to come apart, as access into the room is through a very small doorway. To achieve this, the pedestals are the full height of the desk, with removable top, top rail, back panel and mid-frame section. All of these are screwed together *in situ*.

We discussed whether it should be a rectangular or corner desk and I designed and costed both. I was, however, keen to go for the rectangular version because I wanted to avoid the fitted 'home-office' look. Other factors in favour of the rectangular version were that the person sitting at a corner desk would obstruct the drawers, there would be a loss of usable space in the corner, and it would be more expensive – though that wasn't a primary concern.

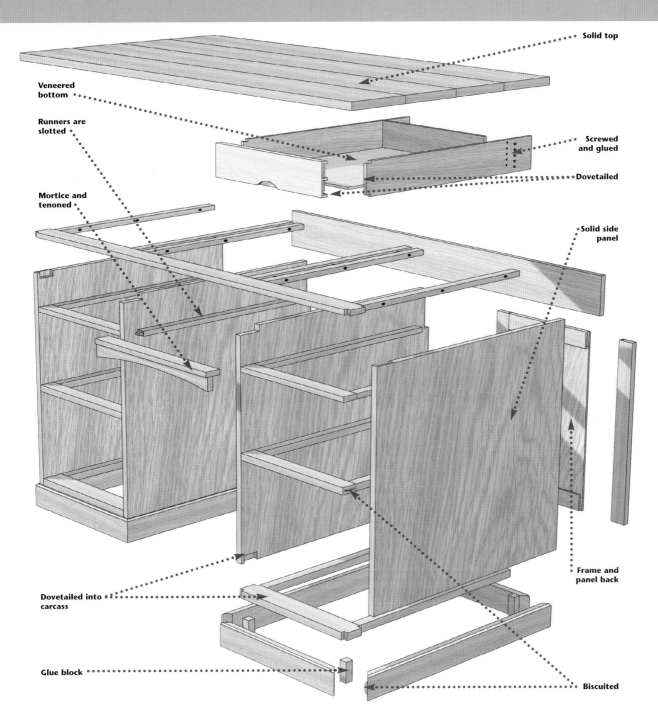

Solid top

Veneered
bottom

Runners are
slotted

Screwed
and glued

Dovetailed

Mortice and
tenoned

Solid side
panel

Frame and
panel back

Dovetailed into
carcass

Glue block

Biscuited

The reason for considering a corner desk was the
need to lay large-format books adjacent to the
work area, for study. The issue was resolved when
I suggested a pull-out flap above the top right-hand
drawer, adding a 23³⁄₁₆ x 15²⁵⁄₃₂in (600 x 400mm)
extension to the top.

The chair made to go with this desk was of laminated
construction (page 30), made in oak with ash wedges.
A small bookcase in ash and oak completed the suite.

TIMBER

Many years ago a gallery owner advised me that
contrasting woods should be of similar grain – for
example, ash, oak, elm and chestnut are all coarse-
grained with open figure, while cherry, maple and
walnut are close-grained – and this works well
for me. I try to avoid using more than two woods in
one piece, and prefer subtle contrasts such as white
and brown oak, or ash and olive ash, as they are
naturally complementary.

• A combination of dovetails, biscuit joints and counterbored screws allow the piece to be knocked down

CONSTRUCTION

The construction becomes clearer when broken down into various elements: two pedestals, two plinth assemblies, central frame, top rails and top. The pedestal backs are frame-and-panel construction, screwed and plugged to solid sides.

The base rails dovetail into the ends and the dividing rails separating the drawers are biscuit jointed. The top front rail is dovetailed at the ends and notched into the central dividers. These joints are dry and screwed, the screws being concealed by the top.

The back rail is the full height of the drawers and extends to meet the top of the back panels, which are in line with the underside of the kneehole, and again this is screwed in position and counterbored. As the desk was to be in front of a window, these holes were left unplugged, but they could be filled if it were located in the middle of a room.

The central drawer runners form the sides of a U-shaped frame, and the front rail is mortice and tenoned to the runners, which are screwed to the cabinet sides through slotted holes. Finally, the top is screwed through the front rails through slots in the drawer kickers, and to expansion plates fitted to the back panel.

• Note batons for attaching the top

• The front rail has dry-fitted dovetails that screw into place

• A pull-out flap extends the usable space

I believe this contributes to the harmony which, in the simple designs I produce, is so important to success. The ash for the desk is French, as is the oak. I have only recently come across French ash, and I think the qualitative difference between it and American ash is as pronounced as between American and French oak. This relates to consistency of colour, board width and drying. All of those are supply factors rather than a comment on the quality of the trees themselves. Unless one is actually prepared to source one's own trees, English hardwoods seem to have all but disappeared commercially. The drawer bottoms are made of ash-veneered MDF.

• Pedestals and connecting frame

• The left-hand drawer acts as a support for the extension

GETTING STARTED

My first job in preparing the cutting list was the drawer linings (sides) and backs. These were resawn from 1⅝in (42mm) stock and thickened to ⅝in (15mm). The lower drawer linings had to be jointed to make up the width, and these were put in stick to condition. Luckily my new workshop is very dry, and I have barely used my dehumidifier since moving in.

The ash drawer fronts had to be jointed rather carefully as I aimed to make the joins virtually invisible. The panels for the top and ends were selected, prepared

and glued up, while the rails were prepared during intervals between glue-ups. With the end panels glued up, sanded and dimensioned, the next stage was the back panels. These are frame-and-panel constructions with ¼in (6mm) veneered MDF panels. The rails are machined with a stub tenon the same thickness as the groove for the panel – rather than morticed and tenoned – and prepared on the spindle moulder (but you could use a router). This method is strong enough in this context, and it saves time.

RAILS

The bottom front rails are lap-dovetailed and the sockets scribed off them straight onto the cabinet sides. It is best to do the top rail dovetails at the same time, as the process is the same. The socket sides are sawn with a dovetail saw, and the waste removed with a router and chisel. Notches are marked and sawn for the front and back rails to join the central cabinet sides. They are bored to take screws, and the back rail counterbored for pellets. The cabinet sides are likewise bored and counterbored for fitting to the frame and panel backs.

Biscuit joints are cut to take the dividing rails between the drawers. The positions of the rails are marked across the full width of the panels to aid aligning the drawer runners later.

• The runners are slotted to allow for expansion

• Runners for the extension and the drawer that supports it

DRAWER CONSTRUCTION

Drawers are traditionally constructed at the front with lap dovetails. Although the sides extend almost to the back of the cabinet, the drawer backs are screwed and plugged about two-thirds of the way back, because the cabinet is about 27⁹⁄₁₆in (700mm) deep and so full-depth drawers would be too deep for practical use. It also means that the drawers can be extended to their full usable depth without falling out. The top right-hand drawer sides fit underneath the pull-out extension, and so are narrower than the others.

The bottoms run under the drawer backs and project about ⅜in (10mm). The material chosen for drawer bottoms will depend on personal preference and budget. I normally choose veneered MDF, for structural as well as economic reasons. Structurally, veneered panels are stiffer for the given thickness and can be glued in place, significantly strengthening the drawer. Although the camphor smell of the cedar traditionally used in drawer bottoms to repel moths is useful in clothes or linen cabinets, it is probably less important in desks. In any case it is not a smell that everyone likes, so it is worth checking with the end user if you are considering cedar of Lebanon.

• **Lapped dovetails are used for the drawer fronts**

The handles are recessed into the underside of the top and middle drawers, and the top edge of the two bottom drawers. A simple template is cut and sanded in MDF, and clamped to the drawer front. A router fitted with a template follower and ¼in (6mm) twin-flute cutter is used to cut the recess. With the template left in place, a dovetail cutter is used to rout the undercut. Generally, the undercut is deepened with a carving gauge to give better grip, and the handle is sanded. The drawers are set back from the front edge of the cabinet by ⁵⁄₆₄in (2mm). The edges of the drawer fronts are lightly chamfered to create a more definitive shadow line. Stops are screwed to the rails and, when accurate fits have been achieved, glued in place.

• **Drawer bottoms are veneered and glued in, adding strength to the construction**

• **The backs are screwed and plugged**

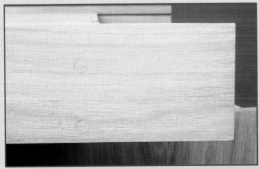

• **The back of one of the pedestal units**

which locate in grooves in the panels' sides. As flatness is essential to the easy action of this, the panel was veneered and lipped and a finger-pull slot was routed to the underside of the front lipping. The runners are prepared with routed slots, to allow for movements in the cabinet sides, and screwed in position. Those at the top are also slotted to take screws to fit the top.

After assembly, the cabinets are trued-up with a hand plane in readiness for fitting the plinths. The plinths are mitred and biscuit-jointed at this stage. My usual practice is to glue 45° clamping blocks to the outside corners to allow each joint to be G-clamped. These clamping blocks are made from the offcuts left from sawing the mitres. After assembly, the blocks are sawn off and the assembly sanded.

Although this is a bit laborious, I have not found a more reliable way to glue mitred joints. The top edges of the plinths are chamfered. The runners and kickers of the centre drawer are prepared like the others, but the runners are tenoned into the centre front rail. A curved sub-rail is screwed to this. The whole piece can now be assembled with plinths, top rails, centre frame and, finally, the top. With the piece set up level and true, drawer fitting can begin.

Prior to gluing up the carcasses, the inside surfaces are sealed with thinned polyurethane and cut back with a palm sander, providing a base for the wax finish. It is important to seal the surfaces of solid wood components even when they won't be seen, as ambient moisture variations will affect the finished and unfinished surfaces differently, possibly causing distortion.

FINISHING

To finish, the piece was sealed with two coats of matt polyurethane varnish thinned 50/50 with white spirit, and cut back with a palm sander to provide a base for several coats of Danish oil.

ASSEMBLY

With joint making and finishing complete, assembly may begin. It would be easier in some ways to fit the drawer runners at this point rather than after assembly, as the panels are still easily accessible. Against it is ensuring that they line up precisely with the front rails, and I decided to fit them after the pedestals were glued up.

The majority are a traditional runner-and-kicker arrangement. The right-hand top drawer is on applied runners – which run in grooves routed in the drawer sides – to accommodate the pull-out work area extension above it. This slides out on wooden runners,

• **The front of one of the pedestal units**

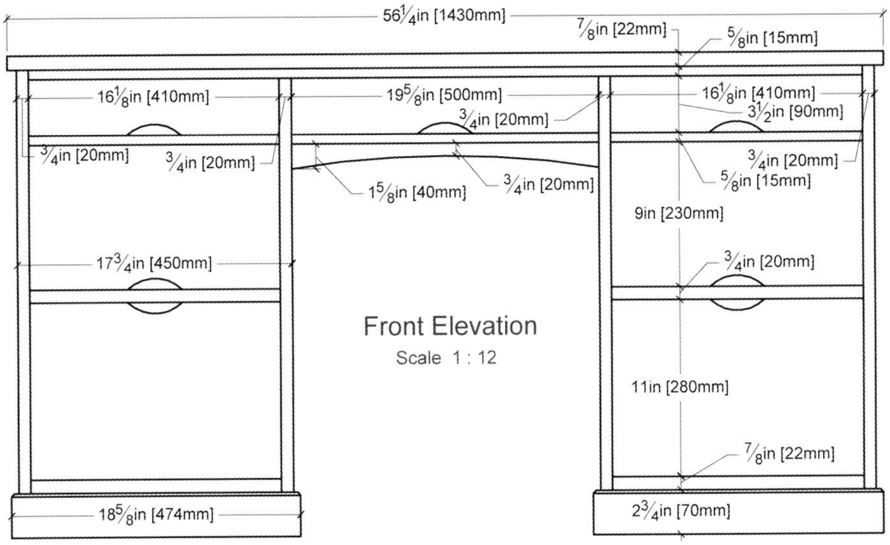
56 1/4in [1430mm]
7/8in [22mm]
5/8in [15mm]
16 1/8in [410mm]
19 5/8in [500mm]
16 1/8in [410mm]
3/4in [20mm]
3 1/2in [90mm]
3/4in [20mm]
3/4in [20mm]
3/4in [20mm]
1 5/8in [40mm]
3/4in [20mm]
5/8in [15mm]
9in [230mm]
17 3/4in [450mm]
3/4in [20mm]
Front Elevation
Scale 1 : 12
11in [280mm]
7/8in [22mm]
18 5/8in [474mm]
2 3/4in [70mm]

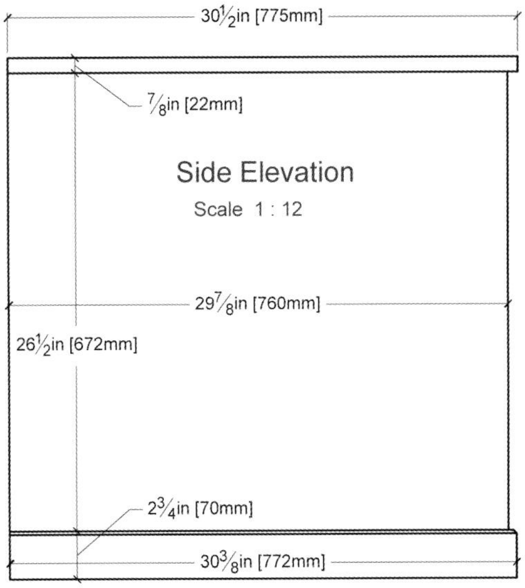
30 1/2in [775mm]
7/8in [22mm]
Side Elevation
Scale 1 : 12
29 7/8in [760mm]
26 1/2in [672mm]
2 3/4in [70mm]
30 3/8in [772mm]

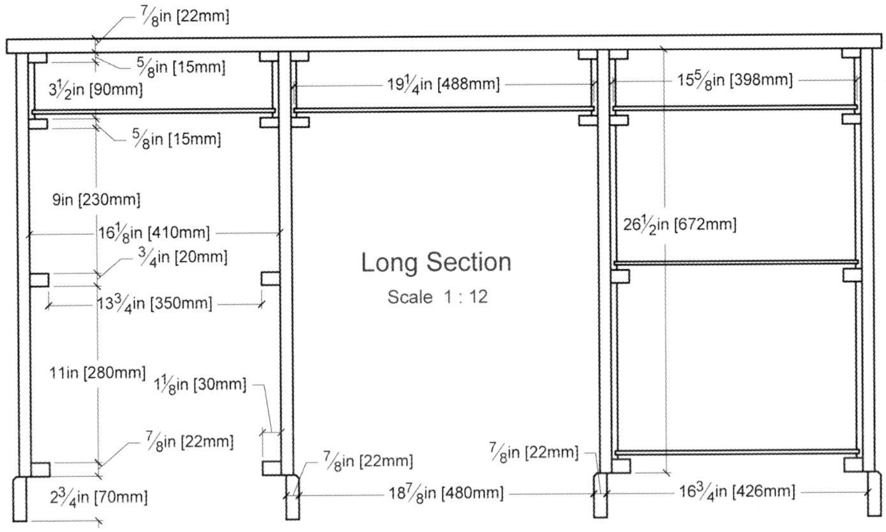
7/8in [22mm]
5/8in [15mm]
3 1/2in [90mm]
19 1/4in [488mm]
15 5/8in [398mm]
5/8in [15mm]
9in [230mm]
26 1/2in [672mm]
16 1/8in [410mm]
3/4in [20mm]
Long Section
Scale 1 : 12
13 3/4in [350mm]
11in [280mm]
1 1/8in [30mm]
7/8in [22mm]
7/8in [22mm]
7/8in [22mm]
2 3/4in [70mm]
18 7/8in [480mm]
16 3/4in [426mm]

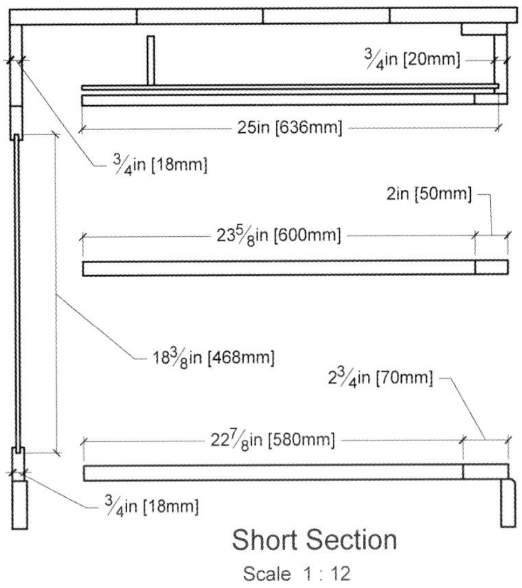
3/4in [20mm]
25in [636mm]
3/4in [18mm]
2in [50mm]
23 5/8in [600mm]
18 3/8in [468mm]
2 3/4in [70mm]
22 7/8in [580mm]
3/4in [18mm]
Short Section
Scale 1 : 12

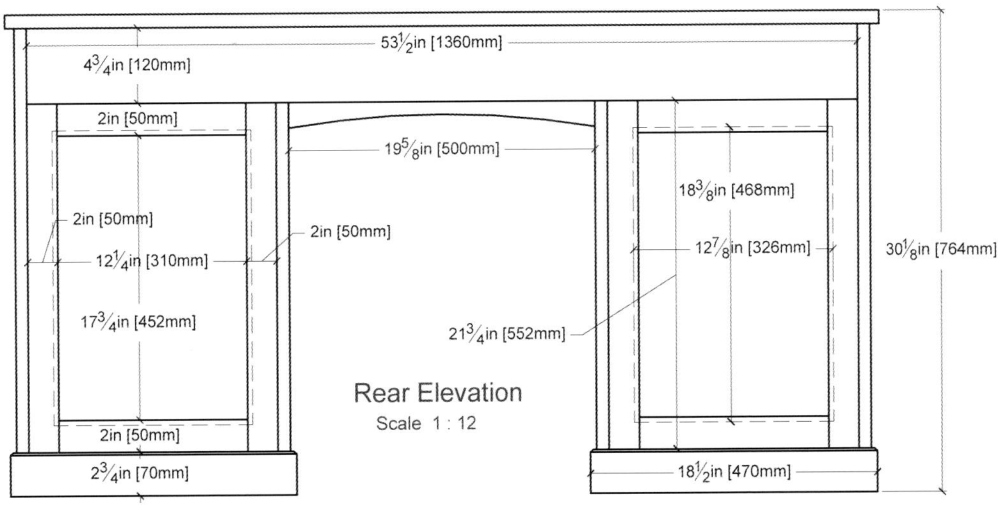
53 1/2in [1360mm]
4 3/4in [120mm]
2in [50mm]
19 5/8in [500mm]
18 3/8in [468mm]
2in [50mm]
2in [50mm]
12 1/4in [310mm]
12 7/8in [326mm]
30 1/8in [764mm]
17 3/4in [452mm]
21 3/4in [552mm]
Rear Elevation
Scale 1 : 12
2in [50mm]
2 3/4in [70mm]
18 1/2in [470mm]

SOLID WOOD is a raw material and buying good quality timber takes some care and a bit of research – even seasoned professionals are sometimes caught out. Wherever you live in the world, you will probably have to travel a bit in search of a good timber merchant unless you are fortunate enough to live close to a large, reputable yard. I would not generally advise buying solid wood unseen, so look for a company that is prepared to let you select, is happy to deal with small buyers and preferably offers a machining service. A large yard will probably have an offcut stock that will be part prepared, making it easier to select wood for your required cutting list. Always check that wood is kiln-dried as air-dried stock is never ready for indoor furniture and requires careful further conditioning. Local cabinetmakers will know about local suppliers and are usually happy to respond to requests for specific advice, providing you don't try to use them as free technical support centres!

Some suppliers sell good quality prepared oak as well as sheet materials. Although this is expensive relative to through-and-through sawn boards, it is an easy way to buy solid wood and negates the need for your own machinery.

Items such as fittings can be purchased by mail order from reputable suppliers, while abrasives and adhesives can often be bought much more cheaply from specialist suppliers than they can from tool suppliers.

A list of recommended suppliers follows, but obviously Internet research is your most useful research tool.

SOLID WOOD

Arnold Laver
478 Basingstoke Road
Reading, Berkshire
RG2 0QN
Tel: +44 (0) 1189 751100
www.timberworld.co.uk

Timberpride Ltd
Quercus Road
Tetbury, Gloustershire
GL8 8GX
Tel: +44 (0) 1666 504436
www.timberpride.co.uk

W. L. West and Son Ltd
Selham
Petworth, West Sussex
GU28 0PJ
Tel: +44 (0) 1798 861611
www.wlwest.co.uk

FITTINGS

Hafele UK Ltd
Swift Valley Industrial Estate
Rugby, Warwickshire
CV21 1RD
Tel: +44 (0) 1788 542020
www.hafele.com/uk

Isaac Lord
185 Desborough Road
High Wycombe, Bucks
HP11 2QN
Tel: +44 (0) 1494 835200
www.isaaclord.co.uk

ABRASIVES AND ADHESIVES

Adkwik
57 Ditton Walk
Cambridge
CB5 8QD
Tel: +44 (0) 1223 412373

SUPPLIERS

Woodcraft Supply, LLC
1177 Rosemar Rd
P.O.Box 1686
Parkersburg, WV 261082
Tel: 1 800 535 4482
E-mail: custserv@woodcraft.com
www.woodcraft.com

Hafele America Co.
3901Cheyenne Drive
Archdale, NC 27263
Tel: 1 800 423 3531
www.hafele.com/us

GarrettWade Co., Inc.
5389 East Provident Drive
Cincinnati, OH 45246
Tel: 1 800 221 2942 (toll free USA and Canada)
      (513)346-2258 (International calls)
E-mail: mail@garrettwade.com
www.garrettwade.com

BIBLIOGRAPHY

Becksvoort, Christian
The Shaker Legacy
The Taunton Press, Inc. Newtown CT, 1998
ISBN: 978 1 56158 357 7

Carruthers, Annette
Gimson, Ernest and the Cotswold Group of Craftsmen
Leics. Museums, Art Galleries & Records Service,1978
ISBN: 978 0 85022 038 4

Fine Woodworking Magazine, Editors of
In the Craftsman Style
The Taunton Press, Inc., 2001
ISBN: 978 1 56158 398 0

Joyce, Ernest
The Technique of Furniture Making
Fourth edition, revised by Alan Peters
B. T. Batsford Ltd, 2003
ISBN: 978 0 71348 814 2

Knell, David
English Country Furniture, 1500–1900
Antique Collectors' Club, 2000
ISBN: 978 1 85149 302 9

Martensson, Alf
The Woodworker's Bible
A & C Black, 1985
ISBN: 978 0 71362 685 8

Nakashima, George
The Soul of a Tree: A Woodworker's Reflections
Kodansha International, 1988
ISBN: 978 0 87011 903 3

O'Donogue, Declan
The Hamlyn Book of Woodworking
Hamlyn, 1997
ISBN: 978 0 60059 214 3

Peters, Alan
Cabinetmaking – The Professional Approach
Second Edition, Linden Publishing, 2009
ISBN: 978 1 93350 226 7

in	mm	in	mm	in	mm	in	mm
1/64	0.3969	5/8	15.8750	2¾	69.8501	33	838.202
1/32	0.7937			2⅞	73.0251	34	863.602
3/64	1.1906	41/64	16.2719	3	76.2002	35	889.002
1/16	1.5875	21/32	16.6687			36 (3ft)	914.402
5/64	1.9844	43/64	17.0656	3⅛	79.3752		
3/32	2.3812	11/16	17.4625	3¼	82.5502	37	939.802
7/64	2.7781	45/64	17.8594	3⅜	85.7252	38	965.202
⅛	3.1750	23/32	18.2562	3½	88.9002	39	990.602
		47/64	18.6531	3⅝	92.0752	40	1016.00
9/64	3.5719	¾	19.0500	3¾	95.2502	41	1041.40
5/32	3.9687			3⅞	98.4252	42	1066.80
11/64	4.3656	49/64	19.4469	4	101.500	43	1092.20
3/16	4.7625	25/32	19.8437			44	1117.60
13/64	5.1594	51/64	20.2406	5	127.000	45	1143.00
7/32	5.5562	13/16	20.6375	6	152.400	46	1158.40
15/64	5.9531	53/64	21.0344	7	177.800	47	1193.80
¼	6.3500	27/32	21.4312	8	203.200	48 (4ft)	1219.20
		55/64	21.8281	9	228.600		
17/64	6.7469	⅞	22.2250	10	254.001	49	1244.60
9/32	7.1437			11	279.401	50	1270.00
19/64	7.5406	57/64	22.6219	12 (1ft)	304.801	51	1295.40
5/16	7.9375	29/32	23.0187			52	1320.80
21/64	8.3344	59/64	23.4156	13	330.201	53	1346.20
11/32	8.7312	15/16	23.8125	14	355.601	54	1371.60
23/64	9.1281	61/64	24.2094	15	381.001	55	1397.00
⅜	9.5250	31/32	24.6062	16	406.401	56	1422.20
		63/64	25.0031	17	431.801	57	1447.80
25/64	9.9219	1	25.4001	18	457.201	58	1473.20
13/32	10.3187			19	482.601	59	1498.60
27/64	10.7156	1⅛	28.5751	20	508.001	60 (5ft)	1524.00
7/16	11.1125	1¼	31.7501	21	533.401		
29/64	11.5094	1⅜	34.9251	22	558.801	61	1549.40
15/32	11.9062	1½	38.1001	23	584.201	62	1574.80
31/64	12.3031	1⅝	41.2751	24 (2ft)	609.601	63	1600.20
½	12.7000	1¾	44.4501			64	1625.60
		1⅞	47.6251	25	635.001	65	1651.00
33/64	13.0969	2	50.8001	26	660.401	66	1676.40
17/32	13.4937			27	685.801	67	1701.80
35/64	13.8906	2⅛	53.9751	28	711.201	68	1727.20
9/16	14.2875	2¼	57.1501	29	736.601	69	1752.60
37/64	14.6844	2⅜	60.3251	30	762.002	70	1778.00
19/32	15.0812	2½	63.5001	31	787.402	71	1803.40
39/64	15.4781	2⅝	66.6751	32	812.802	72 (6ft)	1828.80

ABOUT THE AUTHOR

Mark Ripley, BA Hons MSDC, has been designing and making furniture in his own workshops full time since 1991, having gained an Honours Degree in Furniture Design and Production at Leicester Polytechnic in 1980.

He has contributed to a number of books on design and woodworking and he writes regularly for *Furniture & Cabinetmaking* magazine.

Mark's work has been exhibited widely. He is a member of the Society of Designer Craftsmen and the Hampshire and Berkshire Guild of Craftsmen. His present workshop is in Bramley, Hampshire (southern England). He is married to Monika and they have two daughters, Helena & Alice.

ACKNOWLEDGEMENTS

I would like to acknowledge those involved with my work during the ten years that this book represents: my clients, who form a partnership of trust with me when commissioning work; Manny Cefai and David Smith, who have been photographing my work for many years and have become friends in the process; Ian Hall and Simon Rodway for their patient and skilful interpretations of my designs and text; and Colin Eden-Eadon, for his consistent encouragement.

My family who from the earliest days encouraged my creative development, training and the establishment of my career. They have remained supportive in the development of the work and the workshops in which it has grown.

Finally, Monika, who has shared with me the often insecure life of the professional craft world with love and commitment, and whose encouragement and practical involvement over the years have been invaluable. Her faith, unlike mine, has never wavered.

INDEX

To place an order, or to request a catalogue, contact:
GMC Publications
Castle Place, 166 High Street, Lewes, East Sussex, BN7 1XU United Kingdom
Tel: +44 (0) 1273 488005 Fax: +44 (0) 1273 402866
Website: www.thegmcgroup.com
Orders by credit card are accepted